THE MOTOR MAKERS

THE MOTOR MAKERS

The Turbulent History of Britain's Car Industry

MARTIN ADENEY

COLLINS
8 Grafton Street, London W1
1988

William Collins Sons & Co Ltd
London · Glasgow · Sydney ·Auckland
Toronto · Johannesburg

BRITISH LIBRARY CATALOGUING IN PUBLICATION DATA

Adeney, Martin
The motor makers: the turbulent history of
Britain's car industry.
1. Great. Car industries, to 1988
I. Title
338.4'76292222'0941

ISBN 0–00–217787–0

First published 1988
Copyright © Martin Adeney 1988

Typeset in Linotron Bembo by
Wyvern Typesetting Ltd
Printed and bound in Great Britain by
William Collins Sons & Co. Ltd, Glasgow

For William and Thomas

CONTENTS

ILLUSTRATIONS

The small car dream of the forties and fifties – Issigonis'
Morris Minor. *Photograph: Austin Rover Group*
The most profitable British car ever was the Cortina.
Sir Terence Beckett led the team that produced it.
Photograph: Ford Motor Company
This is how Minis were advertised when they appeared
in 1959. *Photograph: British Motor Industry Heritage Trust*
1965 – The celebration of the millionth Mini.
Photograph: Austin Rover Group
Robot welding on the Ford Sierra production line at
Dagenham. *Photograph: Ford Motor Company*
One of the first Austin Swallows and the latest post-
Lyons Jaguar XJ6. *Photograph: Jaguar Cars*
In the fifties British patriotism celebrated the
performance of Jaguars at Le Mans.
Photograph: Jaguar Cars

PREFACE

I set out to write this book to answer the question why? Why should it be that my street is full of foreign-made cars when the British, as I was brought up to believe, are one of the greatest manufacturing nations on earth? Looking for the answer has taken me on a longer journey than I expected. But not so long as to foil my objective that people who ask, 'Whatever happened to the British motor industry?' should be able to find some answers in a single volume.

It is not a frivolous question. I was struck by the number of men who had spent their lives in the industry who asked me as I went round, 'What happened?' – 'What went wrong?'

It's been a fascinating and dismaying experience. With some notable exceptions, the British have never been the best at *making* cars, especially in large numbers. The British car makers depended on the French and Germans for their first models, and many of their parts; on the Americans to teach them the skills of mass production and on huge import charges for half this century to prevent their British customers buying foreign. Even when they did show their marks of genius, like the Rolls-Royce or the Mini, they often lacked the basic commercial disciplines to turn them into proper success.

Throughout the industry there seems to have run a doctrine of divine right – that Britain makes better cars – if only everyone else would appreciate it; a belief which seems to exempt British firms from following the kind of practical business disciplines which you expect to find in foreign companies.

As the Red Flag Act, which held up the birth of the British motor industry was repealed back in 1896, the patriotic engineer, Sir David Salomons, proclaimed that he was 'quite sure that the

English engineer could easily beat the Continental ones if only allowed to do so.' Sadly, 90 years on, there has been remarkably little evidence to support that view. Most of the major advances in automobile design have come from other countries, from the internal combustion engine onwards, and while it may be true that the British are often very good conceptual engineers, they take a very definite second place when it comes to the kind of production engineering which makes cars efficiently and effectively.

One sentence of the Jaguar Chairman, Sir John Egan, still rings in my ears. 'By the seventies,' he said, 'the standard performance for a British car company was to do badly and go out of business.' In these pages I have tried to set out why that was, and to see what lessons might be learnt for the future of this and other industries.

There are lots of books about cars, and many about the companies; this is a history of the British industry, trying to weave together the various strands of companies' different experiences and relating it to what was happening in the outside world at the time. As such it is very partial, so I have attempted to indicate in a bibliography where an interested reader might go to take things further.

I started off with the deliberate intention of affording a major space to the Ford Motor Company in Britain, as without it, effective motor manufacture might have disappeared from Britain years ago. It has regularly been looked on as an interloper from abroad and its products disparaged – 'What's the time when one Ford overtakes another?' they asked in the 1930s – 'Tin past tin'. Yet the products of Ford's management philosophy and training have spread expertise and effective management throughout British companies, many far removed from motor manufacture. Like Ford or hate it, its sheer professionalism leaves most other companies standing.

Yet the more you examine Ford the more dominated by Americans it appears to be. Granted that in Ford of Britain, hardly an American is to be found. But these days Ford of Britain is little more than the sales arm – the real power is with Ford of Europe, headquartered in Essex, but with four of its six top officers, including the chairman, made in the USA – a proportion that looks unlikely to change significantly.

Apart from the necessarily limited specialists, Jaguar and Rolls-Royce, there is only one company which consistently makes and exports more cars here than anyone else by a long way, and that is the Rover Group. Without it British manufacturing and our balance of trade would be in ribbons. Which is why, I guess, successive British Governments have continued reluctantly to support it at a price which as I write is still something like £20 a week per worker. So thank God for Ford but God save the Rover Group.

This is a book about the car industry but I am conscious that that is an artificial description. The making of commercial vehicles – buses, vans and lorries – cannot be clinically separated off. It is obviously true of Leyland. Vauxhall's progress was importantly affected by the Bedford truck operation and Ford tractor and commercial vehicle production has been a huge money spinner. But one has to draw the line somewhere, and the success of a combined car and commercial vehicle manufacturer has never absolutely depended on its commercial vehicle section in the same way as it has on its cars.

I have tried to go back to first-hand sources as far as possible. That means quoting what people said or wrote at the time and also carrying out lengthy interviews with about 40 key people. I have quoted as much as possible verbatim so that the reader can see what the participants in this drama thought – although the benefits of hindsight are apparent in some cases.

What I have perhaps failed to bring out sufficiently is the sense of excitement and good fortune which so many of these people felt in being involved in the motor industry at all. 'The good old, bad old days' as one man put it. It remained an industry for enthusiasts even when it had outgrown its interwar reputation as the adventurous industry of the future.

A large number of people have helped me at different stages of this project. My thanks go to Erik Johnson and Dr Reiner Karnowski who set me on the way at the Daimler–Benz archive; to Mrs Joan Innes-Kerr for permission to inspect the Simms and the Pollitt papers of the Veteran Car Club at the London University Library and to Helen Young for sorting them out for me; to Gordon Morrison, the librarian of the Institution of Mechanical Engineers; to Anders Clausager, the archivist of the British

Motor Industry Heritage Trust, for statistical information and advice, and to a whole range of public relations officers in different companies including Martyn Watkins at Ford; Neil Gardner and Miriam Carroll at Vauxhall; Brian Johns and John Pullen at Rover Group; Colin Cook at Jaguar and Brian Llewellyn at Peugeot–Talbot, both of whom gave me the benefit of their experience in a range of different companies.

My special thanks however are due to Christopher Leftley, the librarian of the RAC, for allowing me to use the library and finding me a range of material some of which I, and he, did not know existed.

To Lilla Byrne and Duncan Aitchison of the Department of Employment Library who produced a wide range of sources on labour and employment questions, and whose generosity even extended to marking the references for me.

To David Burgess-Wise, the manager of the Ford of Britain archive, who guided me through Ford's extensive material, including the company's unpublished history *Wheels of Fortune* by l'Estrange Fawcett and a series of interviews done by Norman St John Stevas in the early fifties. I am also indebted to him for his wide knowledge of other companies, particularly Clyno, on which he is an expert.

To Sir Pat Lowry, who gave me the benefit of his vast experience at BL and ACAS and elsewhere and went to enormous trouble in providing me with names and addresses.

To Professor Garel Rhys, who read through part of the manuscript; to Christopher Ford and Suzanne Hinton at the Society of Motor Manufacturers and Traders who sought out information and answered innumerable questions; and to Margaret Dowson who transferred my mucky and much-altered manuscripts into impeccable typescript with enormous patience and good humour, and did not hesitate to give timely advice on spelling and sense; without her these pages might never have got to the printers.

Lastly my great gratitude goes to my long-suffering family who paid the price for the toll which writing this book took of my time and my temper in the first half of 1987.

MARTIN ADENEY

1987

The Beginnings
'Faster than a Man Could Walk'

It was perhaps the very success of British invention in pioneering steam power and all that went with it – the railways reaching across even the most trackless parts of the world's land surface, the reliable steamers cleaving inexorably through its oceans – which led to lack of interest in the other nineteenth-century invention which was to have as revolutionary an impact – the internal combustion engine.

The great inventors of the steam age had early turned their attention to road transport. Richard Trevithick, the Cornish mining engineer, had built a steam coach which had driven up a hill 'faster than a man could walk' on Christmas Eve 1801 and had bumped a later model over the rutted track which was then London's Oxford Street, but without finding commercial takers. Later a series of businessmen did begin regular services. In 1828 Sir Goldsworthy Gurney's steam diligences could travel as fast as fourteen miles an hour and carry over twenty passengers, while in 1831 Sir Charles Dance's steam coaches plied four times a day between Gloucester and Cheltenham, and had carried three thousand passengers before the end of June. In London, an obvious proving-ground, a series of routes were opened up.

But it was not to last. The country grandees, opposed at first to the noisy intrusion of steam in all its forms, quickly saw the advantage of railways, selling the companies their land and investing in their booming shares. Self-powered transport was straitjacketed; confined to the narrow, if smelly, corridors of the railway cutting and embankment. The roads, potholed and muddy, reverted to the horse, and as the century advanced and the stage-coach gave way to the iron schedules of the express and the railway timetable, the carriageways crumbled away.

The symbol and seal of all this was the Locomotive Act, passed in 1865 to the great delight of both railway and horse-drawn coach interests, and better known by its nickname – the Red Flag Act. It was the death warrant for the steam-coach and for almost any serious attempts in Britain to develop powered road vehicles for 30 years.

Its key provisions were that 'at least three persons shall be employed to drive or conduct such a locomotive' and that 'one of such persons, while any locomotive is in motion, shall precede such locomotive on foot by not less than 60 yards and shall carry a red flag constantly displayed.'

Just in case the point was missed, speed-limits were imposed – four miles an hour in the country; two miles an hour in the town. Although it was slightly amended in 1878 with local authorities being given discretion about the flag and lantern and the distance they preceded the vehicle being reduced to twenty yards, the result was to suppress the enthusiasm in Britain for experiments in powered road transport.

It was a temporary but devastating setback, whose effects would be felt for years to come. A breach of sorts in the attempt to dam progress and preserve the road for the horse was soon made by the invention of the bicycle and the pneumatic tyre. From the 1870s increasing numbers of cyclists took to the roads, thousands pouring out for weekend excursions, disturbing the horses and stoking up a demand for improvements in the roads which was given concrete form by the Roads Improvement Association set up by cycling associations in 1886.

Huge factories were soon set up to cater for the bicycle boom, making fortunes for the founders and prosperous places such as Coventry. It was from this industry, untrammelled by the Red Flag Act, that much of the money and enthusiasm for the founding of the motor vehicle industry came. Names like Rover and Humber, later to be synonymous with the British motor industry, came from cycle companies, while others like Lucas and Dunlop owed their early prosperity to the bicycle boom.

But it had other consequences too. The engineering require-ments for making cycles were far less exacting than those for the early development of the internal combustion engine. The unhappy results of the best British engineering brains being concentrated on the refinements of steam and heavy engineering and largely neglecting the experiments being carried on in the continent of Europe and the United States were to be felt until well into the twentieth century.

When the *Illustrated London News* struck a souvenir edition to commemorate Queen Victoria's Golden Jubilee in 1897, a full eleven years after the German inventors Daimler and Benz had run their first cars, it was the triumphs of 'Steam and Electricity' it chose to commemorate in its article on technical progress. The motor car received only a single sentence mention.

Thomas Edison, the American inventor, wrote in 1901: 'The motor car ought to have been British. You first invented it in the 1830s. You have roads only second to those of France. You have hundreds of thousands of skilled mechanics in your midst, but you have lost your trade by the same kind of stupid legislation and prejudice that have put you back in many departments of the electrical field.'

The effect was lasting. Writing a treatise on 'The Automobile Industry' in 1904, Geoffrey de Holden-Stone said of the early years of the industry that 'lack of qualified persons engaging in this branch of engineering even among the otherwise technically qualified compelled the few who had taken up automobile construction to take every detail of practice at second hand from the Continent.'

A year later, a manufacturer giving evidence to the Royal Commission on Motor Cars agreed that most of his component parts still had to come from the Continent.

In Europe, the breakthroughs had come from Benz and Daimler. They had both run their first cars in Germany in 1886, but their success was even more enthusiastically exploited in France. While the German industry temporarily faltered, the French rapidly expanded with cars built round the Daimler engine for which Emil Levassor held the manufacturing patent. Both Panhard–Levassor and Peugeot–Levassor cars were produced in France in 1891. The French rapidly devised what was to become standard automobile lay-out with the engine at the front and all seats facing forward, calling it 'le système Panhard'.

By 1894 there were sufficient vehicles for a trial to be run between Paris and Rouen to evaluate the best designs, and by

June 1895 22 petrol, steam and electric cars were setting out on the first ever motor-race over an ambitious seven hundred mile course from Paris to Bordeaux and back.

The huge public enthusiasm they engendered rapidly gave birth to a clutch of highly competitive manufacturers on whose products the British were to rely for the first decade of car ownership. But in Britain the Red Flag Act not only prevented races but discouraged would-be inventors by ruling out road tests.

Even so, there were some early attempts. In 1884 Edward Butler of Erith in Kent applied for a provisional patent (No. 13541) for a motor tricycle, a form which was to be popular among early manufacturers on both sides of the Channel. Drawings were exhibited at the Stanley cycle show and three years later the machine was built. The driver sat between large cycle-type wheels which were steered with upright handles while the contraption was powered by a third wheel at the rear driven by cylinders on each side. It was never put into commercial production.

A more prominent pioneer was James Henry Knight of Farnham. He had first built a steam carriage in 1868 and in 1895 he produced a petrol-engined tricycle. Adapting it to four wheels, it was the only British-made vehicle which could be found to be exhibited at the 1896 Crystal Palace Exhibition of self-propelled vehicles.

At the same time more significant inventors such as Lanchester and Austin were working on their first designs.

By 1896 times were changing even in Britain. The Crystal Palace show was part of a movement to bring in vehicles with the object of captivating public opinion to bring about the repeal of the Red Flag Act and the start of an indigenous British motor industry.

It was, however, late in the day and the Red Ensign which Knight's vehicle bravely carried could not disguise the fact that it was inferior to the vehicles Benz and Daimler had produced a full ten years before. But some groundwork had been laid. From the early 1890s a number of forward-looking British engineers had been attempting to educate the country about the virtues of the new ways of propulsion being developed on the Continent.

Their efforts plus those of the unashamed money men who saw the birth of a new industry as a chance to make their fortunes combined to achieve the political objective of replacing the Act in a remarkably short space of time. But founding the industry in Britain brought them into a conflict which was to cripple its beginnings. As one famous motor engineer was to write twenty years later: 'The motor-car started as the rich man's toy. As a business proposition, it drifted largely into the hands of charlatans and ignorant men who regarded the application of scientific techniques to business as a dangerous innovation.'[1]

A prime mover among those engineers was Frederick Henry Simms, one of the few Englishmen to have made major technical contributions to the development of the internal combustion engine and the man who most qualified for the title of founder of the British motor industry.

It was no coincidence that Simms was himself born on the Continent, in Hamburg, where his grandfather, who came from Birmingham, had established a supply business for fishing trawlers. Simms had started by making aerial cable-lifts for which he needed suitable motors. It was in 1890 when he was only 27 that he came across Gottlieb Daimler at the Bremen International Exhibition where the Daimler engine was powering a rail truck. He was immediately impressed. He formed a close association and friendship with Daimler, later helping him reorganize his Stuttgart factory and making various technical improvements to the engines. He swiftly saw the potential of the engine, which by then had been employed as much to power launches as cars, and was writing to an associate in Worthing in February 1891:

We have started a department for *petrol-motor boats and cars etc.* i.e. we have made an agreement with the Daimler Motor Co. Ltd which has just been turned into a Ltd Co. having grand results.

Now I am going to exhibit a motor car at the German exhibition at Earls Court and then I want to run a beautiful motorboat on the Serpentine to show the grand thing which I have secured.

The motor is unequalled, i.e. quite dangerless, no smell,

50 per cent cheaper than all other motors and very small consumption . . . the petrol motor is the best thing that I ever came across.

Simms had taken a licence to develop the engine throughout the British Empire (excluding Canada), but he was to face considerable difficulties before he could even exhibit the engine in Britain.

He abandoned the idea of getting a car to Earls Court because of the difficulties, proposing instead to exhibit a Daimler engine driving a chocolate and cocoa making machine. But the organizers panicked about the risk of explosion from the machine and forbade it. Similar alarm frustrated his plan to run a launch on the Serpentine or the Crystal Palace lake, but by the summer of 1891 he succeeded in demonstrating the power of the Daimler engine in a launch on the Thames. He swiftly followed that up by establishing a workshop to fit Daimler engines into boats in an arch next to Putney railway station, renting it from the District Railway Company for £25 a year. The sales brochure for Simms and Co., Engineers, described 'The Daimler Patent Gas and Oil Motor' as 'the cheapest, lightest and most reliable motor ever invented'.

Simms' enthusiasm for the engine was widely shared. The French motor industry had been established round it. But it was obvious to Simms and others that until the Red Flag Act was repealed, a similar British industry was a non-starter.

Besides Simms' qualities as an engineer, he was also to demonstrate a liking and a knack for setting up organizations throughout his long life. In 1895 he became a founder member of the Self Propelled Traffic Association with the aim of getting the law changed.

The man behind this was Sir David Salomons, the Mayor of Tunbridge Wells, who was a keen amateur engineer. He had devised an electrical installation to power his house and invented an electric car. There were also strong commercial interests represented, particularly from manufacturers who had made small fortunes in the cycle boom and could now see that being repeated on a much larger scale if the motor car was freed from restriction.

They were led by the protean and publicity-seeking figure of Harry J. Lawson, the son of a Puritan preacher in the East End, a man who spent most of his life contradicting all the tenets of his upbringing. He was the first of the larger than life figures of the British motor industry – the incarnation of 'the man you would never buy a second-hand car from', making his appearance before the industry had got off the ground. It was this man who was to dominate and distort the first efforts to form a British Motor Industry.

There were always two views of Lawson. One was set out by the Stock Exchange Gazette on February 15th 1896 on the day of the flotation of the British Daimler Motor Company. 'The fact that Mr H.J. Lawson is the controlling spirit is a very bad omen for the company and augurs a speedy acquaintance with the Bankruptcy Court rather than the success the patent deserves.'

The other was held by W.O. Duncan, an associate of Lawson's in the cycle business, who wrote sentimentally of the 'little man' commonly seen in his smoking jacket, and styled him 'the founder of the motor-car industry in England and the world's cycle and motor trade'.[2]

Lawson was a financial wheeler-dealer whose speciality was to buy up companies and then to float shares to the public for a price far beyond what he had paid. In three years in the cycle boom he and a partner, Ernest T. Hooley, had promoted 26 companies, which had produced for them about £5 million profit.

Many of the companies interlocked in a way familiar to readers of city scandals in the later twentieth century. His firms transferred business to each other and were wound up when the going got difficult. At one stage he himself claimed to have set up thirteen public companies and 21 others which he said 'had never got beyond the stage of registration'.

He was a tireless self-publicist. In one of the many pamphlets advertising his achievements, he declared his philosophy:

> As to companies, there is no other way of exploiting new inventions of much novelty. For private firms will not experiment and even losses are inevitable. I have invested money in syndicates, with bankers, brokers and city men for the founda-

tion of new industrial companies and the majority of these companies have been successful. . . .

These industries have put, as I can prove, millions of pounds into the British pocket and employed hundreds of thousands of British workers.

Lawson had made his fortune out of the cycle industry, which by this time was employing over ten thousand people revitalizing Midlands centres like Coventry. A keen amateur in the Watford club, he claimed to have invented the first 'safety bicycle', getting away from the awkward penny-farthing. There was sufficient doubt about it for him to go to the lengths of arranging a public ceremony at a Coventry hotel where the Mayor presented him with an illuminated address to prove the fact years later.

He had indeed registered a safety bicycle (patent No. 3934), the Lawson Bicyclette in 1879. Described as more like a penny-halfpenny than a penny-farthing, with its back wheel rather larger than its front, it had a rudimentary chain drive. But the mechanism restricted the turning angle of the front wheel, and caused the manager of the Rudge company where Lawson worked, to fall off when he tried it out. The company rejected the design as a result. It was then overtaken by Rovers and others.

Lawson had helped found the Humber bicycle company. But his most successful enterprise was the recapitalization of the Dunlop Pneumatic Tyre Company, increasing its capital from £75,000 to three million pounds. It made his fortune and encouraged him to launch yet another company, the Beeston Tyre Company with a capital of one million pounds.

The key element in the Dunlop company's success was the strength of its patent rights and the remorseless way in which any possible infringement was pursued. Lawson now saw another opportunity. His plan was nothing less than to corner the market in all motor car patents and snap up any new inventions as they became available, whether foreign or British. A broadsheet for his British Motor Syndicate to be issued in 1896 was headed 'The coming revenue of the British Motor Syndicate, sole owners of the master motor car patent in this country' and was decorated with fanciful drawings of policemen on motor tricycles and horse carriages proceeding without their horses. It declared:

The object is to obtain in this country a complete monopoly to the Syndicate of all Motor Car patents deemed of any value .... The Directors are of the opinion that no such sums of money have ever been received from any Patent Monopoly as the payments now beginning to be made to this Syndicate for Royalties and Licences from manufacturers of motor vans and carriages under the original Motor Car patents, all of which, of any known importance – belong solely to this Syndicate.

Lawson's hucksterism upset many of his allies, particularly Salomons, but his energy swept them along. His strength was that he made things happen and made it all intensely exciting. He was also, one contemporary wrote, 'extremely generous and quick to spot ability in others'. His failure was that he diverted public enthusiasm and available investment into his own self-aggrandizement and up technical blind alleys. The speculative cash available for what others beside Lawson could clearly see was likely to be 'a very great industry which will not only be profitable in itself but will augment the profits of innumerable other industries' was first swallowed and then discouraged by the eventual collapse of his projects.

But for the moment, his energy and enthusiasm for propaganda galvanized the early pioneers. He founded a campaigning magazine *The Autocar* to be edited by a business associate, Henry Sturmey, who had run the *Cycling Times*. A Motor Car Club was set up with Simms and a spattering of peers. Most important, arrangements were set in hand to break down the public ignorance of what was still variously called the horseless carriage, the self-propelled carriage or the autocar by bringing more into the country and exhibiting them.

The early pioneers were a small band, their names, their companies and even their individual vehicles recurring in a variety of places and settings.

Nobody knows for sure which was the first motor-car to be imported into Britain. It was probably a small 1½ horsepower German Benz brought in by Henry Hewetson in 1894. Hewetson, a London tea-merchant, had seen Benz cars on a visit to Mannheim where Karl Benz had first run his 'patent Motor-wagen' eight years before, and ordered one. (An early Benz tricycle now in the Science Museum in London may possibly have been imported earlier but no records remain).

But the most significant arrival was what was probably the second car to be brought in, a Daimler engined Panhard–Levassor from France.

Through the agency of Simms, who controlled the Daimler patent, the car was bought by the Hon. Evelyn Ellis, another enthusiast, and in July 1895 Simms went down to Micheldever near Winchester in Hampshire to help him drive it back the 56 miles to his home at Datchet near Windsor. The Red Flag Act still applied, but it was not enforced on this occasion, as Simms' account of the drive makes clear.

We passed through Datchet and arrived in front of the entrance hall of Mr Ellis' house at Datchet at 6 o'clock thus completing our enjoyable journey of 56 miles – the first ever made by a petroleum motor carriage in this country – in 5 hours, 32 minutes, exclusive of stoppages. The average speed we attained was 9·84 miles per hour, the usual travelling speed being between 8 and 12 miles per hour.

In every place we passed through we were, not unnaturally, the object of a good deal of curiosity. Whole villages turned out to behold, open-mouthed, the new marvel of locomotion. The departure of coaches was delayed to enable their passengers to have a look at our horseless vehicle, while cyclists would stop to gaze enviously at us, as we surmounted with ease some long and to them, tiring hill.'

Mr Ellis' Panhard–Daimler motor-carriage is a neat and compact four-wheeled dog-cart with accommodation for four persons and two portmanteaux. The consumption of petrol is a little over one half-penny per mile and there is no smoke, heat or smell. The carriage runs smoothly and without vibration. The simple and ingenious gear puts the carriage under complete control. The steering is likewise extremely simple, and either of the two powerful brakes can bring the carriage to a complete standstill within a little over a yard.

Simms' account, which appeared the same month in the *Saturday Review* was the first example of the glowing prose of the motoring salesman in Britain. The vehicle was to prove a popular advertisement of the new motoring age.

In October, Salomons, who with his political and society connections was leading the campaign for the repeal of the Red Flag Act, persuaded the organizers of the agricultural show at Tunbridge Wells to accommodate what was called 'a horseless exhibition'. It was highly successful but it demonstrated just how little progress the motor vehicle had made in Britain. There were just six exhibits in the programme, and only five materialized. There was Ellis' car; a Peugeot with Daimler engine fitted, again by Panhard–Levassor, which Salomons had bought, and a French de Dion-Bouton motor tricycle ridden by its inventor, Georges Bouton, which circled the enclosure of 'soft, rough turf' and was said by the *Autocar* to be 'obviously a tricycle and not for running over rough pastures.' The other two vehicles were a steam engine attached to a carriage and a fire-engine belonging to Ellis which used a Daimler engine only to power its pump, and was propelled around the showgrounds by a team of jogging firemen. It was scarcely the kind of display to shake Parliament into action.

However the movement was growing. In November, George Johnston had driven his own autocar through the night-time streets of Glasgow. It was described by the *Autocar* as 'a four-wheeled dog-cart without the shafts' and the first car 'on this side of the Border' while at the annual Stanley cycle show, Ellis' car had been joined on the exhibition stand by another French vehicle, a Roger, imported by Leon l'Hollier of Birmingham.

On December 10th three to four hundred people gathered in the Pillar Room of the Cannon Street Hotel in London to form Salomons' Self-Propelled Traffic Association to campaign for a change in the law. Salomons spoke of an 'outlet for capital and labour which the creation of a new and huge industry means everywhere', and Mr H.J. Knight claimed a hearing as 'the maker of the first oil motor carriage in the country'.

A week later Simms was entertaining about a score of press-men from the principal journals to lunch in the Garden Restaurant at Crystal Palace and giving them the opportunity to try a Daimler imported from Germany. It was a public relations operation which was to excite the admiration of the Daimler Benz public relations department 90 years later. 'Simms showed

the way to every subsequent motor manufacturer how to get the
Press on their side. In other words, he offered a synthesis of hard
news together with some hospitality and a personal experience'.[3]

Attacking what he called 'the absurd restriction which at
present prevented enterprise in autocar manufacture' he said he
hoped their papers would be unanimous in supporting the change
in the law.

Salomons meanwhile was proceeding along more establishment routes. In February he led a deputation to see the President
of the Local Government Board, Henry Chaplin, the Government minister who would be responsible for any changes in the
law to end the Red Flag Act.

Salomons struck the patriotic note which runs throughout
British motor history. He felt 'quite sure that the English
engineer could easily beat the Continental ones if only allowed to
do so.' It was, he told Chaplin, 'the duty of the Government to
encourage any form of industry which would find employment
for the coming generations.' The Government's reply was better
than the motor enthusiasts could have dreamed. Mr Chaplin told
them that he was 'fully in sympathy with everything that had
been said and a bill dealing with the subject was now in an
advanced stage.' He expected it to go through without any
formidable opposition. The Walls of Jericho had fallen at the first
trumpet blast. It was probably the first and last time that a motor
industry delegation ever got such a whole-hearted response from
Government.

Salomons himself was closely consulted about the bill and was
to claim that the Government accepted the various points he had
put. He declared when the bill was passed nine months later that
'for the great freedom given in this measure, I feel that I am in a
large way responsible.'

But his detached lobbying had been accompanied by a storm of
propaganda and agitation from Lawson, whose unabashed commercial intentions were soon infuriating the fastidious Tunbridge
Wells engineer.

On November 2, 1895 the first edition of the *Autocar* had
appeared, styling itself 'a journal published in the interests of the
mechanically propelled road carriage.'

Its editorial declared, 'Every new movement is fostered and

encouraged by publicity and the free letting in upon it of the light of public opinion.' The automobile carriage movement had come suddenly before the British public although for over a year it had been making steady headway on the Continent, and it pointed out that the cyclist and the cycle maker had paved the way for the autocar. The editorial continued:

> To those who would revile the British engineer with having allowed both France and America to be before him, we point to the legacy of the past which throttled all enterprise at its birth . . . We have no fear that Great Britain will find herself in any way behind as soon as the inventive talent of her mechanics has had time to develop herself.

They were brave words, and if editor Sturmey was echoing the views of his friend and backer, Harry J. Lawson, why not? Mr Lawson was already planning ways to find work for inventive mechanics.

Two weeks later, the magazine carried a headline 'Autocars to be manufactured in England; a large company forming for the purpose.' Mr H.J. Lawson, it said, was 'busily engaged in organizing the company! He recognizes the immensity of the business before him and has had the foresight to secure agreements with the owners of the principal motors.' Already some £16,000 had been paid out as deposits to secure contracts.

That autumn Simms had been approached in his office by one B.B. Van Praagh, a solicitor. He explained that he was representing a private syndicate which was anxious to buy the Daimler patents from Simms and offered him £25,000 for them and said he was prepared to leave a cheque for £5,000 there and then. Simms, whose syndicate had paid £18,750 for the rights, sensibly held out. Negotiations continued and in the end Simms agreed to do business for £35,000 of which £15,000 was to be paid on account. The syndicate of course consisted of Lawson and two associates.

Their British Motor Syndicate showed a quick profit. When they floated the Daimler Motor Company in early 1896, its £100,000 capital was £10,000 over-subscribed, and one of its first acts was to pay the Syndicate, not £35,000, but £40,000, for the Daimler patents for manufacturing only. Lawson's construction

of interlocking companies continued. Later in the year he was to
float the Great Horseless Carriage Company which promptly
paid two thirds of its capital in turn to the Motor Syndicate.
Arrangements were made with the Daimler company to supply it
with the engines, while Daimler was committed to having its
bodies built by the Great Horseless Carriage Company.

The effect of Lawson's commercialism on the prospects for
changing the law began to alarm Salomons. There had been a
row at the inaugural meeting of the Self-Propelled Traffic Association when he had resisted appointments to the council of
those whose wish was 'to make the Association little more or less
than a Company promoting concern.'

But for the moment the alliance held. The *Autocar* circulated a
petition to the Commons declaring that the laws relating to the
highways were 'obstructive to the users of all horseless carriages
and that thereby the industry of manufacturing such carriages is
retarded.' Its 8,027 signatures were backed up by resolutions
passed by nineteen councils including those of Coventry and
Birmingham asking for the law to be changed.

In February Lawson and Simms' Motor Car Club was organizing a display of vehicles at the Imperial Institute in South
Kensington to impress members of Parliament and other influential people, with the importance of changing the law. A few days
before it was due to open, a message was received from the Prince
of Wales (soon to be Edward VII) that he would like to visit. He
was duly shown round on the day before the opening and given a
ride, inevitably in Evelyn Ellis' car, accompanied also by Simms.
The *Autocar* reported that 'The Prince expressed himself as highly
pleased at his experience, giving vent to the hope, however, that
autocars would not entirely supersede horses of which animals he
is a great admirer, which we are inclined to think was another
way of expressing a decided belief in the extensive use of the
vehicle in the near future.'

The same edition carried a furious letter from Salomons
announcing that it was a source of satisfaction to him that he was
not connected in any way whatever with either the Motor Car
Club or the Daimler Motor Company. He had no financial
interest in the motor question and 'any part I have played has been
done purely out of patriotism.'

The rupture was final. Salomons went on to organize another Crystal Palace exhibition with his own car, two Daimlers, a car imported to Scotland and Knight's old invention. Lawson described it as 'a failure' and pressed ahead with plans for a much bigger show at the Imperial Institute round which he could build his latest money-raising scheme for equipping what he intended to be the first motor vehicle factory in Britain.

On April 4th 1896 the *Autocar* had announced the Daimler company's purchase of 'perhaps the finest manufacturing property in the Midland counties, this being the estate and building of the Coventry Cotton Spinning and Weaving Company Ltd.' The reality was a starkly traditional mill with two large blocks set in about twelve acres close to a canal. It had been gutted by fire and the top three of four storeys rebuilt by the insurance company. The ground floor was still full of spinning machinery. The prediction that the company would be able to supply motors, 'at any rate of one or two types, within a month' was simply bogus. It was not until July that any operations started.

Much more accurate was the prediction that 'This looks as if Coventry, which is already the head centre of the cycle industry and one of the principal centres in England of the watchmaking and weaving trades may also be looked upon in the future as the chief centre of the autocar industry.'

Lawson was by now engaged in drumming up more support both for the industry and his schemes. The centre-piece was the opening of a new exhibition at the Imperial Institute whose summer season ran for three months from May 9th. Posters advertising the 'International exhibition of Motors, Horseless carriages, Self-propelled cycles etc.' to the strains of the 'famous Monte Carlo orchestra' were plastered all over London. Two weeks later the *Autocar* was carrying the prospectus for the latest scheme, the Great Horseless Carriage Company which was intended to occupy the Motor Mills (as Lawson had smartly termed his new Coventry factory) and make use of the patents being exhibited at the show.

Organizing the show had presented some familiar difficulties. There were not enough vehicles available, and some of those on which Lawson was prepared to pay large sums of patent money were just not practical. To try to improve matters, Lawson employed an old cycling acquaintance, W.O. Duncan, who had just sold his own cycle business in France and knew the French motor trade. His job was to look for vehicles and promising patents.

It was a difficult situation. As Duncan explained,

As there were only a few petrol motor-cycles or cars for demonstration in the Institute grounds, I was instructed to go to Paris at once and buy or send or bring anything back that would help to astonish the crowd. 'What I want is some motor-cycles or motor-cars that will run for half an hour or so, and they must not break down in the middle of the exhibition,' Lawson said to me.

As a matter of fact we could only show (actually running) the Benz petrol car, the de Dion-Bouton motor tricycle, the Hilderbrant and Wolfmuller motor-bicycle and brief appearances of the Pennington light quadricycle. Lawson was reserving his steam and electric vehicles for other financial ventures. For obvious reasons, some exhibitors objected to their vehicles being demonstrated in the grounds. Many of them were merely dummies, while others might develop too much speed or otherwise be difficult to drive in a very limited area.

However, Duncan soon heard of a new machine, another tricycle, but called a tandem, being made in Le Mans by Leon Bollée. Impressed with a trial he offered to buy the British patents and Bollée agreed to travel to London to meet Lawson. After a twenty minute trial at the Imperial Institute Lawson's mind was made up.

Bollée wanted £30,000 for his patents. The following day according to the account of Duncan who acted as interpreter, Lawson offered £20,000 for the machine with working drawings and all British rights. ' "Il n'y a rien à faire," said Bollée jumping up. I told Lawson he would not accept the offer and that the business was at an end. "I will give them until 12 o'clock to make up their minds as I'm off to Coventry this afternoon," replied Lawson.'

After an hour's animated discussion, Bollée finally agreed to accept £20,000. However, he then accompanied Lawson to Coventry after receiving a cheque for £4,000 and postdated bills for the remainder. In the train, he noticed that the bills were not signed by Lawson and believed he had been tricked. Bollée sat up most of the night at his hotel discussing it with Duncan until he finally burst out that he would give £1,000 to have the bills signed by Lawson.

Duncan seized his opportunity. Groping his way down to the hotel writing room, he persuaded Bollée to sign a letter to that effect, and as soon as Lawson appeared for breakfast, Duncan got his agreement to replace the bills with promisory notes. Lawson insisted that Duncan keep the £1,000. Such was the atmosphere of the early industry.

Bollée's tandem was at least moderately successful. But the same could not be said of the invention for which Lawson paid as much as £100,000 and which was to prove a star of the Imperial Institute show but a disaster for the Lawson companies.

This was the patent of an American inventor, Edward Pennington. Lawson's closest partner, Martin Rucker, who was closely associated with the Humber cycle company, had been greatly impressed with Pennington's prototype motor-cycle in the United States. He had persuaded Lawson to purchase the patents for the astonishing sum of £100,000. The machine was advertised in full page spreads throughout the first year of the *Autocar* and Pennington came over to England. Here he disguised the shortcomings of his machine for months by his mastery of public relations.

At the Imperial Institute show, both he and his good-looking wife appeared in diamonds and their stand was opposite the tea gardens where the fashionable took their afternoon tea. Pennington had a glossy catalogue printed, which contained a number of designs, most of which had never been built, and a seriously intentioned but entirely comic picture of what was described as the 'Flying Pennington cycle'. It showed the cycle leaping over a river complete with startled rowers in a boat beneath. The caption explained that by means of an inclined plane, the cycle had travelled 65ft with the rider able to keep his seat without trouble.

The French inventors, the Comte de Dion and Leon Bollée,

burst into laughter when Pennington handed them a copy, and de Dion challenged Pennington to repeat the stunt for a wager of the fee Lawson had paid Pennington for his patents. Pennington wisely refused. After the exhibition Lawson then installed him as a great inventor on one floor of the Motor Mills to carry out experiments, using him to dissuade the growing number of doubters amongst his investors. His machines were never a commercial success.

Duncan was one of the few experts who eventually managed to inspect a Pennington machine closely. He described it as having no carburettor and attempting to put the spark directly into the combustion chamber.

It was the clearest example of what another enthusiast at the show, S.F. Edge of the Dunlop Company described as Lawson's 'weakness'. 'Instead of making a careful study of what was proving itself successful on the Continent in competitions and concentrating on that particular design he was open to purchase the patent rights for any so-called improvement . . .

'A short trip in some motor vehicle was quite sufficient to influence him to purchase the so-called patent rights for some fabulous sum of money.'[4] Edge himself was soon to show with the successful Napier cars how differently things might be managed.

But the Institute show was a great success and Lawson followed it by organizing the first London to Brighton Run on the day the Red Flag Act was finally repealed in the following November.

Fifty-eight vehicles had been booked to start, but only 33 actually got away. Edge who kept up with the run on a bicycle described the scene:

Burners had to be lighted and starting handles swung, not once or twice but for half-an-hour or more before the engine would fire . . . mechanics not understanding a single word of our language were running about and tearing open toolbags to find spanners that they required. Engines would suddenly burst into song when drivers least expected them to do so, making a noise like a number of field guns going off. . . .

Even at the start there were a number of lame ducks. One I

recall, captained by a Frenchman, was particularly stubborn. The engine would fire for a short time; the crew would get in and tuck themselves up with rugs and then the engine would promptly stop. Several times this occurred until the driver was almost frantic with rage. My last recollection is of seeing him waving a starting-handle above his head and giving vent to what were, doubtless, the most fearful French expletives.

Of the 33 which did manage to start, no more than ten definitely finished, though nobody could agree on the number. The two first home were Bollée tricycles ridden by their inventors. It was scarcely the most convincing demonstration of the unstoppable progress of the motor car, but it was the start of the motor industry in Britain. From now on, there was incentive for British firms to build cars, a chance to test them on the roads, and at last a market for them. Lawson's attempts to restrict others by fierce legal action over patents would for a time retard progress and manufacturers would need a lot more experience before they would catch up with the reliability of both the French and the emerging Americans, but the industry could now be launched.

The Pioneers
'Hideous Noise and Wretched Dust'

The London to Brighton run on November 14 1896 had been labelled the Emancipation run. At the banquet in Brighton which followed it Lawson described it as the 'day of the great deliverance of our roads and highways from the reign of quadrupeds and the rule of – well, other animals. We are today witnessing the dawn of a great prosperity for all kinds of mechanical trades.'

But others were to be less easily persuaded. While it took the brake off the industry, and off the importers, the Locomotives on Highways Act which disposed of the Red Flag Act did not give the motorist carte blanche. There was a maximum speed limit of fourteen miles an hour, which the Local Government Board reduced to twelve miles an hour. More important, the public still needed to be persuaded of the merits of the motor-car. This was particularly difficult when its most obvious characteristics were that it was expensive, unreliable and sprayed out noise and dirt on the inadequate road surfaces, especially when driven, as it frequently was, at speeds well above those permitted by the Act. The problems of cars and roads, their speeds and effect on others were to be the subject of the 1898 Locomotive Act, the 1903 Motor Car Act and the 1904 Motor Cars Order as well as the 1905 Royal Commission on Motor Cars.

Edge wrote of 'immense public prejudice' against motor vehicles:

On more than one occasion I have had drivers of horse-drawn vehicles slash at me with their whips as I have passed them on the road. I have had stones hurled at my head and broken glass bottles deliberately placed in front of motor tricycles I have been riding . . . In driving through London, for example, one was bombarded by jeers and insults from practically every bus-driver and cab-driver one met, and this bombardment increased tenfold if a car or motor-cycle happened to need adjustment, or should break down at the roadside.

The battle between rich motorist and truculent pedestrian was pointed up by a story of Edge's return from Brighton to London on a moonlit snowy night in 1900.

Near Crawley, he was struck on the head by a piece of ice hurled by one of a group of what he called 'country yokels'. Edge braked sharply and pursued him into the middle of a field covered in snow. Confronting him, he ordered him to remove his coat, jacket, waistcoat and trousers. The man complied and Edge tucked them under his arm and strode off leaving the other 'in the middle of the field in a semi-nude condition on one of the coldest nights I can remember.' A few miles down the road Edge handed the clothes to another group to be returned to his attacker.

A view from the other side comes from a contemporary newspaper report of a speech at a Northern agricultural show which described the car in these terms. . . .

They were a hideous sort of thing and the occupants were generally dressed up in a manner more resembling monkeys than anything else. They travelled along at what they con-sidered their legal rate – he supposed 20 mph – killing and maiming men, women and children, and driving everyone else from the road with their hideous noise and wretched dust. Still farmers were obliged to contribute largely towards the cost of maintaining the roads, which these hideous things did so much to destroy.

The antagonism was to continue until the First World War. It had a distinct class flavour about it, as motoring continued to be largely the prerogative of the moneyed. In varying forms the clash of interests continues to this day.

In 1896 however, the main problem for the would-be motorist was how to get his hands on what was soon to be christened the motor car.

In 1895 the *Hardwareman* had complained that 'so sudden has been the appreciation of the possibilities of the new type of vehicle that no satisfactory English generic name has so far been adopted. In one paper we may see them vaguely referred to as horseless vehicles, in another more descriptively as "self-propel- led" carriages.' There was obviously a need, it said, for some- thing 'short, euphonious and convenient for general use . . . to this end we suggest the adoption of the word "autocar".' But it was to be the phrase 'motor car' for which Simms claimed responsibility which was ultimately to triumph.

Lawson had preferred another favourite expression when he established his Great Horseless Carriage Company. This was floated in May 1896 but only about half the £750,000 capital was subscribed. Two thirds of that was soon paid over to Lawson's British Motor Syndicate. The Company then purchased from another Lawson company, Daimler, part of the Motor Mills complex. The four storey central works building was bought for £20,000 which, according to Duncan, was more than Daimler had paid for the whole estate. He estimated Daimler made £12,000 on the deal.

Lawson had by now sold his patent for Bollée tricycles for which he had paid £20,000 to Humber. The company had started to prepare for manufacture when a fire swept through their plant consuming the prototype. Duncan was sent to France to purchase another machine plus working drawings, and once again was entangled with the excitable Leon Bollée. Lawson, characteris- tically, had still not paid the £16,000 outstanding on the original contract. Bollée refused to send another machine until he did so. Duncan was sent out with a cheque to collect the new machine. But once again Bollée let his distrust of Lawson show through. He told Duncan that he would hold him hostage until the bankers confirmed that the money had been paid. For five days, Duncan was not allowed to leave the Bollée house and his door was locked at night. Finally the money arrived and Duncan returned to Britain with a new machine whose noise he described as 'wicked' and 'worse than any machine gun'.

Lawson turned the Humber disaster to his profit. The Motor Mills building was far too big for what he could produce. So he let out the bottom floor to Humber stipulating that they should install machinery suitable for motor manufacture and leave it behind them afterwards. On the first floor he set up Pennington to do 'experimental work' while the top floor was given over to the Beeston Pneumatic Tyre Company, another Lawson creation. Manufacture was slow to start. In April 1896, the *Autocar* had talked of the Daimler company being in a position to supply motors 'of one or two types within a month'! But it was not until July that the firm was described as 'running for the actual manufacture of motors'.

In September the magazine carried a report about 'good progress' at the Great Horseless Carriage factory but the contents seemed to contradict its title. 'All the tackle has been on order for some time and is being installed as quickly as received', adding ominously, 'only those who have had to wait know what time is often wasted between the planning and execution of an order for machine tools.' In a complaint which would echo down the years, it went on: 'We regret to say it has been found considerably quicker to order, say, a milling machine from America than to wait until a British firm completes the order.'

Then when the first statutory meeting of the Great Horseless Carriage Company was held in September, the Motor Mills appeared to have been further subdivided, with both Merry-weather fire engines and Humber occupying part of the second floor and Pennington's accommodation now said to be hired by the British Motor Syndicate, the company at the centre of the Lawson patent web.

An impressive picture of the Motor Mills at lunch-time appeared in the *Autocar* and was subsequently much reproduced by Lawson in publicity material. But of the large crowd of workers, many were accounted for by other companies such as Humber, and the Beeston Tyre Company. The magazine claimed that even at this stage the industry was an important one, 'employing already over 1,000 hands.'

In October Lawson was writing to say that it would be 'impossible for a considerable time to supply the quite enormous demand that had arisen.' But ominously the same edition contained an advertisement from 'S.J.T. in Coventry' offering to sell 145 fully paid £10 shares in the company for a knockdown £1,000.

By mid-December Lawson was admitting that they did not expect to be able to place motors in any quantity until the following May or June.

Meanwhile he was responding to growing concern among shareholders and sniping from articles in journals outside his control, by giving shareholders in the British Motor Syndicate and Great Horseless Carriage Company a visit to the Motor Mills. He passed off a decline in the value of the shares to the wish of poor shareholders to make a quick profit, suggesting that the company would stabilize as it got more substantial shareholders.

Meanwhile existing subscribers were met at the Motor Mills by the great inventor Pennington who demonstrated a two horsepower engine, and then were taken to view the recently equipped Daimler factory.

The work was now said to be extending so rapidly that 'accommodation cannot be found for the workpeople engaged and many families are camping out in gipsy caravans in the fields.' Accommodation was so short that a number of other workers were being allowed to sleep in the casual wards of the workhouse.

It was heady stuff. The *Financial News*, watching the public relations trick disarm the shareholders declared, 'Verily they believe in motors and in Motor Lawson too, as far as appearances go.'

Eventually some British built vehicles began to appear, though few ever came from the Great Horseless Carriage Company. A version of the Bollée tandem was produced at a separate Coventry works, and known as the Coventry Motette. Bollée himself was brought over to advise on its production. More important, the first Daimlers appeared in the summer of 1897.

They were a primitive vehicle described as a wagonette and steered by a tiller. They were driven by two-cylinder vertical engines and developed about five and a half horsepower. Their design was a straightforward crib of the French Panhard which, of course, was built round the Daimler engine.

It was a none too ambitious start, and the company was to be dogged by financial difficulties into the twentieth century. But the cars, if crude, were effective.

So the first British-built production cars had finally appeared with imported German engines and built to a French design which had already been superseded on the Continent. The numbers were tiny; in the following year, 1898, Daimler production only amounted to about 50.

One of the first Daimlers was owned by Major General Montgomery, who lived near Winchester. A workman was sent down to show his groom how to operate it, and in August the local paper was describing the general's satisfaction as he chugged for 50 miles, a journey that took six hours.

But the car's reputation was established by two experienced publicists who had been placed on the Daimler board. Evelyn Ellis soon took the car for successful hill trials and in October Sturmey drove a Coventry-built Daimler on a 900 mile marathon from John O'Groats to Land's End, laying in stocks of fuel at strategic points and handing out publicity cards as he went. It was a tribute to the engineering skills of the manager of the new works, J.S. Critchley. Although at ten miles an hour, the journey was slow and unexciting by existing standards on the Continent, it had established the Daimler marque.

Sturmey soon took over from Lawson as chairman, as the financier now saw better opportunities elsewhere. By now his hopes of huge profits were concentrated more on licence royalties than on manufacturing. The Great Horseless Carriage Company was to be wound up in 1898. In the meantime his office at 40 Holborn Viaduct on the edge of the City of London was the centre of patent activity.

A contemporary, St John Nixon, described it as a 'Tom-tiddler's ground for every charlatan in Europe'. Amongst those who offered their inventions was a watchmaker whose vehicle would have been powered by a huge clock spring, which would have had to be rewound every fifty yards. The Syndicate turned him down.

Meanwhile it defended its own patents vigorously. In October 1898, as Emancipation beckoned, Lawson had written to the *Autocar* that as it would be impossible to supply the enormous demand that had arisen for motor-carriages, the Syndicate was 'prepared for twelve months to give to individuals desirous of purchasing foreign-made motor vehicles a licence on payment of a royalty of £10 per cent on the purchase price.' More threateningly, he warned that 'owners of any unauthorized motor cars' would have the company's patent rights enforced against them 'with all the resources at our command.'

What that meant was that even French cars made under French patents with Daimler engines were to be regarded as somehow under the control of the Syndicate.

One of the first victims was the Hon. Charles Rolls, a younger son of Lord Llangattock who was to give his name to the most famous English car of all. Rolls, an avid enthusiast, had brought in a Peugeot from France. Lawson and the Syndicate, trying to maintain that both Peugeots and Panhard–Levassor cars were covered by their patents, threatened proceedings.

Rolls, who had previously written to Lawson asking who represented Peugeot and had failed to get a reply, paid over £15 for a perpetual licence. He was then outraged to find his name being used in Syndicate propaganda which suggested that he had been ordered to pay damages. In a pained letter he insisted that he had not been 'inclined to incur the trouble and expense of disputing the validity of their patents (which were therefore not "upheld")'.

The problem of patents also affected other founders of the industry. In 1895, a certain Herbert Austin of the Wolseley Sheep Shearing Machine Company who had already shown his talents for innovation by establishing a number of patents for the company's machinery, turned his hand to building a motor car. It was a slack period at the works which was diversifying into machine tools and bicycle parts to keep going.

He went over to inspect French vehicles but thought them too heavy and clumsy with the exception of the Bollée.

On his return he set out to build a similar three wheel model but adapted it in an attempt to compensate for its famous noisiness and ill-balance. Asked later why he had chosen a three wheeler and not something more substantial, he said it was 'because it was simpler.' Austin was, however, conscious of the brooding shadow of Lawson's patent threats, and never attempted commercial manufacture of his first design.

But by the end of 1896 he had a second car ready to exhibit at the National Cycle Exhibition at the Crystal Palace. The Christmas edition of the *Engineer* described it as being 'in the form of a dogcart, the seating being arranged for two people back to back. It has three wheels, the one steering wheel in front being similar to that of a bath chair. The engine is arranged in the body of the car under the seats and is entirely hidden from view by light wooden panels which are lined with thin sheet iron to prevent the oil soaking into the wood.' The price was £100 or, for a four-seater, £150.

Herbert Austin was to be the most enduring figure of the industry's history, still actively involved in the firm which bore his name until his death in 1941. A gruff, severe-looking man with a reputation for obstinacy, he lived for engineering, fascinated alike by his cars and the machine processes for making them. In his autobiography, John Moore-Brabazon, later Lord Brabazon, described his first impression of Austin in the very early days: 'His dark clothes and bowler hat, his brusqueness and inability to suffer fools gladly, his directness and the patent fact that stood out – that he was a mechanic, nothing more nor less.'

Even at the weekend he could not keep away from his factory, and on weekdays he would prowl round the drawing office inspecting designs before the draughtsmen arrived.

Early pictures of Austin with his rudimentary cars have a slight flavour of Laurel and Hardy films, perhaps because of the way he wore a bowler pushed to the back of his head. It was his trademark – he was never seen in the factory without a hat, though on occasions it could be a grey trilby or, in hot weather, a panama. There was little amusing about him; he rarely smiled his dry smile, and the most fun the works got out of him was one day when he walked down the production line past the men in pits painting exhaust pipes, in the company of a French woman friend and her black poodle. When they reached the end of the line, the dog's private parts were painted a tactful silver.

One of his supervisors described him as 'brusque but very well-respected and a hardworking chap.' Freddie Henry, the chairman of the Austin ex-Apprentices, who went onto the company's central staff, was one of the few to penetrate the Austin family circle where he says, 'he was quite different, just like any other family man. Certainly he had determined ideas, but if you could prove he was wrong he was fine.'

Austin managed to remain on good terms with both com-

petitors and his staff, which was not the case with contemporaries
such as William Morris. Henry's first sight of him was on one of
his typical rapid walks through the factory, bowler pushed back,
staff fluttering to keep up. 'He hadn't time for idle talk; he just
rushed from one job to another.'

'I was working in the machine shop where Drummonds of
Guildford were installing a crank shaft turning machine when the
old man suddenly appeared as he usually did when there was any
interesting machinery about. He jumped up on the platform and
pushed off the man from Drummonds and started to operate it
himself. Then he dashed off at high speed.'

Austin was a punctilious attender at the apprentices' annual
dinner at the Birmingham Grand Hotel, but was obviously bored
by the popular entertainers hired to cheer the company, doodling
mechanical diagrams on his programme instead. But Henry
remembers, 'One day we had a fellow who did conjuring tricks;
he did these rings and the old man suddenly looked up and was
interested. It was a mechanical problem you see. The conjuror
walked up to him and Austin did the trick in about two seconds.'

Austin was never off duty, whether sitting at his desk looking
out at the gate of Longbridge, the top of his bald head just visible
to those arriving, or on business in London. Again Henry recalls,
'I was once in a taxi with him to the RAC Club. The commis-
sionaire always used to pay the fare because the old man never
carried much cash. As he left, he said, "You need your shock
absorbers adjusting." ' His dedication was to carry him through
for nearly half a century as a leader of the industry.

Austin's experience was typical of what was to be the first wave
of indigenous British motor manufacturers. They took their
inspiration from Continental models and often a good many of
their parts, and they built their cars as adjuncts to existing
businesses. These varied from relatively unsophisticated cycle
assembly to, in the case of Henry Royce, electric crane manufacture, to technically advanced engineering such as engine
manufacture on which successful early companies like Napier,
Crossley or Vauxhall were already engaged.

But at the beginning they were only a sideshow, a makeweight
and useful diversion when business was slack elsewhere. Austin,
for example, found himself having to build his cars largely at the

weekend. Wolseley, which was to be the most prolific manufacturer before the First World War, was not to split off until
1901.

The most inventive of the early British pioneers was Frederick
Lanchester, the first and one of the only Englishmen to have
made a major contribution to automotive design. Lanchester had
been at the Royal College of Science and then, in 1889, he became
assistant works manager at the Forward Gas Engine Company in
Birmingham. The company made gas engines on the model
developed by Otto in Germany, a successful engine from which
Otto developed an oil engine which, in turn, became the basis of
the petrol fired internal combustion engine.

Lanchester early showed his inventiveness, patenting a
pendulum governor in 1889 and announcing in the *Autocar* in
November 1895 a patent for 'improvements in the driving
mechanism of motor vehicles'. By now he was launched into
what was his first car designed 'from first principles' and built
with £700 provided for development by James and Allen Whit-
field. It was a big sum, the equivalent of the combined annual
incomes of the eight men he was soon to employ in his first
factory.

It was a full-scale four-wheeled car, not a tricycle like those
built by Bollée or Austin or Knight's primitive attempt. It had
electric ignition which was rare and unreliable in those days when
the proven Daimler engine employed a platinum hot tube system
which required the 'chauffeur' to warm it first with a separate gas
burner. Later Lanchester was to pioneer disc brakes and a live axle
drive which replaced the primitive chain drive generally used.

Lanchester was not pleased with his first car, although it ran
continuously for 68 miles. Later he was to say that all the early
pioneers had 'underestimated both the speed at which cars could
be driven and the power required.'

It had cost about £1,200 to develop, money met again by the
Whitfields. He was faced with finding another £1,400 for buildings and plant. Again the Whitfields put up the money.

He set up a workshop with his brother George as chief assistant
and employed eight men in a galvanized iron shed. His annual
outgoings were between £1,000 and £1,200, of which over half
went on wages.

Lanchester, later nicknamed 'Doctor Fred', was, like many of the engineers who founded motor companies, a quiet man fascinated by the technical challenges of design and production but temperamentally badly equipped to run a big firm. He relied heavily on his brother George to manage the business and in 1909 he abandoned the firm which bore his name to become the chief engineer of Daimler.

His restless mind was always searching for new problems to solve. By the First World War he was to devote himself not merely to the design of aero-engines – an obvious development – but to drawing up elaborate military strategies for the fledgling RAF, the Royal Flying Corps. While other pioneer motor-makers became engrossed in business policies, Lanchester most determinedly stuck to his role as a creative thinker.

By 1899 Lanchester had registered ten British and twenty foreign patents; he had rebuilt his 1895 car and made two others, one of which was to be the surprise of the 1899 show at Richmond.

This was organized by the Automobile Club, the ancestor of today's RAC, which had been set up by Frederick Simms in 1897. He had by now broken with Lawson, resigning as consulting engineer to the Daimler Company. He had been worried about the obvious hucksterism of the old Motor Car Club which Lawson had established in his own office and for which he had even designed a uniform. (It was a dark blue serge suit with gold braid, topped off with a white-topped navy cap. Bollée, highly amused, described it as like a Swiss Admiral's). Simms had withdrawn and set up instead the Automobile Club with offices in two rooms at Whitehall Court. He proposed to bear the cost himself and installed an old colleague, Charles Harrington Moore. Lawson still badgered them to do deals. In October 1897, Moore wrote an anguished letter to Simms about Lawson's latest plans to bring together 'all the hostile parties', and a 'large amalgamation in which all his companies and later on the Daimler, would join'. 'My impression,' wrote Moore, 'is that I would personally much prefer to steer clear of Mr Lawson and all his schemes.'

The awards for the 1899 Automobile Club Show included gold medals for the Daimler Motor Company, the Delahaye Motor

Carriage Company and what was described as a three seater Phaeton made by F.W. Lanchester. 'This carriage,' the programme said, 'exhibited many novel features and a wider departure from stereo-typed forms than any other vehicle shown. The working of this carriage was smooth and quiet, largely due to the use of the worm-gear and absence of chain-gear. The workmanship throughout is of a very high class and although the consumption of petrol was not so low as by other carriages of even larger size, its excellent performance, the absence of water cooling, the novelty of its leading features and the possibility of their further development led the judges to award it a gold medal.' The industry had found a winner, but was scarcely in the position to exploit it.

In spite of the success of its products the Daimler Company, the first manufacturer, was perpetually teetering on the brink of disaster. By the end of 1898 a committee of shareholders had reported that the directors were incompetent and that the £40,000 paid to Lawson for the patents was 'excessive'. Its report was rejected and the company staggered on to record a surplus of £1,045 in fifteen months' trading to the end of 1899. It had cut back so much on its few skilled men that when orders had picked up in the spring it had had difficulty in meeting them. Its principal success had been the production of its first light car designed by its works manager, Critchley, to make use of 50 imported Daimler engines of four horsepower for which there had been no previous use.

But if these were the problems of an established company, Lanchester was eloquent on the problems of starting from scratch.

The difficulties of management were very great, partly owing to the fact that no ancillary trades had then developed, and we had to do everything ourselves – chassis, magneto, wheels, bodywork etc., everything except the tyres. Moreover for many purposes I had personally to train my labour.[1]

Worse still for the industry at large, there was still no agreement about some of the most basic design questions. Should it be steering wheels or tillers, water or air cooling, electric or hot tube ignition, solid or pneumatic tyres, even steam or petrol engines?

They were questions endlessly debated by the enthusiasts, and in 1899 Alfred Harmsworth, who had just started the *Daily Mail* and was a keen motorist, proposed a thousand mile endurance run from London to Edinburgh and back; its purpose to test vehicles and to publicize them. As one of the participants, the journalist St John Nixon, wrote 'At the end of 1899 the industry was highly unstable, hundreds of thousands of people had still to see a motor car for the first time in their lives.'

However, by the end of the run in 1900 he could say, 'It was the means of deciding many points of design. Tube ignition received its *coup de grace*; as did tiller steering. Water cooling became universal and the necessity of improving pneumatic tyres rather than extending the use of solids became apparent.'[2]

Thirteen out of thirteen Daimlers finished, and the company's pride swelled further when later in the year the Prince of Wales ordered a two cylinder six horsepower model. The year brought a profit of £4,430.

For Wolseley and Austin it was even more of a breakthrough. The car driven by Austin himself won the first prize in the B Class. It completed the rally with only two replacement parts needed – a new bell and a new wire to the carburettor.

It was the first four-wheel car Austin had built and its success opened the way for the company's expansion. The American, Sir Hiram Maxim, inventor of the famous machine-gun, was on the board of the big Vickers armaments company. A motoring enthusiast, he had used Wolseley for the construction of parts for a folly – a huge steampowered flying machine. Now he persuaded Vickers to put up the money to register a separate company, the Wolseley Tool and Motor Car Company Ltd. with Austin as general manager. It was the only case of one of the huge industrial combines of the period backing the motor business. It did not delight Vickers; Austin was to be scandalized after hearing the company secretary of Vickers complain later that Wolseley's 'had not pulled up any trees.'

The new company offered two cars. They were basic models and extras had to be paid for. Like all cars of the period their brakes only prevented them rolling forward. To stop them rolling backwards downhill, a sprag had to be fitted and that cost extra. The five horsepower Phaeton cost £270; the ten horse-power Tonneau £380.

Progress was slow. The company's first ten months saw a loss of over five thousand pounds; about a quarter of its entire turnover. Profits were made in 1902 and 1903 but for the next five years the company ran at a loss. Austin was partly to blame. He had insisted on sticking with horizontal engines, and after refusing to change the policy he left in 1905.

Austin then started up his own company with the help of a cavalry officer, Frank Kayser, who put in £4,000 to augment Austin's money and patents.

The Austin Motor Company was just one of a huge number of companies which sprang up between 1901 and 1905. By one estimate there were as many as 221.[3] Few survived, as engineers' enthusiasm was rarely matched by hard-headed commercial judgement. Austin was one of the few to last. By 1914 it was estimated that almost two hundred companies had gone to the wall. Most of the companies were built round imported parts. In particular de Dion and Aster engines were brought in from France while another French firm, Lacoste and Battmann exported a small chassis to various British agents.

The enthusiasm for the products of the infant industry can be judged by the letters from all over the country which poured into just one small company, the Yorkshire Motor Company, which had been established in Bradford in 1897. Its founder, Reginald Jackson, produced a doctor's car which was made by a local cycle dealer.

The car was advertised in June 1899 in small sixteen-page brochures with a tear-off back cover for placing an order along with £5 deposit on the £140 vehicle. They explained why the car was directed at medical men.

> There is no class of men who are more anxious to use motor-cars when the right one is found and so do away with the expenses and worry of horse-keeping and we know that when we have produced a car which shall meet the needs of the doctor, we shall also have one which will appeal to the large number of persons of all classes who desire a pleasure or

business carriage and who yet cannot afford the continual
expenses of horses.

The economy of the car was such, the brochure stated, that
'renewals and wear and tear should not be more than the upkeep
of the horse-drawn carriage and the shoeing of the horse' with the
result that 'the cost of stabling, of veterinary fees, of fodder and
seven eighths of the horse's feed are all saved.'

From the middle of June 1899, letters were coming in at the rate
of three or four a day. But when the firm got into its stride in 1900
it could only produce one car every three weeks.

One of the first enquiries on June 15, 1899 came from one K.D.
Wadia of the Bombay Cycle Agency enquiring about the terms
of an agency for India. Other agents from up and down the
country and even from St Petersburg were among the corres-
pondents. There was a letter from Isaac Silverthorne of The
London Horse Agency, 36 Cambridge Street, Hyde Park. He
explained that after being in the horse business for 30 years trade
had now fallen off greatly owing to the motor coming in and he
was therefore intending to change to a motor agency. On June
19th H. Sanford-Burton of Cornmarket, Oxford, was asking for
details and enquiring whether the company would take his
MMC tricycle (a Lawson relic) in part exchange. On July 7th,
Mr C.J. Brooks, an estate manager, wanted to know whether he
could drive a Jackson car with an artificial leg.

On this wave of excitement the Yorkshire Motor Company
expanded, taking in premises in Halifax and Hipperholme, but it
died in its infancy in 1901. However, among the more lusty
infants were many future household names.

In 1899 the cycle makers, Sunbeam and Humber, turned their
energies to motor car manufacture. Sunbeam produced its first
car for sale in 1902. Humber had had the misfortune of being
saddled with the Pennington patents by Lawson but exhibited its
first four-wheel car based on a de Dion engine in 1899. After the
company was reconstructed in 1900, breaking with the Lawson
connection, it began to produce a light car, the Humberette,
which proved very popular.

In 1902 the first car was built by the Vauxhall Iron Works
company which had been making marine engines on the banks of

the Thames since 1857 at Vauxhall. Designed by F.W. Hodges and J.H. Chambers, the five horsepower production model was described by the *Autocar* as a 'neat effect and cheap'. The same year also brought the first quadricycle from the Guildford firm of Dennis. Its founder John Dennis had again been a small-time cycle maker after starting out as an ironmonger. His early vehicles were built round a de Dion engine. When he moved up to a fully-fledged four-wheel car in 1904, he pulled in £30,000 of orders at the Crystal Palace Show.

In 1903 the Manchester firm of Crossley Brothers which built oil engines produced its first car, designed by J.S. Critchley, the first general manager of the Daimler company who had resigned in the face of the company's in-fighting. The same year saw the birth of the specialist A.C. company with an engineer, John Weller, producing the car and a butcher, called Portwine, putting up the money.

The most significant arrival however was to be Standard. It was started by R.W. Maudslay who had followed a public school education with an engineering apprenticeship constructing docks. His idea, which gave rise to the name, was to build a cheap car using standard parts, an almost revolutionary concept in an industry of custom-built vehicles.

In 1904 the venerable Rover Cycle Company created an eight horsepower single cylinder car which became the basis of one of the most successful and reliable pre-war light cars. In the same year, an American, Wilbur Gunn, who had come to Britain to be an opera singer, built the first Lagonda at Staines, naming it after a creek in the American mid-West.

But the biggest event of the year was the production of the first three cars by the electrical engineer, Henry Royce, in Manchester. The ten horsepower car greatly impressed the enthusiast Charles Rolls. Rolls had won the 1,000 miles run on a Panhard and had been patriotically looking for a British car to add to his agency for Panhard and Minerva imports. On December 23, 1904 an agreement was signed whereby Royce would supply Rolls with four different models – the two cylinder ten horsepower car of the type already made, a fifteen horsepower three cylinder, a twenty horsepower four cylinder and a six cylinder version producing thirty horsepower which would sell at £890, more than double the price of the smallest car, which cost £395. The key features of the deal were that Rolls guaranteed to take Royce's entire production, and that the cars would all be called Rolls-Royce.

It was an unlikely partnership. Royce, the awkward genius, was the son of an impoverished Lincolnshire miller who moved to London and died when the boy was nine. The young Royce missed school to work as a newspaper and a telegraph boy to support a family so short of money that some days his only food was bread soaked in milk, starting a pattern of malnutrition which was to stay with him.

At fourteen he was apprenticed to the Peterborough works of the Great Northern Railway, staying with the father of a fellow-apprentice who taught them painstaking skills on a lathe in his garden-shed.

But once again lack of money forced Royce to leave and to tramp the country for better paid work. He ended up working long hours in a Leeds toolmakers. His break came when he got a job in the infant electrical industry, eventually setting up his own firm in Manchester.

Royce, addressed by his workers as 'Pa', was an obsessive, awkward man living only for his work – lodging above his workshop, sometimes working through the night as he started on his own. As the business grew, he refused to move into an office, working from a table in the workshop, subsisting on an erratic diet of sandwiches and sausages cooked on the works boiler, while his worried foreman sent apprentices to chase him with glasses of milk.

His cars reaped the benefits of his obsession, testing and re-testing every engine part, concentrating on silence and smooth running, exploding at a mechanic who announced that something was 'good enough' and demanding, 'Who is the author of this sinker?' if he found a component too heavy. He worked impossibly long hours, demanding the same from his workers.

Even after success, life remained painful – serious illness and an unpleasant colostomy operation – and for the last twenty years of his life he was kept away from the factory, designing in far away Sussex under the care of nurses, and still measuring everything by how silent it was.

By contrast, the aristocratic Charles Rolls was born with a

silver spoon in his mouth – the epitome of the gallant, gilded
youth of Edwardian times; a charmer who could commend his
cars to his personal friends amongst the senior officers and smart
society set of early twentieth century London. The first undergraduate with a car at Cambridge, he was described by S.F.
Edge as 'an exceedingly nice fellow and a great sportsman, an
excellent racing driver though rather reckless'. He shared with
Royce a fascination for tinkering with engines, but his thirst for
new experience early took him away from motor-cars to
aeroplanes.

He first flew, naturally, with none other than Wilbur Wright,
and became the first man to fly the channel consecutively in both
directions. He expressed his delight like this: 'After experience
with every form of locomotion including cycling and motor-
racing, a voyage in a dirigible balloon of the French army and
over 130 trips in an ordinary balloon, there is nothing so
exhilarating as flying . . . it gives one an entirely new sense of
life.' On July 12, 1910 it cost Rolls his life; attempting too abrupt
a manoeuvre for the experimental tailplane he had fitted, he was
killed when his aircraft crashed. But by that time the odd couple's
names were inseparably linked in a title which had become a
synonym for excellence the world over.

By now the industry was at last free of the shadow of patents
controversy. The Lawson empire, now flying the banner of the
British Motor Traction Company, had been attempting to
enforce them in a reckless way, in some cases trying to charge
royalties which were more than the cost of the item itself. For
example it attempted to take ten per cent of the cost of a car
(which could be as much as £40) on the basis of the patent on a
carburettor developed by Gottlieb Daimler's engineer,
Maybach, which cost only two pounds. An Automobilists'
Mutual Protection Association was formed to fight patent cases,
and in July 1901 Charles Friswell took the Lawson British Motor
Traction Company to court over the Maybach carburettor and
won. He did so with publicity worthy of the old promoter
himself, taking advertisements in advance in the papers declaring, 'Wait until Friswell fights the British Motor Traction Company. One spot on a lump of sugar will kill an elephant; Friswell
has a barrowful.' It was the end for the Lawson scheme. In 1907

all remaining patent rights were sold for a thousand pounds, a far cry from the million pound flotation a decade before.

The demand for cars was spiralling. In the first eight months of 1904 the huge number of 4,662 cars and chassis had been imported from abroad – which the British makers could not match. In 1906, the Royal Commission on Motor Cars reported that by May of that year the number of cars on the road had increased by 80 per cent in sixteen months, to 44,908. It estimated that the capital invested in the industry had reached £5 million by October 1905, 'since greatly increased' while the 'hands therein employed' numbered 17,000.

There had, it said, been 'a great advance in the use of motor cars for trade purposes such as the carrying of goods in light vans or heavy lorries and for professional purposes, e.g. by medical men and by surveyors and public officials whose duties include the inspection of large districts. Moreover horses have rapidly become familiarized with cars in places where they are much used and it may fairly be said that in London and its neighbourhood, motor cars and even the noisy omnibuses have ceased to be a special cause of alarm to the horse-drawn traffic.' By 1907 nearly a third of the Fleet Street omnibuses were to be motor-driven.

Doctors were particularly good customers. The secretary of a committee of doctors using motor cars gave evidence to the commission. Estimating a doctor's net annual income at £300, he suggested that it cost £50 a year to run a car compared with £100 for a horse and trap, although that appeared to exclude wear and tear.

The way the industry had developed may be illustrated by the contrasting fortunes of two of the major pre-First World War carmakers, neither of whom were to last much beyond the end of the war.

As London manager of the Dunlop Pneumatic Tyre Company, S.F. Edge was well placed to be one of the early enthusiasts. Pedalling his bicycle among the starters in the London to Brighton run; travelling to Paris to get his first ride on an automobile; he had arranged with Lawson to test the various patent machines which were stored in the basement of his offices.

Almost every weekend and in the evenings, he and Charles Jarrott, who, like Edge, was to become one of the early racing drivers, tinkered with the machines, covering themselves in grime. A six horsepower Panhard which had come second in the 1896 Paris–Marseilles race, one of a series of contests in which continental manufacturers were honing their designs, particularly interested Edge. Buying a used car from Lawson he inevitably had to pay a high price. But the plan was to use it as a test bed for his ideas of improving performance.

Edge then approached Montague Napier, an old cycling rival with a family business making precision weighing machines in Lambeth in London. He found he was already attempting to build his own car but Napier agreed to modify the Panhard by fitting first a steering wheel and then a radiator. Then came the crucial breakthrough. To Edge's delight, Napier suggested a new engine design, which proved highly successful.

Edge then persuaded his boss, Arthur du Cros, to put up the money to establish a company to distribute Napier cars, prudently linking it with an agency for two French makes, Clement–Panhard and Gladiator. It was this arrangement with agent and manufacturer closely linked which was to be copied by Rolls and Royce.

The deal was made in 1900. Edge guaranteed to take all Napier production and 396 cars were to be delivered by 1904. The principal model was to be a sixteen horsepower four cylinder car. Edge called the new company The Motor Vehicle Company and was soon receiving orders. He stated: 'The small car-purchasing public which then existed seemed to be impressed with the object of the new company, i.e. to build a British car which would not only bear comparison with the best the Continent could produce, but, as we hoped, would turn out to be a considerable improvement thereon.'

Within days of being completed the car came second in the thousand miles' run of 1900.

Edge left a revealing description of the conditions at the time:

With electric ignition, the car ran on one battery and a second one was carried as a spare, which meant disconnecting the terminals from the exhausted battery and fitting them to the spare one. It was also common to find that by some mysterious means the spare one had exhausted itself when it was most needed. The driving chains ran in a constant bath of grit, mud and water, as they were unprotected.

The slightest incline, unless it could be 'rushed' meant a change of gear and to miss one's gear on a steep hill nearly always resulted in the car running backwards as brakes would only operate in a forward position. They consisted of nothing more substantial than a brass brake-drum attached to the rear sprocket, round which was wound some wire rope, with numbers of wooden blocks attached to it, which rubbed against the drum when the brake lever was applied.[4]

This success was followed by the first British victory in a Continental road race, in the 1902 Gordon Bennett race. The races had been started by an American newspaper magnate, James Gordon Bennett. They were to be contested by national teams each entering three cars, which had to be constructed entirely from components made in that country. Britain, of course, had been unable to take part. But Edge and Napier resolved to change this, seeing it as the only way to prove their cars' merits against foreign competition.

In 1901 a huge 50 horsepower Napier had been prepared for the race, but it was scratched when it became clear its tyres would not stand the wear. The following year, a modified version came in first after its last rival, a French car, broke down on the final stage.

Britain never again won the race, but it made the reputation of Napier. It was to vie with Rolls-Royce as a well-engineered high performance motor.

By 1904 Napier were employing 500 men at a new factory in West London and had launched the first successful six-cylinder engine, and were styling their cars – 'The best car in the world'. A contemporary report in 1906 stated: 'The man of moderate means is not the class of client for whom the Napier motor is intended. It is essentially a rich man's luxury.' Prices for chassis only started at seven or eight hundred pounds, over twice a doctor's annual salary, and a succession of clients which included Dukes, generals, Indian princes and politicians like Arthur Balfour and Winston Churchill were invited to visit the works and 'see the cars in every stage of construction', and no doubt increase the price by custom-made additions.

Napier increased their profits by building taxis, a thousand in 1909 and 1910 and later on they added a small car to their range as the popularity of smaller vehicles increased with growing affluence and the introduction of horsepower tax in the 1909 Budget.

By contrast an attempt to establish a mass market car came from a company which was briefly to claim to be the largest manufacturing unit in Europe. This was the Argyll company of Scotland.

The Scots had been active early in the history of the industry. George Johnston had driven his own car through the streets of Glasgow by night in 1895, later establishing the Arrol-Johnston Company.

In 1896 the *Financial Times* had complained that members of the Civil and Mechanical Engineers Institute had had 'sent up with their ham and eggs' a prospectus headed 'Autocars' which invited members to subscribe towards the £150,000 capital of a new company. It had come from an address in St Vincent Street, Glasgow, which the paper thought 'more suggestive of church-going on foot' than 'the speculative excursions of the autocar'.

In 1899 one Alexander Govan of the Scotland Cycle Manufacturing Company in Hozier Street, Glasgow, built a small motor car described as 'not the cycle-type nor yet the highly powered car, but a neat moderate powered carriage.' It was enough to convince Warren Smith of the National Telegraph Company who put up the money to form the Hozier Engineering Company to manufacture the vehicle which he called Argyll.

The first Argylls used a small two-and-three-quarter horsepower imported de Dion engine and had a difficult system of steering – a horizontal bar. One early customer, a Mr G. W. Cox of Southsea, made three attempts to drive his car back from the dealer in London. The third time, he took a corner too fast for the vehicle and tore both tyres off the back wheels. The car completed its journey by train being manhandled on its side into the guard's van.

Nonetheless the company prospered. In 1902 its car was described as 'meeting the demand for a light, serviceable car for clients who do not wish to retain mechanics.' By 1903 there was a choice of three 8 horsepower engines and two, three and four cylinder propulsion.

By 1904 production workers, including a night shift were at full stretch producing fifteen cars a week. An Argyll appropriately broke the John O'Groats to Land's End record.

The company seemed on the edge of a breakthrough. In 1905 Govan gave evidence to the Royal Commission about the new factory they were building at Alexandria, sixteen miles from Glasgow: 'We have spent just about £220,000 in putting down buildings and plant and we will employ certainly not less than 2,000 men. At the present time we have about 350 employed there and making parts, but the buildings are only just being erected.' Already, he claimed, there were orders for 1,500 cars in the following year worth about £400,000.

This was at a time when the infant industry was struggling to match foreign imports yet Govan could say, when asked whether foreign competition was severe, 'Yes, but I could not ever say we have felt it because we have never been able to supply the demand.' As for his component parts however, he agreed most had to be imported. He depended particularly on French engine cylinders because he had not been able to get British ones which were more than 75 per cent reliable.

He described his experience like this:

In the early days, we had any quantity of trouble. We had axles breaking, wheels breaking, gears wearing out too quickly, and cylinders cracking. In fact we had everything going wrong with the car which could possibly go wrong with any make and it has only been by gradually overcoming the difficulties one by one that we believe now we have a vehicle – I am speaking generally of motor cars and not only our own – which is practically perfect.

Argyll did not stint themselves on the new factory, particularly when you compare Napier's investment in Acton, which, at £32,000, was a fraction of the cost. Opened by Lord Montague of Beaulieu on June 26th, 1906 the offices had marble floors and staircase and were topped by three gold-leafed domes. For the workers there were 500 washbasins with hot and cold water and clean towels provided.

There was even a poem composed by one Fred Gillet.

'Motor Mary of Argyll,
in thy home among the Highlands,
in the new ancestral halls,
where the staircase can outmarble
even Pall Mall clubhouse walls,
I have gazed upon thy workshops
and thy silent golden domes.'

But it could not last.

In 1906, the company produced 800 cars, an increase, but only half the number Govan had claimed as ordered. By 1907 it was offering five models and 25 styles and received the Royal Warrant of the King of Spain. But in the summer, Govan died and the slump of 1908 combined with the company's over-ambition to bring it down. It went into voluntary liquidation and 1,500 men were sacked.

Argyll was reconstructed the following year and by 1913 was back in reasonable production, producing 600 cars in a year. But in 1914 it finally collapsed with debts of £80,000.

The failure of Argyll demonstrated clearly the hopelessly un-commercial methods of many early British manufacturers. While what were effectively one-off designs could be built for the wealthier at the top end of the market by companies like Napier provided they kept their reputation, the proliferation of models and lack of standardization at medium car level sealed the fate of many companies.

Amongst the Argyll apprentices had been Harry Ferguson, who was to develop a successful tractor, and J.L. Baird, the inventor of television. Another, J.P. Christian, provided this account of the methods the firm used:

The chassis frame was brought to the erecting shop and fitted with springs and front axle. Both the gearbox and rear axle were built in their own departments and run in under power, tested and adjusted and then sent down to the chassis. Steering columns (brass plated by hand with sheets of brass 'wrapped' round the column) and boxes were assembled . . . the engine was hand-built (even the oil grooves in the bearings were cut by hand with home-made chisels) and was tested in the engine test shop and then stripped down, adjusted and reassembled before being fitted on the chassis. The car was than run on a test track and given a hundred mile test drive.

The body which was to be fitted had previously been upholstered with leather and horsehair and had been given 30 to 35 coats of paint and varnish, and the car was then carefully polished ready for delivery.

The same rigid inspection took place at every stage of all parts made in the factory and there was no doubt that the car was genuine value. Too much so perhaps . . .[5]

Argyll was only an exaggerated example of the general situation prevailing among British motor manufacturers at the end of their first decade. They were still far behind the Continental manufacturers and depended heavily on them. It was to be left to another foreign car maker, this time American, to show them the way forward.

Mass Production
'Sell it and Buy a Ford'

The American motor industry had been slow off the mark, although not as slow as the British. Its early years were hampered, however, by an attempt to corner the patents as Lawson had done in Britain. It was not until 1906 that American production exceeded that of France.

But what the Americans provided, almost from the start, was a different way of doing things; one which allowed for much more standardization and for component manufacture to be extensively farmed out to sub-contractors. In part this was because of the patterns which already existed in American engineering; in part, for men like Henry Ford, it was a necessity due to lack of capital; in part it was due to a cast of mind which looked for the simplest way of doing things and a concern for production engineering which throughout the twentieth century was to single out American manufacturers.

Among the first American cars to appear in Britain were those made by the Duryea Brothers. Sturmey of the *Autocar* had visited them in 1899, securing the distribution rights in 1902 and following that by opening a small factory to manufacture in Coventry. Engines and other parts were made by the firm of Willans and Robinson in Rugby.

The Duryeas were medium sized to large cars, from fifteen horsepower upwards. The 'colonial carriage' sold for £425. At the 1904 motor show however the company placed a new advertisement. 'If you can't afford a Duryea, GET A FORD – two cylinders eight horsepower, £195.' It was the first appearance of the company which would dominate the British industry.

The *Motor* commented:

There will be a light two-seated Ford car with which the (Duryea) company hope to attract the 'man of moderate means'. This car, although making its appearance for the first time in England, is widely known in America where it has accomplished some sensational speed performances, and we shall be very much surprised if it does not make many friends on this side of the water.

The car was a Model A, first made in the United States in 1903. Soon the Central Motor Car Company was being formed to sell Fords, including the new ten horsepower Model C, with the selling point that it 'starts from seat' with a starting handle located on the outside of the car so the driver could reach it.

In 1904, the new company took on as a technical advisor, and then manager, the 26 year old Percival Perry, a man who was to be as important to the British motor industry as his contemporaries Austin and Morris.

Perry was another from the Lawson circle. He came from Birmingham and had been a solicitor's clerk when he saw an advertisement in the *Birmingham Post* for a young man who was 'willing to do hard and useful work, drudgery, if necessary' in a London office for £1 a week. He bought a cheap ticket to London, supposedly selling his stamp collection to find the ready cash, and found himself working in Lawson's office. He made the most of the experience, returning to the Midlands to work for a Coventry engineering firm and getting to know the business so well that the new Central Company called him in as a technical expert to give an opinion on the new Fords.

Percival Perry, later Lord Perry, was to be the founder of Ford's manufacturing operations in Europe, a personal friend of Henry Ford, summoned back to save the company in the 1920s when American management failed. His guiding hand was to set it on course to be the most successful British-based motor manufacturer.

In his youth Perry was known for a liking for bright socks and champagne – a contrast to some of the glummer British motor engineers; by the end of his life he was writing improving pamphlets with titles like 'How many beans make five?' with homilies about the philosophy of work akin to the sententious

The four-page broadsheet issued to entice investors into the British Motor Syndicate – its purpose to own the patents of every kind of motor vehicle in Britain. The vehicles illustrated were mostly imaginary.

Harry J. Lawson and his wife in Brighton on the day after the 1896 Emancipation run. Lawson is wearing the uniform he invented for the Motor Car Club, unkindly described as being like 'a Swiss Admiral's'.

The Coventry Motor Mills – centre of Lawson's erratic attempts at manufacture. The first British motor-car factory.

The Rootes Group started as motor dealers, only later buying factories. This was where they began in Kent.

The first British production car. The 1897 Daimler built at Coventry was a version of the crude early German Daimlers; already superseded by more sophisticated versions when it was built. In the driving seat is Evelyn Ellis, one of the first to import a car into Britain. Second from left is Wilhelm Maybach, a German engineer who came from the Daimler factory in Stuttgart. The works manager, J.S. Critchley, stands at the front.

Another early production vehicle was the Coventry motette based on a French patent by Leon Bollée. It is advertised in the Diamond Jubilee procession for Queen Victoria in 1897 in Coventry where it was built. The clown is Percival, later Lord, Perry who set up Ford's operations in Britain.

S.F. Edge in the 1901 Napier. Intended for the international Gordon Bennett race, it was so powerful that no British-made tyres could stand the pace, and it had to scratch from the race. French tyres were fitted.

Frederick Lanchester, the most inventive of the English pioneers in the car which won the gold medal in the 1899 Richmond show. His brother George is nearest the camera.

Henry Ford. In between he was twice called on to sort out government production in two world wars, and developed a willingness to devolve responsibility, which was rare among the motor magnates in Britain who designed their own cars like Austin or Morris.

In the early years, a Ford manager spent fifteen minutes explaining to Perry just how a new plant would be laid out, when he felt a hand on his shoulder, 'Haselden, I thought you were building this place, you are responsible, not me. There is only one thing I want to know – is that what you want to do the job I asked you – are you satisfied with it ?" ' In the Second World War, a production manager was turning out Ford tractors when he received a telephone call asking if he made a vehicle for a particular customer. Protesting that the batch was committed to Government contract, he heard Perry's firm voice, 'Just do it.'

Perry was enthusiastic and soon joined the board of the new company. His early advertisements stressed the virtues of the American imports, above all their simplicity and reliability, but glossed over their spartan aspects – they had for example, no doors and only two gears forward and one in reverse.

In March 1905 he advertised the Model B in the *Autocar*. 'It is inexpensive to buy and economical to maintain. It is easy to drive and manage. It has only one quarter of the working parts required by other types and yet it is the most perfect car of its type and power upon the market.'

Perry imported three of these cars and turned them into some of the first taxi-cabs. It was partly a publicity stunt – London cabbies had a reputation of being rough and tough and to get a licence, as Perry himself put it in the *Ford Times*, 'knowledge of the machine was of no importance. Driving skill did not greatly matter.' Instead what was important was 'that he knew the latest haunt of vice, the mustiest club and the absolutely shortest route from the Toad in the Hole Saloon, Hoxton, to the Tripe Dressers Arms, Chelsea.' Perry put three cabbies (called Crew, Chambers and Clarke) into the three cars and they rapidly picked up the simple skills needed to control the vehicles.

But business did not prosper. The cars were regarded as unsophisticated and noisy and, as Henry Ford pointed out, there was another problem too. The introduction of the car into Britain was somewhat difficult on account of the failure of the American bicycle. Because the American bicycle had not been suited to English uses, it was taken for granted and made a point of by the distributors that no American vehicle could appeal to the British market.[1]

Perry described a 'five years' war' with 'impregnable prejudice'. 'The public, its opinions fostered by an anti-American press could not be induced to vacate its position of insular indifference. In externals it [the car] conflicted with the accepted canons of motoring form. In internals it was regarded as of string and hoop-iron and fitting food for the scrap heap to which it must certainly go after a few weeks of inglorious life. The car was given no opportunity of showing its mettle.'

In 1903 the company sold only a dozen cars, and few more in 1904. In 1905 Perry turned to the well-tried technique of entering the car for a trial – the 800 mile Scottish reliability trial in which a Model C distinguished itself.

The following year, however, the company still only managed to sell 50 cars – less than one a week – and the burden of having to pay cash in Detroit for the cars was putting a mounting strain on the business.

Perry decided that he would go to America and try to persuade Ford to set up a branch of his own organization in Britain. He found the Ford business in a state of disarray. A move into a huge new factory had been followed by board-room resignations over Henry Ford's determination to concentrate on a single model; the decision which was to make the company's fortunes. Perry stayed in Ford's home and had a friendly competition with his son, Edsel, to get to the bathroom first in the morning. He gained Ford's agreement. But it was not till 1909 that Perry opened a showroom in Shaftesbury Avenue in London as Manager of the Ford Motor Company of Detroit, on the basis of a commission of 25 per cent for himself.

In his first year he sold about 400 cars, mostly Model Ns but soon the Model T. The cars arrived built up in crates with only wheels, windscreens, and tops packed separately. They were landed at Vauxhall on the Thames and then driven off, some being sold directly to customers, who were often conspicuously ignorant of their workings. The Lord Lieutenant of Hampshire filled the engine instead of the radiator with water; a chauffeur jacking up one side of his car thought the back wheel had seized up because it would not spin freely.

Perry lost many of the first consignment of Model Ts when the ship carrying them, the *Minnehaha*, ran aground on the Needles and the vehicles were off-loaded. While the dealers sent to rescue them from the beach were having lunch, the cars were sold off for spot cash prices as low as £55. The first Model T to be unloaded at Vauxhall was dropped from the crane, its front axle bent and it was taken by horse and cart to the showrooms. But the strength of the vanadium steel which Ford had employed to make it was demonstrated when the axle was straightened without any form of heat treatment.

In 1910 600 cars were sold, much the same as Austin or Napier, but fewer than Wolseley. Perry then arranged an amazing stunt. He had one of his cars driven to the summit of Britain's highest mountain, Ben Nevis. Success in other, less extraordinary trials continued but it was all leading to one end, the opening in 1911 in Trafford Park in Manchester of the company's own manufacturing plant, the first in Britain to make use of the assembly line.

British manufacturers had themselves been making some attempt to rationalize their production techniques. There was some batch production, introduced for example in 1912 at Rover, which was one of the largest manufacturers, when Owen Clegg arrived from Wolseley, then the biggest producer with about 2,000 vehicles that year. By 1914 Wolseley was assembling engines and chassis by sections with specialist groups of men on each section.

At Daimler gangs of twenty or so were divided into groups of three or four and given the frame and the components to fit together to construct a chassis. Austin also had groups assembling a chassis but the whole process was extremely complicated with test bodies being fitted on temporarily and then being removed while a final body was fitted later.

The most advanced manufacturer was Sunbeam. There a girder tramway was suspended from the roof. The car frame began at one end of the shop and was then attended to by a specialist gang, before being hoisted up and onto the following station for the next operation.

An early works guide to Daimler gave this description of their 'works, its organization, method and products'.

Throughout the works it will be frequently noticed that design, size and general plans have been dictated by necessity . . . the money had to be earned first and improvements made gradually in one department at a time . . .

At the present time there are in use at the works approximately twelve acres of floor space, nearly all on the ground floor. The main machine shop was originally a three storeyed cotton mill, but this has been altered somewhat and a high speed lift and store accommodation on each floor make it a very efficient shop. The erecting shop and foundry on the Radford estate are built on somewhat more extensive lines with wider bays while the erecting shop is equipped with two electric travelling cranes.

It described the works as divided into five departments – a foundry; machine and fitting shops for producing all components including engines, gear-cases, steering brakes etc; erecting and fitting where the chassis were built up; coach building which included sawmills and plating where it noted 'the modern trend for customers to prefer the complete vehicle from one firm'. A fifth department covered testing.

By contrast the *Ford Times* in 1914 described the assembly of the parts it imported. Making clear that engine and transmission (which included gears, magneto and carburettor) arrived in a single unit, already tested, it stated:

In our Manchester plant, the frame members are riveted together, the rear spring attached and thus with nothing else they are placed upon the conveyor. This conveyor is a sort of moving endless bench. It is 114 feet long. It moves very slowly even at the top of its three speeds. [At its fastest it went two feet three inches a minute, and reached the end of the line in 50 minutes, producing 21 chassis an hour.]

First the axles with the springs are attached . . . then the engine unit comes aboard. Next the dash assembly comes sliding down the slope arriving just at that point in the travel of the conveyor where the partly-built chassis is ready for it. The hand-brake lever, control shaft and truss rods, both the latter made in Manchester, follow. Down another slide from above come the petrol tanks (made in Manchester) and are immediately ready. Exhaust pipes and muffler and silencer (made in Manchester) come next and while they are coming the wheels are being added.

When it comes off, what started as a bare frame, plus one spring is a complete chassis, wanting only body, hood, screen and accessories. And these are added as the chassis on its tyred wheels travels over the remaining 90 ft of the shop.

The bodies had been brought to this point on trolleys after arriving by train from the coach-building works. They were complete except for hood and side curtains.

The article went on to describe how wheels were submerged in pans of paint and then revolved at high speed and how varnishing which would have taken an hour and a quarter by hand was carried out in three minutes by paint sprayers.

Under the heading 'An Essay in Order' it described the assembly line. 'No man had hurried himself unduly. There is no suggestion of the "hustle" that is popularly supposed to be inseparable from intensive production. There is less stir, more leisurely movement in the Ford factory than probably any other works can show. "Hustle" in the usual sense of the word is an expression of incoherency. Organization is coherency, order, regular movement.'

It was a view not all agreed with. Just after the First World War, writing about the same line, one Horace Wyatt described the Ford workman. 'He is almost a part of the machinery of the factory. He is engaged on repetitive work and he is expected to do those jobs that cannot conveniently or more economically be done by the machine itself. The tendency must be to crush individuality or resourcefulness.'[2]

It was an argument that was to continue throughout the industry's life. But in 1912, the *Times* had no doubt that the way ahead for the industry was to encourage a great deal less individuality. British manufacturers were already embarked on the course they would follow for most of the century, of a very large range of models, too large for the long production runs necessary to become economical and compete with the American techniques. By now factories had many machine tools, but they were not organized properly.

In 1904 the Cycle Engineers Institution, which had been set up to discuss the industry's technical questions, had resolved to change its name to take in automobile engineers. The reason was obvious. The men and the companies who made cycles were now turning to car production. The first President of the New Institution of Cycle and Automobile Engineers was Herbert Austin. His Presidential address demonstrated just how far the industry had to go in rationalizing production at a time when even standard screw threads could not be taken for granted.

'We cannot too carefully consider the necessity for standardization,' he said. 'The confusion that has existed with such items as wire and sheet gauges, screw threads, pipes and flanges, joints and girders is, I am glad to say, giving place to something like a state of orderliness. Few realize what a boon Whitworth screw threads have been to us.'

With general engineering in such disarray, the path of rationalization was to be painfully slow for the motor industry, and one whose importance it consistently downplayed.

In June 1910 the first edition of the magazine *Automobile Engineer* described itself as 'a technical magazine devoted to the theory and practice of automobile construction'. Its editor was soon stressing the need for comparative studies of the industry. 'What has surprised us more than anything else is the extraordinary lack of knowledge which the managers of one motor manufacturing firm have of the practice of another.' Up to 1902, he said, this had not been so, but now designers and engineers concentrated simply on their own make and its development.

By now British industry was turning its eyes less across the Channel and more across the Atlantic. The United States had overtaken France as the leading producer, and its manufacturing techniques had clear lessons for the British.

In 1911 the American Society of Automobile Engineers under their President, the inappropriately named Mr Coffin, had taken action to try and rationalize production. Noting that 1,500 different sizes of tubing were being employed to construct cars, it devised a plan to reduce them to little more than 50 within a year. The approach was viewed with interest but some alarm by the British *Automobile Engineer*. Warming to a theme which was constantly rehearsed by manufacturers at the time, it took the view that 'the average excellence of British cars is as great as, or even greater than that of any foreign ones.' It had been the high quality not the cost which had distinguished the industry, and it warned that 'this country should not make too great haste to copy the American example. It is of far greater importance to maintain that reputation than to reduce costs of production at the expense of ever so little merit.'

But the transparent success of the Americans could not be ignored. By mid-1912 the Institution of Automobile Engineers was establishing a Committee of Manufacturers to discuss standardization, while in late 1911 *Automobile Engineer* ran a series of first-hand reports from the American industry which abandoned the patronizing tone and gave some remarkable insights into the condition of the British industry.

Its correspondent addressed the question which was being forced on the British carmakers by the evident success of Ford which had started to manufacture in Britain that year and was poised to overtake all British manufacturers within two years. At the cheaper end of the market, was the American rough and ready approach producing more effective and saleable cars than the English devotion to polish and quality? Up to now the standard English answer had been to rubbish the Americans, but now this was to be challenged.

The *Automobile Engineer* noted the rough finish of popular American cars with 'no time wasted by sandblasting castings' but also the practicality of the design. Ridiculing those who suggested that cheap American cars would fall apart in a few weeks, it stated firmly, 'The American way of producing cheap cars is better than the European. In every case the engine and transmission of the cheap car are rather heavy and large and it is intended to keep the engine so inefficient that it can never overload itself or any portions of the vehicle.' The result was a smooth running car which did not need such high quality material or accurate workmanship.

By contrast with Britain, it noted, unsurprisingly, that there were few cramped factories and as far as machine tools were concerned, things were much the same. But with one difference. There were almost no old tools in American factories; they were 'scrapped quite ruthlessly'.

The journal also recorded a highly significant development. There was 'a very large class of manufacturers who assemble instead of actually making the cars'. In what could equally be a description of late twentieth century practice it set out the steps whereby engineers would design a vehicle and then various general engineering firms ('of which there are an enormous number throughout the United States') were asked to quote for each individual part, given a very rigid specification for materials and then had inspectors checking production at the works.

In Britain by contrast 'the manufacturer who buys finished parts and puts them together has been generally regarded somewhat contemptuously and it is usual to assume that cars made in this way cannot be really good.'

The writer, however, acknowledged one major drawback in copying the American pattern – the lack in Britain of a network of good quality engineering firms which could undertake the manufacture of parts.

Also, as the *Times* put it in 1912, 'there is no firm at present which has been sufficiently enterprising to lay down a large enough plant to make small cars in sufficient numbers to make their production really cheap.'

By now, demand for cars was snowballing. The total number of motor vehicles in use in 1904 was about 17,000 of which over 8,000 were cars. By 1905 both figures had nearly doubled. The number of vehicles on the road rose by between 10 and 15,000 a year until 1911 when growth accelerated again. The numbers of cars on the road had jumped from 8,465 in 1904 to 53,196 in 1910 and then more than doubled again to 132,015 in 1914. About a third of these were taxicabs. In 1904 the Metropolitan Police in London had licensed one solitary motorcab as against 585 horse-drawn cabs. In four years, the position was reversed. In 1908 a mere 21 horse cabs were registered compared to 1,715 motorcabs, a figure which doubled to 3,956 the following year. It was a lucrative market for the manufacturers. In 1910 Napier's production of 617 cars was almost matched by the 562 hackney carriages it built. But the demand was only met by continuing large-scale imports.

The earliest figures for imports of motor vehicles, including motor cycles, are those for 1902. They show 3,742 coming in with exports of 415, a pattern not unlike that of the 1970s and 1980s. By 1903 both figures had doubled with 6,134 vehicles coming in and 955 being exported. By 1904 the Board of Trade was showing motor vehicles separately from motor cycles and counted 5,378 imports as against 700 exports. At this point the motor industry was probably importing almost as many vehicles as it was manufacturing.

But by 1907, the first year for which production figures are quoted by the Society of Motor Manufacturers and Traders, imports at 4,819 were between a third and a half of indigenous production of 12,000 cars and commercial vehicles. However, in the slump year of 1908 the import share again rose sharply. The British industry produced 10,500 vehicles while imports amounted to 7,200, about half of them in the form of chassis for final assembly in Britain. This proportion of imports, equivalent to roughly two-thirds of the home industry's own production, continued until 1913 when there was a huge jump in British production, doubling from 22,000 to 44,000 in a year. At the same time exports rose steadily to a peak of 8,829 in 1913. By the time war broke out Britain was exporting about half as much as it was importing, counted either by number of vehicles or value. Including parts, exports came to just over three and a half million pounds worth compared with imports of six and a half million.

The number of people working in the industry was growing at a similar rate. In 1905 the Royal Commission had estimated that there had been 17,000 in the industry. Two years later in 1907, the Society of Motor Manufacturers and Traders calculated subsequently that double that number, 34,000, had been employed in the construction and repair of road motor vehicles. Four years later, in 1911, it had almost doubled again at 66,000, while a decade after that, in 1921, it had nearly trebled, to 159,000.

The new industry brought new forms of social organization with it as well. Although many concerns were based on small workshops which expanded piecemeal, the industry was produc-

ing factories of a size for which there were not many parallels in
Britain at the time. Apart from Argyll's gigantic extravagance,
the employment by Wolseley of about 4,000 workers in 1913 or
Austin with 1,900 put them among the largest manufacturing
complexes in the country. They were only exceeded by places
like the huge railway building works, some shipyards and arma-
ment works and a few big heavy engineering centres, while they
surpassed individual coalmines and textile mills. At the same
time they had started to spawn and swell an emerging component
industry which was eventually to surpass the employment provided by assembly plants.

Carmakers still tended to make most of their component parts
themselves, but a trend was developing of relying more on
specialist manufacturers for some parts. The argument about
whether it was better to have as much as possible made outside to
reduce costs or to produce everything yourself to ensure quality,
which was never to be entirely resolved for the rest of the
century, was already surfacing. While, as the Daimler works-
guide makes clear, there was a shift towards firms making more
bodies themselves, eroding the traditional preserve of the old
carriage makers, the tendency with mechanical parts ran in the
opposite direction. It was to be given impetus by the arrival of the
first British mass-production enthusiast, William Morris, later
Lord Nuffield.

Amongst the companies to benefit from the demands for
components were the established Midlands firms of Joseph Lucas
of Birmingham, Thomas Sankey of Bilston, Rubery Owen of
Darlaston, and of course Dunlop, with its plants in Birmingham
and elsewhere. All were to survive and grow although many of
the companies they serviced went under.

Sankeys (now part of GKN) had been producing pressed steel
mudguards and after an approach from Herbert Austin, had
started to make metal body pressings to go onto wooden frames.
In 1908 they produced the first all-metal body, and a practically
designed metal wheel, made in two halves and welded together.
By 1913 they were turning out 30,000 wheels a year at a new plant
at Wellington in Shropshire and 3,000 bodies, including some for
export.

Rubery Owen were specialists in chassis frames, starting

experiments as early as 1896, and using methods of pressing out steel developed in the American industry.

Lucas had started making binnacle lights for ships and then successfully diversified into lamps for the booming cycle business in the 1880s. Its 'King of the Road' trademark was soon extended to petrol and then acetylene lamps for motor cars under the heading devised for Joseph Lucas shortly before his death in 1902 of 'Motoralities'. It also included horns and patent oil ('no gum, no char, no stick, no acid, no dirt'). Lucas was another large concern, employing about a thousand at its Great King Street building in Birmingham in the early years of the century. From 1909 electric lighting systems were available, and from 1912 dynamos. The company also moved into self-starters and batteries.

Engine manufacture was another burgeoning business. The almost standard procedure for would-be car manufacturers had been to buy a foreign engine and build a car around it. But, increasingly, British firms were now producing engines, often developed from foreign prototypes. So the Jowett company had begun in 1901 to make an engine to replace the French Aster and moved into car production in 1905.

White and Poppe were founded in Coventry in 1900 to make motorcycle engines, but soon turned to motor engine manufacture, while a steam engine maker in Rugby, Willans and Robinson, built engines for Rover as well as Duryea.

Frederick Simms, too, the virtual founder of the industry, friend of Daimler and original holder of his patents had found time, along with founding the RAC and the SMMT, to move into component manufacture. Here he made an important advance in the unresolved riddle of the first car – a reliable starting system. Together with Robert Bosch of Stuttgart, he developed the early magneto, an achievement for which he never felt he gained full credit. In his late seventies he had privately printed a *History of the Magneto* in which he told the story of how he first met Bosch 'who never invented anything himself, cleverly using others for that purpose' in 1895, and built on an idea from Bosch's foreman to produce the first successful Simms–Bosch magnetos.

Simms continued to deal with Bosch, taking him to shoot chamois in the Alps, in a kind of missionary spirit. 'I advised him,' he wrote, 'that it was necessary when working hard to play hard at least once a year.' But returning one day from his shooting he was rewarded by finding Bosch poring over his blueprints for rotary-magneto and rotary-armature magnetos. He was dismayed to find a fortnight later that Bosch had left early to construct one and apply for a German patent. After hard words, it was registered under both names.

Simms, who was described even in his own company's history as suffering from 'excessive breadth of outlook', had at various times developed armoured motorcycles and mobile forts, engines, lorries, buses and engines. Now in 1907 he decided to concentrate on magneto production forming the Simms Magneto Company Limited. But he faced bitter competition from Bosch who first forced him to sell his share of their joint company in France and then undercut his prices in Britain. Although the Simms company produced 43,000 units in its career, it could not survive against the Stuttgart imports and closed its doors early in 1913. Eighteen months later the British motor industry's heavy reliance on imported German magnetos was to provoke a crisis when supplies were cut by the outbreak of war.

So, by 1914 the British industry was still not self-sufficient. But it was developing at a rapid rate, and in some independent directions.

In 1909, after years of agitation from the public about the noise, dust and damage motorists caused, paralleled by motorists' complaints about the state of the highways, the Chancellor of the Exchequer, Lloyd George, introduced motor taxation in his Budget. Two forms of duty were to be levied – a petrol tax, and a tax on vehicles with the proceeds being used for the improvement of roads.

The Government had been at pains to discuss the possible changes with the RAC which, with royal patronage, had now emerged as the establishment body to represent motorists as opposed to the more aggressive Motor Union and the Automobile Association, which was essentially a motorists' relief organization, even running patrols to warn them of police speed traps. As a result of its discussions with the RAC, a formula was agreed for the vehicle tax which would profoundly affect both

British car design and the progress of foreign imports and British exports. The new tax was to be based on horsepower. Its effect was to be two-fold: the egalitarian one of making those who could afford the more expensive cars pay more, and the technical one of encouraging British manufacturers to concentrate on small-bore and long-stroke engines in distinct contrast to the products of the even more rapidly expanding American motor industry.

The effect of the horsepower tax on limiting British design was to be the source of endless controversy, but the advantage with which it appeared to provide manufacturers on the home market was sufficient to blunt the force of the motor industry's complaint and prevent it ever coalescing to the point where it embarrassed the Government.

The argument over the horsepower tax paralleled many of the arguments which the industry was to have with Government, marked characteristically by disagreements among the industry's leaders which enabled Ministers to deflect their representations and not take the industry as seriously as they might.

However, the first impact of the horsepower tax was relatively small as the variations in the tax itself were limited. Between six and a half and twelve horsepower a tax of three pounds a year was payable; up to sixteen horsepower, four guineas; up to twenty-six horsepower six guineas, and so on to the top rate of forty-two pounds a year for cars of over sixty horsepower.

By the end of 1912, the catalogue for the Motor Show at Olympia was listing 129 makes of car on exhibition. Of these 54 were British or made in Britain. At the same time J.S. Critchley was bringing out his yearbook of British motor vehicles for 1913. Inside its union jack cover it listed 64 British makes, but significantly did not count Ford which had exhibited its cheap runabout at the show at £135 plus six guineas tax a year.

In his list of models Critchley found the cheapest to be a two-cylinder 9·2 horsepower GWK; four cylinder vehicles ranged from a ten horsepower Pilot complete at £150 to Lanchesters and Argylls at £650 and £690. The bigger cars included a 59·9 horsepower Napier at £1,135 and a 41·6 horsepower Rolls-Royce at £985 for the chassis only.

But the tax, carefully listed against every model in the show was already having an effect on models unlisted by Critchley, boosting the sales of what came to be called light cars.

In October 1913 a new magazine entitled *Light Car* was spun off from the *Autocar*. It declared that twelve months before there had been scarcely a light car (which it defined as a 'big car in a miniature' as opposed to a cycle car) on the market. Now there were dozens, including the Humberette (which sold for £115), the Wolseley Stellite, and the Morris Oxford. 'The British small car,' it said, 'seems to be a separate "creation" of our engineers, while the French light car is more often an adaptation of old notions.' Some of the cars were very small with single seats in tandem. There continued to be confusion with cycle cars and three-wheelers, but the British penchant for the small car which was to mark out the industry was now established.

At the top end of the range Napier had been losing ground to Rolls-Royce. Henry Royce was a perfectionist. In his workshops at Cook Street in Manchester he had built up a business from making electric bell sets to designing dynamos and later electric cranes. But by the early years of the twentieth century his electrical business came under pressure from American imports, some of which had made use of his ideas without paying patent rights, and he became increasingly fascinated by motor cars.

Just as Edge and Napier, he started by modifying a French car, a Decauville, before announcing in 1903 that he proposed to build three experimental cars. The precision of his engineering was such that the first ten horsepower cars were remarkably quiet, smooth-running and reliable. Charles Rolls, who had been unimpressed by ten horsepower vehicles in his search for a British manufacturer to supply him, was an immediate convert. Rolls' reputation as a motorist was an enormous boost for the car and his society connections made him an extraordinary salesman, driving generals at manoeuvres and encouraging fellow Old Etonians to present one to a retiring headmaster.

The first Rolls-Royces were quickly followed by a fifteen horsepower model and a twenty horsepower series and were rapidly successful. The fastest non-stop run in the 1905 Isle of Man TT; the Monte Carlo to London record; victory in the 1906 Scottish reliability trials, the 1906 TT and successes in a New York race; the world non-stop reliability record.

Yet even with so technically successful a product commercial disaster was only narrowly avoided when the company was publicly floated at the end of 1906. A last minute appeal to a friendly Yorkshire businessman had to be mounted to prevent it from being under-subscribed and failing.

Rolls himself was to be killed when his Wright aircraft crashed in 1910. He had largely lost interest in the motor company already and turned instead to experimenting with aircraft. The company was only saved by the third partner, Claude Johnson, who was able to give it the stability and business direction which neither Rolls nor Royce could provide, and which many other motor firms lacked.

He concentrated, like Henry Ford but unlike other British manufacturers, on a single model, the 40 horsepower Silver Ghost. He got rival bids for a new factory from the cities of Derby and Leicester and chose Derby because it offered cheaper power. When Royce was taken seriously ill in 1910, Johnson drove him abroad and arranged for him to live in future in a French villa in the winter and in an English south coast house in summer with designers and draughtsmen working with him to translate his plans into action for the next twenty years.

Meanwhile the Royce standards were maintained and the cars defeated Napiers in a 1910 speed and fuel consumption trial and won spectacular victories in Alpine races.

But even with the Rolls-Royce established, there was still plenty of money for other manufacturers at the top end of the market. Napier had its best three years between 1909 and 1911; its profits going from £28,485 in 1909 to £67,062 in 1910 and dropping slightly to £57,407 in 1911.

Of the other pioneers, Frederick Lanchester failed to find a commercial brain to match his engineering genius. Some of his ideas, for example for interchangeable parts, were just too early for the technology and market available, and he was not to find a Claude Johnson to bring the commercial coherence to the business it needed.

In 1903 Lanchester had made a profit of £8,669 on a turnover of under £80,000, but his cash flow was always a problem and he often had to rely on the £10 deposits placed for new cars to pay the weekly wages bill. An attempt to get a share subscription going failed, and Lanchester fought against the idea that they should make a small car too. In March 1904 the company went into receivership, but was re-formed in 1905 as the Lanchester Motor Company. But in 1909 'Dr Fred' gave up the struggle and became consulting engineer to the Daimler company, leaving his brother George to continue with the design and running of the company.

Lanchester's influence at Daimler was soon obvious. The company had never quite shaken off the rather rough and ready image of its early models, whatever its association with royalty, and both Napier and Rolls-Royce were producing smoother and more polished products. In 1909, however, Daimler decided to adopt the new sleeve valve six cylinder engine of the American designer Charles Knight. It came to be nicknamed the 'Silent Knight' engine and with modifications by Lanchester became a standard feature on Daimler cars. More Lanchester ideas were put to work on subsequent models, with the characteristic worm-driven rear axle featuring in 1910 models. Daimler itself had been wound up in 1904 after orders in hand had sunk to only £1,530 worth in the autumn of 1903. But its profits rose sharply to over £80,000 in 1905 and 1906, after it had been re-formed.

By 1910 Daimler's shaky financial future seemed assured as it was taken over by BSA, the Birmingham Small Arms company, which had already been building some small cars of its own. By the time war broke out, Daimler employed 4,000 workers at its factories, and was turning out over 1,000 cars a year. By 1914 those figures were to be surpassed only by Ford, Wolseley, Rover and Singer while they were roughly matched by Austin and a fast-rising new entrant, William Morris of Oxford.

Austin's departure from Wolseley had been followed by a period of rapid growth for the company. Besides its own cars where its twelve and twenty horsepower ranges were to sell 7,500 before the war, it also manufactured Siddeley cars designed by J.D. Siddeley while its light car, the Stellite, was designed by Wolseley but produced by another Vickers company, the Electric and Ordnance Accessories Company Ltd at Aston in Birmingham. The company also turned out hundreds of taxicabs and some extraordinary purpose-built vehicles including vacuum cleaner cars for the British Vacuum Cleaner Company which would call at houses and offices and pass long vacuum hoses through their windows to carry out the cleaning. With its Vickers connections, the company was involved in submarine engines, motor sledges for Captain Scott's ill-fated Antarctic expedition, and perhaps most extraordinary of all a huge gyroscopic car which ran on wheels like a motorcycle, but was kept upright by gyroscopes. It was designed by a Russian Count, and only the prototype was ever built.

Austin had started by taking over a factory at Longbridge in Birmingham which had been standing empty for six years, together with eight acres. It cost him £7,750, and he expected to spend as much equipping the place. Running costs were estimated at £600 a week, and he did not expect to produce his first vehicle for four months. He hurriedly produced pictures of the factory for the 1905 motor show, together with drawings and designs for the first cars under his name, which were enough to win orders before any car had been built.

Austin slowly built up. He made 23 cars in his first year, mostly 25 and 30 horsepower models, but eight years later he was employing over two thousand men and making nearly 900 cars in the year.

Austin cars had various rally successes, including some in Russia, but progress was steady rather than spectacular and hampered by a proliferation of models which the company only attempted to simplify in 1913.

There was no production line but Austin, who prided himself on 'the value of dependability', modified the design of some of his extensive range of machine tools to make production more efficient. Once again most of the components were made in-house, although Austin did not think the operation big enough to warrant its own foundry.

In 1913 the Austin works, established seven years before, produced nearly 900 cars. But in the next two years its production was to be almost matched by a newcomer to the business who had started from scratch, but was the first British motor manufacturer to take to heart the lessons of the American industry which had been spelt out in the *Automobile Engineer*.

On October 26th, 1912 the *Autocar* reported that 'a new miniature light car has been put on the market by W.R.M. Motors Ltd of Longwall Street, Oxford.' It gave a rating of ten horsepower and described it as 'a two seater torpedo' and noted that 'its springs are exceptionally long for this type of car.'

The Morris Oxford was the first product of William Richard Morris, who was to become Lord Nuffield, and who, with Austin and Perry, was to shape the British mass production car market for good, and sometimes ill, for the rest of the century.

Morris had set up as a cycle repairer, working from his parents' home as early as 1893. By the early years of the century he was making both bicycles and motorcycles in his own central Oxford premises. He then became a motor car agent garaging undergraduate cars, carrying out repairs and holding the franchise for a large number of companies including the big-selling Humber, Singer and Wolseley makes.

By 1910 he had decided to make his own light car, but to follow the practice of his cycle and motorcycle business by having the main component parts made for him by outside firms, so becoming an assembler on the American model. 'As long ago as 1912,' he was later to write, 'I became convinced that the best way for the small concern to manufacture was to get specialists on every separate unit of the job. The work is better and more cheaply done, while the cost and worry of more plant is avoided. Money is conserved for better use in other directions.'[3]

Therefore Morris was able to start his company with very little extra capital – £4,000 in preference shares from the Earl of Macclesfield. His practicality extended to the design of the car. It had a completely enclosed transmission, an idea copied from the American Hupmobile car for which he was an agent, and intended to stop the dust and mud which early motorists like Edge had identified as a major problem. An early catalogue declared that while it was 'expensive to produce, its advantages are so great that we have not allowed the question of cost to prevent its adoption.' He advertised the car's characteristics as simplicity of control, ability to start and 'absolute freedom from trouble.' It should need 'the minimum attention . . . both when driving and when in the garage.' By the end of 1913 the car had been so successful that few modifications were necessary for the next model.

Morris had gone to the Midlands manufacturers for his parts, spending days in Coventry inspecting and negotiating. Engines came from White and Poppe, axles from E.G. Wrigley of Birmingham, while he was the first motor manufacturer to make use of Sankey's new steel wheels. His bodies were built in Oxford by a coach-builder called Raworth and assembly took place at an old military academy at Cowley just outside Oxford which had been derelict for twenty years, and where Morris' own father had once gone to school.

Morris had marketed the vehicle at the 1912 Motor Show on the basis of the blueprints alone. The car itself was not ready. The *Autocar*'s description of it was inaccurate in that it had an 8·9 horsepower engine and the price turned out to be only £165, which compared with the rock-bottom £135 for the Model T from the Ford company which Morris was to see as his greatest rival.

The business was assured by an order for 400 cars which Morris took at the show from a London car dealer, Gordon Stewart, who paid a crucial deposit.

But although the Morris advertisements made much of his reliance on British component manufacturers, embodying 'the joint productions of the greatest British experts', his experience of them was far from satisfactory, and he was soon to turn away from them.

When Stewart came to collect the first of the production cars, its universal joint, made from brittle cast iron, snapped after only a few yards. A replacement carried him only another thirty miles or so. Morris is said to have raged at White and Poppe, 'Are you all mad, you engineers in Coventry?' and insisted that replacements were made in phosphor-bronze which could absorb sudden shocks.

A more serious problem emerged when he prepared for the next model – the Morris Cowley. Morris found that White and Poppe were short of capacity and other possible manufacturers had no experience of the quantity production he wanted. So he took a radical step; he went to America. British manufacturers had long been using foreign parts to the extent that there was a deficit in foreign trade on motor parts throughout the early years up to the First World War. But they had largely come from Europe (with the obvious exception of Ford). Morris was now the first large-scale manufacturer to turn to the United States with its more efficient and economical production for components, and was to demonstrate just how much cheaper American production was.

During his first visit he placed no orders, but returned with blueprints and quoted prices, which included £25 for the engines he wanted. Turning once more to White and Poppe he was quoted £50 for the same engine, which would be nearly a third of the price of the car. Morris then went back to America and ordered not only engines (which came from the Continental Motor Manufacturing Company in Detroit at just over £17 each) but also gearboxes, transmissions, axles and steering gear.

And that was nearly the end of the story. A few days later the ship which Morris was booked on, the *Empress of Ireland*, left for England and sank in a collision in the St Lawrence. She took with her 1,011 people, the majority of her passengers and crew. It was the worst maritime disaster since the *Titanic* but Morris, delayed by a late train, had fortunately missed the sailing.

He had ordered 1,500 engines from the United States. But before they could arrive, a much more widespread calamity had occurred. The First World War had broken out in August 1914. It was to prove a watershed for the industry; at last concentrating its mind on the techniques of mass production. But it was to bring economic consequences which would wipe out many of the pre-war carmakers and soon concentrate large scale production in the hands of a few big companies, largely protected from foreign rivals in the United States or elsewhere.

4

The First World War
'Desperately Behind the Continent'

The First World War was a watershed. Before it the industry was
still heavily dependent on foreign imports of cars and parts,
unconvinced about the necessity for mass production, and still in
the process of change. Up to 1914 an estimated 393 British motor
manufacturers had been founded, of which nearly a third (113)
were still in existence.

By the end of the war the industry had learnt many of the
lessons of mass production through turning out a wide range of
armaments, many far removed from its traditional product; its
major firms had become established and the death warrants
written, if not quite signed, for many of the unsuccessful companies. The industry as a whole had been forced to turn to its own
home-built resources, a development sealed by the imposition of
a swingeing import duty on foreign parts and cars which was
both to delight and distort the industry for the next half century.

At the same time the war was to see the motor industry
overtaken as the most exciting frontier of engineering technology and design. The fledgling aircraft industry, which had
already seduced pioneers like Charles Rolls from their first love of
motor cars, was now to occupy the energies of some of the most
innovative designers and companies and to take over from the
motor industry as the most powerful magnet for the ambitious
technical innovator. Lanchester, Royce and Napier were all to
become absorbed with the questions of aero-engine design.

War was declared on August 4th 1914. Almost simultaneously
the War Ministry moved to impose its demands on the factories.
At the Daimler plant in Coventry, which was officially on
holiday, production was immediately directed. Between August
7th and the 18th 60 vehicles on twenty horsepower chassis with

special box backs were turned out. Production, planned at 25–30 cars a week pre-war, was stepped up to 50 and eventually 60 a week. Daimler depots were directed to send their vehicles for requisition to London and 200 were assembled in Hyde Park. Daimlers in private hands were commandeered and sent to Coventry for overhaul and modification. An order for 150 staff cars was placed.

Rolls-Royce, with its extraordinary reputation for precision and reliability, was to be another standby for the forces. At the start of the war the RAC, following home-based Motor Volunteer Corps during the Boer War, had compiled a register of 13,000 cars and their owners. On August 20th, 1914 it arranged for 25 owner drivers and their cars in the Royal Automobile Club Corps to cross to Le Havre to chauffeur the top brass of GHQ about the rapidly shifting battle-lines. Soon another 46 cars accompanied the Royal Naval Division in an unsuccessful thrust from Antwerp, while at the same time a scratch collection of vehicles was fitted with rudimentary armour-plating to assist the deployment of Royal Naval Air Service squadrons at airfields in Belgium near Ostend. Rolls-Royce were prominent in all these expeditions and when (as a result of the Belgian experience) the Royal Naval Armoured Car Division was established, it was on Rolls-Royce that armoured car production was standardized.

The cars were fitted with armour-plating and a turret for a machine gun. With strengthened springs, they were found on test to maintain speeds of 45 miles an hour. Mechanics from the works at Derby were attached to each squadron.

The vehicles saw service throughout the battlefields, in North, West and East Africa, in Mesopotamia and in Lawrence of Arabia's campaigns. Rolls enthusiasts treasured Lawrence's description of armoured cars running at 65 miles an hour after 'months of ploughing the desert with only such running repairs as the drivers had time and tools to give them. The cars came steaming and hissing along, dangerously fast to avoid getting stuck, rocking over hummocks in a style which looked fatal for the springs. However we knew it was nearly impossible to break a Rolls-Royce and so we were sorrier for the drivers.'

A motley collection of cars was pressed into service. Miles Thomas, later to become one of Nuffield's managers, served in an armoured car squadron in the East African campaign and described the arrival of their vehicles – four Rolls-Royce armoured cars, Napier transport vehicles, Model T Fords and Douglas motor cycles.

But it was to be the workaday Fords, designed for American farmers, which were to be the military's favourite, the First World War equivalent of the jeep.

As the largest manufacturer, Ford poured out a huge number of vehicles during the war. In the four years to 1918 it sold 48,883 vehicles and 30,000 Model Ts were supplied to the British forces for use in all theatres of war. Some were ambulances, the first built to an extraordinary design with a bell-tent on bare boards placed across the chassis. By 1915 100 ambulances a day were being turned out.

Other Ford vehicles included basic Model Ts used for troop transport and patrol cars and lorries. Ford enthusiasts pointed to the remarks of General Allenby after his successful Middle Eastern campaign that one of the three keys to his victory had been the Ford car along with the camel and Egyptian labour.

Model Ts became light patrol cars in the desert, occasionally equipped with Lewis guns, while on the Western front they were sometimes fitted with flanged wheels for use on railway lines.

The Ford factory itself came under Government control as a 'controlled establishment' in December 1914 and was also used for munitions production with women workers being brought in to replace men who had gone to the Front.

But the company also suffered from persistent anti-American-ism, particularly when Henry Ford, who had opposed the war, sent a 'peace ship' to Europe. Coventry council, which could have had more parochial reasons too, refused to buy Ford cars in 1916 because they were not English.

In November 1915 the *Pall Mall Gazette* had refused to publish a Ford advertisement before it got an assurance of support for the war effort saying it opposed advertisements 'calculated to help any firm of anti-British tendencies to expand or maintain their trade in this country.'

Perry had replied both to this and attacks in the papers owned by Lord Northcliffe, pointing out that the Ford plant was controlled by the Ministry of Munitions. He himself was extremely active, first in attempts to improve food production by the supply and use of tractors as the Government's Director of Agricultural Machinery, and later as Deputy Controller of Mechanical Warfare and Director of Traction at the Ministry of Munitions. The Manchester plant turned out some of the first light tanks.

Firms producing the more high powered models competed for staff car contracts. Vauxhall produced nearly 2,000 of its 25 horsepower D type which had first come out as a touring car in 1912. It became a standard army staff car taking General Allenby into Jerusalem on its capture from the Turks, carrying King George V in France and boosting Vauxhall output and profits at the factory in Luton to which it had moved from south London in 1905. Sunbeam also got a contract for its sixteen horsepower car and some had to be sub-contracted to Rover, who built 1,781 during the war.

But military demand was most heavily concentrated on the firms producing the heavy duty commercial vehicles, and with the home market for cars cut away, some manufacturers were soon in trouble. Austin had to give notice to some of his semi-skilled workers by the end of August 1914 because of the cancellation of orders. The company sent a letter to the press under the title 'Business as usual' to explain its attempts to get fresh work and keep men employed. It offered to do subcontracting and to produce machine tools and bought time by building wooden limber wagons and horsedrawn ambulances for the Government, an extraordinary backward step for a motor manufacturer. Then it signed a lifesaving contract, a half a million pound deal to supply vehicles to the extremely backward and hardly mechanized Imperial Russian Army. Ambulances, lorries and armoured cars which were to become prototypes for Austin armoured cars in the British army, were shipped to Russia.

By the end of 1914 the Longbridge works had also started to manufacture shells, and as the shortage of ammunition became more and more critical, the plant was extended with Government subsidies to make ammunition as its main product. Austin himself developed machine tools to speed up the slow manual construction and filling of shell cases which had horrified the Munitions Minister, Lloyd George. By the end of the war the factory had expanded to employ 20,000 people, ten times the number working there before the war.

The old (south) works were extended by the company but Government money financed the bulding of two new works; within six months the company was employing another ten thousand people, with 5,000 women amongst those who came from all over the country to work in the new factories. Hostels and an estate for 7,000 people, some housed in wooden huts, were built. An airfield was also constructed for the aircraft built in the factory.

The huge, almost overnight, expansion of the works brought its own problems. There was a fierce argument which would continue for many years about 'dilution of labour' with craft unions fiercely opposing the increasing reliance on unskilled or semi-skilled workers. Austin in particular had moved in that direction because of the difficulties of finding enough skilled men to travel to what was in the early days a rural site, served only by train. With swelling numbers, the unions became increasingly powerful and a strike at the end of the war in 1918 was a foretaste of things to come.

But by then the company had big profits to fall back on. Austin's most successful pre-war year had been 1912 with a profit of £55,000. After the difficult year of 1914 the company carried forward just £413, but by 1916 it was hugely in the black. A profit of £176,125 was followed by £380,267 in 1917 and £591,081 in 1918.

Morris too was quickly to benefit financially and industrially from the War. With its concentration on assembly, his operation was much smaller, but because it made so few of its original parts, it appeared to have less to offer the war effort. It was not until the Government panicked about the supply of munitions that Morris was able to secure contracts which again depended on others manufacturing the component parts. In the meantime he attempted to keep car production and, more important, sales going, actually announcing a new model, the Morris Cowley, in 1915 which depended on the parts he had ordered from the United States. But it was swimming uphill. In 1914, the company had made a small profit of £13,000; in 1915 it made a £1,000 loss.

However, by then Morris had won a contract for the manufacture of hand grenades followed by casings for mortar bombs. The success of the carefully planned Cowley assembly shops impressed the Ministry and Morris was soon appointed to various committees on production. There he used his contacts to obtain a contract for mine sinkers, a complicated device which paid out cables as mines sank in the sea and then halted them at a set depth. Bringing together the components and organizing assembly was Morris' talent and it gave him valuable experience as well as assured profits. He received a salary of £1,200 a year and part of his works was commandeered by the Ministry of Munitions. For the rest of the war his profits averaged £17,000, ten or twenty times less than Austin's but a reasonable improvement on his own pre-war figures. His chief gain perhaps was to find how small suppliers properly supervised could be found to provide good-quality components.

All vehicle producers large and small faced difficulties as a result of the war, generally over the parts which they imported from abroad and from Germany in particular. While British manufacturers had drawn much of their early inspiration from the design and components of French cars, and their experience of advanced manufacturing techniques from the Americans, by 1914 they were taking a sizeable quantity of their parts from German firms whose factories were already the object of some envious comment for their organization.

Early in the war, in a remarkable speech to the Institute of Automobile Engineers, the able designer and engineer, Laurence Pomeroy, who was responsible for some of the most successful and handsome pre-war Vauxhalls, and later for Daimlers, spelt out some of the shortcomings of the British motor supply industry. He was particularly critical of the standard of British steel-making, complaining that supplying firms asked exaggerated prices for their dies from motor companies and neglected some of the most basic techniques for producing acceptable qualities of steel. He even accused some suppliers of 'lack of knowledge of the physical characteristics' of the materials they were using; he said many firms showed complete disregard for any form of heat treatment after shaping parts and described British methods as 'desperately behind those on the Continent'.

British firms, he criticized, had explained the fact that some firms on the Continent could supply parts at half the price as due to 'cheap labour'. This was not so; the real reason was the output achieved per man. It was difficult, he concluded, to think of a single detail of a car on which there could not be a saving of fifty per cent.

Pomeroy's indictment of the pre-war industry was a shocking demonstration of how far standards had been let slip throughout British industry. The motor manufacturers were but the latest to try to draw on its apparent strength.

Just how crucial these drawbacks were to the war effort was to be seen in the case of magnetos, a joint British/German design which British commercial ineptitude had handed completely to the Germans, as Pomeroy pointed out in his speech. By the time war broke out, Bosch magnetos were almost exclusively used not only for motor vehicles but also for aero-engines. Worse still, most of their component parts had been imported from Germany or America, including both ballbearings and magnets. Indeed the only British company making magnetos was a small Birmingham concern called Thomson-Bennett which produced about 25 a week for industrial, marine and agricultural engines and so did not challenge the all-conquering Bosch in its monopoly of the motor-vehicle business.

At first the Government seemed unaware of the problem. The War Office told Peter Bennett, the joint owner of the company, that it foresaw no difficulty in obtaining magnetos from the American branch of Bosch. Fortunately the growing Birmingham electrical component firm of Joseph Lucas saw the opportunity. In the third month of the war it bought up Thomson-Bennett, installed Bennett in an experimental shop, and by the end of the war had increased production to 2,000 a week, developing new versions and supplying the French and British aero-engine manufacturers as well as the motor vehicle and motor cycle trade. By mid 1915 the Admiralty had realized how desperate the shortage was and put all magneto factories under Government direction controlling both the numbers and types produced by Lucas and the other smaller companies who had also gone into manufacture.

Car production continued throughout the war – but only just.

Morris made 1,344 cars, the largest manufacturer, Wolseley about 4,000 (although it had no staff car contracts from the services); Austin's contribution was 2,342, including armoured cars and ambulances.

But the production and above all the importing of cars for what was seen as pleasure purposes became increasingly unpopular as the war progressed. There were frequent complaints about the use of cars to go to race meetings. In 1916 when the National Organizing Committee for War Savings attacked private motoring as 'selfish or thoughtless extravagance' the *Daily Mail* called for it to be prohibited by law.[1]

It was in this sort of climate that the Budget Speech by the Chancellor of the Exchequer, Reginald McKenna on September 21st, 1915 announced 'a list of articles, the importation of which may properly be restricted by means of duties in time of war on both the grounds that I have mentioned, namely foreign exchange and luxury.' The list on which a huge duty of $33\frac{1}{3}$ per cent was to be imposed included motor cars, motor cycles and motor parts, cinema films, clocks, watches, musical instruments, table glass and hats. But its principal target was plain. Of the £1·9 million it was expected to yield in revenue, it was expected that £1·1 million was to come from motor vehicles.

The move was sharply challenged in the committee on the Finance Bill by Sir Alfred Mond, the prominent industrialist who created ICI. The Chancellor, he said, had 'hit upon of all things, cheap American cars, for the subject of a luxury tax.' Mond said he could have understood if the Chancellor had taken action to prevent the purchase of large and expensive cars, but 58 per cent of American imports were used for commercial purposes while those classified as used for luxury purposes included 'the use of cars by doctors, veterinary surgeons and officers in His Majesty's service' as well as 'men of business who have been buying smaller or cheaper cars for everyday work.' He pointed to the 'large number of ladies' who now could be found driving cars. He then went on to criticize the Government action as protectionism – a blow to the prevailing commitment to Free Trade. He suggested that the tariff might continue for many years to the benefit of the nineteen firms which he counted were at the time making cars for the general public.

In reply, E.S. Montagu, the Financial Secretary to the Treasury, produced another argument for restricting motor imports. There was 'a shortage of ships for all the things we must have'. Montagu went on to reject Mond's suggestion that, once passed, the duties would continue for a long time. The Government won the vote overwhelmingly, by 169 votes to 34.

But it was Mond's judgement which proved entirely correct. Apart from the brief period of the first Labour Government between 1924 and 1925 the duties were to stay substantially unchanged for roughly fifty years. It was not until 1962 that the duty on the generality of foreign motor cars was to fall below 30 per cent; not until 1968 that it was lower than 25 per cent.

It was a high ring-fence of protectionism behind which the British motor industry was to make its huge interwar and postwar expansion, allowing it to maintain and develop its own idiosyncratic and often inefficient ways. It was the most lasting and deepest seated legacy of the First World War.

5

Interwar Years
'The Rise of a New Industry'

When the war ended in 1918, the value of motor transport had become established as never before. Thousands of men and women who had hardly encountered motor vehicles before the war had now had the experience of driving and depending on them. The return from war brought an insatiable demand for motor cars.

Yet even the manufacturers cannot have expected that the inter-war years of the 1920s and 1930s should turn into such a golden age for British motor cars and motormakers. In spite of the terrible dark clouds – the industrial unrest and the lengthening dole queues, the catastrophic rise of foreign dictatorships – the motor industry seemed to cruise onwards and upwards across the sunlit uplands of its own advertisements. Even the slump of the early 1930s had less effect on British manufacturers than those abroad, and it was a small hiccup in a progress which saw a seemingly inexhaustible thirst for cars from those eager and increasingly able to buy them.

It was the age when the car became a symbol of the desirable lifestyle. It was not just the long sweep of the limousine, purring its way to the corniche of the French Riviera with the cloche hats and the smart-brimmed fedoras of the moneyed classes, which captured people's imagination. It was the idea of the 'nice little car', of 'runs in the country' beyond the spreading suburbs and the new ring roads which offered release and independence and became affordable as the price of cars tumbled both absolutely and spectacularly when compared with the cost of living. Even the difference between the romantic dream and the economic reality was partly bridged by the huge range of low-priced models, unparalleled elsewhere in the world, each offering some slight improvement or individuality to cherish.

And the romance spread to the industry too. Ambitious young men trekked to the Midlands to look for work in a modern industry for wages which largely outstripped those in other companies. Dashing ex-officers looked for posts in the show-rooms and, if possible, on the boards of companies. The enter-prise grew and grew, soon to become the third largest industry in the country, the employer of over half a million people by the late 1930s.

The feeling of the modern industry of the future was summed up by the 'luxury river cruises' on board a specially built motor launch from Westminster pier in the heart of historic London which sailed down the Thames to the damp Essex marshes to view the Ford works at Dagenham advertised as 'including a comprehensive tour of Europe's largest motor car factory'. From the jetties of Dagenham cranes swung out the cars which swelled a huge expansion of Britain's export trade, although its reliance on captive Empire markets came increasingly to disturb the thinkers in the industry. Meanwhile, until the pushy German export drive gathered pace in the late thirties under Hitler, the home market was British as never before. The traditional flow of imported vehicles and parts from abroad was repelled by the McKenna duties and the idiosyncratic English style of popular car, its development hastened by a reassessed horsepower tax which penalized larger American-type engines even more severely.

So in December 1935 the *Economist* could hail 'the rise of a new industry' with a special supplement.

The outbreak of the Great War closed the experimental stage of the new means of transport. The end of the war ushered in the period of expansion. After some initial difficulties due to the War, mechanization of road transport in Britain proceeded apace with a rapidity unrivalled by any other major industry. A new industry grew up to satisfy the ever-increasing demand for motor-vehicles. Within fifteen years the British motor industry rose from a position of relative insignificance to third place among factory trades.

Production of motor vehicles increased from 34,000 in 1913 to 73,000 in 1922 and 403,720 in 1935. Similarly the number of vehicles in use in the United Kingdom rose from 207,878 in 1913, to 575,823 in 1922 and 2,047,000 in 1935. This is no mean achievement.

But even the *Economist* was to be baffled by where the huge demand for popular low-priced cars came from. Writing in 1934 about the 'extraordinary growth' in motor ownership, it puzzled:

It has been estimated that about 25 per cent of the private cars registered represents purely business ownership, while a further 100,000 may be taken as representing multiple ownership, i.e. the ownership of more than one car by a single family. Even after making these corrections however, there remain nearly 900,000 car owning families who use their vehicles partly or wholly for private purposes, a figure which is very substantially in excess of the number of incomes known to the Inland Revenue authorities of £400 a year and upwards.

The economics of motor ownership in some of the lower income grades constitutes a puzzle for the cost of running a small car, even if the mileage be very moderate, must be an extremely heavy item in a family budget of £400 a year, while the indirect expenses on meals and refreshments taken away from home and the generally high standard of weekend entertainment induced by the ownership of a private car must also be very considerable in the aggregate.

Still scratching its head a year later, the *Economist* decided that

Many people have become accustomed to spend rather a high proportion of their income on motoring. Judging from the Inland Revenue returns which show some 800,000 incomes of over £400 a year, minimum car-income, which a few years ago was estimated to be not less than £450 a year, has fallen to something below £400 and appears to be rapidly approaching the £300 mark.

The boom was assisted by a huge reduction in car prices; by 1934 retail prices of cars as measured by the Society of Motor Manufacturers and Traders were little more than half of what they had been a decade earlier (51·8 per cent) after a ferocious shake-out of manufacturers which was to leave 90 per cent of business in the hands of the 'Big Six' car makers by the time war broke out again in 1939. It had spelt the doom of dozens of small manufacturers by the early 1920s.

The cornucopia to come, however, was not immediately apparent to the established manufacturers at the end of 1918. Little car manufacture had continued during the war and the expansion of the big companies had largely been in production facilities for making ammunition which was no longer required and they could not be easily or cheaply switched to car production. There was a general uncertainty and restlessness which made itself felt in outbreaks of industrial unrest; the most serious, the strike by 50,000 moulders in the autumn of 1919. Austin estimated it cost his business between a quarter and half a million pounds, while the delay it caused to Napier's first post-war model effectively finished the company as a car producer.

The chief beneficiary was Ford whose American parent company, as British manufacturers bitterly pointed out, had not had to reduce its car production because of the war. In 1919 Ford sold 8,000 cars, as many as it had in 1914, and in 1920 the figure trebled to 26,000. With second-hand cars fetching twice the price they had been sold for when new, even the McKenna duties were ineffective against cheaply produced American imports.

Compared with that Austin managed to produce little more than 200 cars in 1919. The first half of his year had been devoted to a thorough and expensive conversion of the government munition works which had been bought for £240,000. Austin, knighted for his war work, now had the largest motor manufacturing plant in Britain. He laid out his new buildings from scratch according to principles which he had set out. He aimed for complete standardization in both body and chassis building with parts kept to a minimum for each model. He redesigned his jigs and machine tools and went over to spray painting.

It was highly expensive and by 1920 the company had a million pound overdraft and owed as much again to suppliers and customers who had paid deposits but as yet had not received their cars. When the company sought £2½ million more capital in early 1920, the new issue was a failure and had to be rescued by underwriters.

By the time car production began to reflect the benefits of the new manufacturing plant, it was too late. Production of the new Austin 20 costing £695 in the touring version climbed from 34 in January to 641 in July and during the year 4,319 cars were produced. But as Austin told shareholders: 'First the export and then the home markets suddenly collapsed, and by late autumn, output had to be restricted to a point which could not support expenses, in fact, the latter part of the year not only wiped out the profits made in the earlier half but incurred a loss.' Austin was in deep trouble. By early 1920 the General Motors Corporation of America was on the prowl for a British company to take over and entered lengthy talks with the company. But agreement could not be reached and Austin refused to sell them his shareholding. By April 26, a receiver was called in and petitions lodged for the winding up of the company.

The experience of Morris at first paralleled that of Austin, though on a much smaller scale. Whereas the huge Longbridge site accommodated about 20,000 people by the end of the war, the three floors of Morris's old military academy at Cowley plus the new steel building erected during the war only had about 200 workers in 1919. Like Austin, Morris took the opportunity to reorganize the works, but it was an altogether more modest operation.

Previously the limited machining which Morris needed was carried out on the ground floor with assembly taking place upstairs on the first floor. Now all assembly was put onto the ground floor of the new building and for the first time some sort of line production was introduced. The chassis were moved from station to station, but only once their wheels were fitted. They were pushed by hand; there was no moving track of the sort which Ford had introduced before the war.

Even so small a reorganization had put the company into the red. Morris lost nearly £8,000 in 1919. But assisted by the parts imported during the war, he was able to get a production programme going and, unaffected by the moulders' strike in his relatively rural surroundings, he was able to sell 387 cars in 1919 and 1,932 (more than his 1914 total) in 1920. But by the autumn of 1920 depression had set in. The brief post-war boom was over; the price of labour and materials had rocketed, forcing up car selling prices; the government was deflating and it raised taxes. As Morris' sales halved first from 276 cars and chassis in September to 137 in November 1920 and then again to 74 in January 1921, so his overdraft doubled (from £48,120 in September 1920 to £84,315) and he ran up a debt of about £50,000 to his suppliers.

His reaction to the crisis was to be the making of him, establishing him almost overnight as the biggest and most successful British car manufacturer and setting patterns for the industry's cars and the way of selling them for many years to come. Put simply, he cut his prices and found a new market.

In February 1921, the prices of the Morris Cowley were cut by a fifth. (The four seater went down £100 to £425 and the two seater by £90 to £375). There were small reductions on his other less popular model, the Oxford. Then as other manufacturers began tardily to follow, he cut again overnight at the autumn Motor Show, taking almost another £100 off the best-selling models. Sales rocketed. From 3,076 in 1921, they rose to 6,956 in 1922 and 20,048 in 1923.

It was a performance never matched in the industry before or since; comparable perhaps only to the impact of the manufacture of the first Model T Fords in Britain. It was a product of Morris' business skill and bravery, made more possible by his peculiar position as essentially an assembler of other people's supplies. It was assisted by changes in taxation and national prosperity which had sharply shifted the market away from the old pre-war pattern to a degree which even Morris himself probably did not appreciate.

Even so, it only just saved him. He had to increase his bank borrowing; he persuaded suppliers to accept a delay in payments and distributors a cut in commission. He calculated that suppliers' prices would fall in the slump. When his sales manager protested that the cuts would wipe out the slender £15 a car profit they were making, Morris said he replied, 'The place is full of cars and you are not making a profit at all. You are making a loss.'

His drive for volume – the textbook approach for motor companies for the rest of the century – produced a spectacular return. When the figures were totted up after the first price cut, far from making a loss, profit had risen to £50 a car. Even Morris who had calculated his figures carefully had not expected to be back in profit for two years. In the event he made £45,000, his biggest profit to date, in 1920; doubling that to £128,000 in 1921 and almost doubling it again to £225,000 in 1922. In 1923, he was in the really big league with a profit of £852,000 post-tax.

But Morris was lucky as well as astute. The 1920 Finance Act had discriminated even more heavily in favour of small cars. The old duties based on horsepower were simplified so that instead of applying in broad bands to different ranges of cars, they went up by one pound for every horsepower. So the difference between the 11·9 horsepower Cowley and the 22 horsepower Model T Ford went from three guineas to ten pounds a year. At the same time the demand for vehicles was coming from old customers who found themselves much less wealthy than before the war and from a new market – the emerging middle classes who had not thought of the expense of a large chauffeur-driven vehicle before the war. They were particularly attracted by Morris' offer of a car which came complete without endless extra expenditure having to be found for lighting, spare wheels and other parts as had been the case before.

Morris became the patron saint of the new class of popular motorist which was to grow rapidly during the inter-war years, establishing his own 'Morris Owner' magazine for them, setting up the first hire-purchase scheme in conjunction with United Dominions Trust, setting a scale for repair charges. In 1924 he wrote:

One continual source of anxiety to the owner is the cost of running repairs. We are therefore instituting a system of standardizing repair charges. One of the things we have to impress on the dealer is the necessity for holding a sufficient stock of spare parts. Only under these conditions can we give service to the owners of Morris cars. It will be realized that most of the work attached to dealing with complaints falls under the same heading – the giving of services to the man who had once bought the car.

As for his selling policies, he asked:

Is it quite sufficiently realized in this country that every time you make a reduction, you drop down on what I may call the

pyramid of consumption power to a wider base? Even a ten
pound price reduction drops you into an entirely new market.
If the man cannot pay the last £10 . . . he cannot buy the car.
The one object in life of many makers seems to be to make the
thing the public *cannot* buy. The one object in my life has been
to make the thing they *can* buy.

But for Sir Herbert Austin the problem in May 1921 was that
he was producing nothing which the public could buy. His new
Austin 20 was for a limited market and particularly hit by the new
tax structure. However, when the receiver called a meeting of
creditors, the company was given a reprieve. It was decided to
issue £200,000 of mortgage debentures which would be paid off
out of profits. But by the beginning of 1922 the accounts showed
that £380,000 had been lost in two years and the company had
debts of £2 million. Austin shares which had been worth 27s 6d in
January 1920 plummeted to 1s in March 1922.

It was the lowest point in Austin's fortunes. But by the time the
figures came out he had already produced a new car, the Austin
12, the money for the first models only found by selling off stocks
and plant. It made up half the production of 2,559 cars in 1922 and
by the end of the year the company was starting to pay off its
debts. By that time, Austin had added a revolutionary new
model, a car he himself described at the press launch as 'a decent
car for the man who, at present, can only afford a motor cycle and
sidecar and yet has the ambition to become a motorist. It is also
for the vast host of motorists who realize that, owing to taxation
and the high cost of living, they are paying ridiculously for the
privilege of using their car.'

This was the Austin Seven, an obvious successor to the light
cars and cycle cars which had boomed in the immediate pre-war
years. Austin planned it in the utmost secrecy, employing one of
his designers, Stanley Edge, for eight months to work at the
Austin home at Lickey Grange to work out the detailed design
from rough drawings made by Austin.

'My picture of him,' Edge later wrote, 'is of a portly gentleman, wedged against my drawing board, talking and sketching
with a stub of a pencil, or looking straight at me while I tried to
say what I thought. Often after dinner he would ask whether I

had enjoyed it and at times he would bring in some chocolates or crystallized fruits.'[1]

The first drawings were obviously heavily influenced by the current Rover Eight, a highly successful light car of the time. But what emerged from the secrecy of the boarded up section of the works where it was produced was something much smaller – a 'bath on wheels' as someone described it.

It was a short stubby little car, a bit like a motorized pram which was to become the butt of a hundred music hall jokes, yet was to do exactly what Austin intended – to capture the fancy of the new car-owning generation, the people who could just scrape together enough money for something small and manageable and shrank from the discomfort of the motor-cycle and sidecar.

The Austin Seven was the car which most capitalized on the British penchant for small cars, which was to make such a success of the Mini and Morris Minor in later years, a liking that was affected but not entirely caused by the curiosities of the horse-power tax.

The car and its derivatives, with their sentimental names like 'Chummy' or 'Ruby' (quite apart from the nicknames like Popjoy or Ethel which their affectionate owners bestowed on them), managed to appeal both to the suburban middle classes who wanted a 'nice little car' and to the mechanically intrigued enthusiasts who might otherwise have continued to tinker with their motor-cycles.

Austin made no friends when he chose to announce his new car in his brusque way at the Birmingham Motor Cycle Club Dinner of 1922 as a model which 'would knock the motor-cycle and sidecar into a cocked hat and far surpass it in comfort and passenger-carrying capacity.'

What was to commend the car to enthusiasts in addition was the brilliant performance of its small engine. It was soon winning races in special sports and racing versions, ranging from fabric covered variants, to curious pointed tail specials, to what were in effect fully equipped miniature racing cars. In 1923 at the Italian motor-cycle car championships at Monza it produced the first British continental victory since the war, and in the 1930s enthusiasts recorded with delight the defeat of the hare, in the shape of the huge four and a half litre Bentley by the modest, if not quite tortoise-like, Austin Seven in a 500 mile endurance race.

It was one of the few British cars to be made under licence abroad both in France and Germany where it became in effect an ancestor of the BMW – a car with a very different image.

Austin's brainchild came in at first for ridicule. One prominent dealer, Billy Rootes, told him, 'The public just will not stand for it.' Even the directors were sceptical but approved production with Austin confidently claiming royalties of two guineas a car. In 1923 Austin production was 6,417, with each model selling roughly a third. But the decline in the company's fortunes was demonstrated by the way that Morris was now selling three times as many.

Austin was at least back in profit making £176,334 in 1923, though with huge debts of over one and a half million to pay off. It was enough to give the business confidence to continue by contrast with the large number of firms whom the 1920 slump and Morris' aggressive tactics had put out of business for good.

At the end of the war there had been a stampede of would-be car manufacturers into the industry, some attempting to sell cars on the basis of no more than hopeful prospectuses and pictures. According to one calculation 40 new makes of car or proposed car appeared between 1919 and 1920 and 46 more between 1920 and 1925. But the ramp could not last in the recession, and by 1925 there were 35 fewer motor makers than there had been four years earlier, in spite of all the new hopefuls. By 1929 the numbers had halved again.

A company which almost perfectly illustrated the boom to bust fortunes of the small manufacturer was the Clyno company of Wolverhampton. Morris had demonstrated just how rapidly a small firm could expand. Clyno matched his progress to the extent that it became the third largest producer of popular cars, overtaking Ford, but it proved unable to build on that success and in 1929 it was gone for good.

It had originally been begun in the early 1900s as a motor-cycle maker by two cousins, Frank and Alwyn Smith. In the First World War, it had produced motor-cycle combinations which carried machine guns. After the war it built a prototype car, but the slump of the early 1920s finished it off when its backers, Thomas de la Rue, pulled out.

The Smith family managed to reform the company in 1922 as the Clyno Engineering Company, keeping the title which had reflected a patent inclined plane device for varying the original motor cycle's belt drive. The same principle was to be applied later to produce the first constantly variable transmission systems.

The first car came out in 1922. It was highly competitive with the Morris and lived up to the company's slogan, 'a price level as low as any car of like rating in the world – and a value vastly higher.' The intention was to be sorely tested as Morris cut his prices in 1923 – and Clyno matched him – but the car's reliability and success in a string of competitions rapidly established it. It benefitted from a successful Coventry Climax engine and in 1923 the *Motor Trader* announced that 'the agents are receiving the car with open arms.'

In 1924 Clyno produced its most successful model to date which motoring historians regarded as a better car than the Morris equivalent. It had options on four wheel brakes which Morris could not provide, as well as balloon tyres and a sophisticated gear change. Output soared from 623 in the first year to 4,849 in 1925 to 12,349 in 1926 putting the company ahead of Ford. The tiny factory was extended by the simple method of roofing over the yard beside it.

But then, like Argyll twenty years before, Clyno over-reached itself. It borrowed heavily to build a huge new factory; production fell during the changeover and the company's new models were not sufficiently improved for the market. In 1928, a new small, cheap car was rushed out. It only cost £112 10s and had an inexpensive fabric body. But there was little margin for profit and when the 'Century' proved too obviously cheap-skate for public and dealers, it became known as the 'cemetery'. Things went from bad to worse; the Coventry Climax engine was dropped to save money but Clyno had trouble with their own replacement. In February 1929 a receiver was appointed and the company was wound up in September.

Clyno's failure emphasized Morris' achievement in sustaining his rapid success. It was all too easy to be driven to the wall by over-expansion. Clyno also had to face the sharp competition which Morris provided on price. It failed to beat him at his own game. A well-trodden anecdote illustrates the rivalry between the companies. At the Motor Show, it is said, Frank Smith was always the last to put the price on his cars. He knew where Morris had their catalogues printed and would then match their prices. The ebullient Miles Thomas arranged for a wrong, lower, price to be put in the first catalogues. Smith then set his prices at a hopelessly uneconomic level.

Clyno's collapse was a disaster not only for the company but also for the town. In the early 1920s Wolverhampton had been the third largest centre for the motor industries. By the end of the 1930s not a single motor car manufacturer was left. Besides Clyno, Star, Briton, AJS, and most famous of all, Sunbeam, were gone by the time war broke out once more.

It was not just the new boys who suffered. Amongst the venerable names who went to the wall was Wolseley, the biggest British manufacturer before 1914. The company had had a good war, turning out over 4,000 vehicles and becoming a highly successful aero-engine maker. It had designed and built its first engines in only eleven weeks. Its Viper engine powered the successful SE5 which was responsible for many of the British aerial victories in the last stages of the war. As part of the Vickers group the company also turned out shells, gunsights and aircraft. But when the war ended its machinery was in poor repair and huge sums were spent on re-equipping a newly-bought factory and an expensive prestige office on Piccadilly in London.

Wolseley's sales could not sustain its level of ambition. Its ten to fifteen horsepower range, based on an aero-engine, failed and later cars could not protect it from the consequences of the depression. It built a famous model called the 'Silent Six', which Morris liked, but cost it a fortune from baffled customers. They had expected the engine to be genuinely silent and suspected the worse when it made a noise. By November 1926 the company owed two million pounds and was wound up.

Two years earlier Wolseley had been involved in a scheme to merge the three biggest British companies – Austin, Morris and Wolseley in what would have been a forerunner of the British Motor Corporation of the 1950s. Austin, wearied by his long struggle to survive, and Dudley Docker of Wolseley were keen.

Morris, very much in the ascendancy, was less so. After detailed talks, Morris's accountant wrote to Austin that Morris felt that 'his business is entirely his own, to make or break, to mar or improve, and he does not feel he can give up this position of freedom to share, even with yourself and others, the responsibility which he would have to members of the public, if he joined in an amalgamation of the kind suggested.' He believed that even with 'the admirable plant' provided by Wolseley, 'the organization would be so great that it would be difficult to control and might tend to strangle itself.'[2] They were prophetic words.

Morris took over Wolseley on his own terms. In 1926 he and Austin both bid for the assets of the bankrupt company in the office of the receiver in Carey Street in London. After Morris' initial written offer of £600,000 the bidding went steadily higher as each magnate outbid the other by £1,000 a time. Miles Thomas who accompanied Morris said later, 'So it went on, each leapfrogging the other, until I noticed a whispered conversation between a rather tense-looking Paton (Austin's Finance Director) and a very flushed bright-eyed Mr Morris.

'I was able to hear the gist of the whispering which on Morris' part with his chin well stuck out, was to the effect that he was determined to outbid Austin. He repeated the assertion out loud for all to hear. The Morris finances were very sound, and so at £730,000 Wolseley Motors was knocked down to Morris.'[3]

It was a poignant moment for Austin to see the company he had founded sold to his greatest rival.

But there was plenty of room for both of them. By the end of 1929 they shared 60 per cent of the output of the industry. With Clyno gone, the only other company producing more than 10,000 cars in a year was Singer.

The biggest surprise was the collapse of their oldest and deadliest rival, the Ford motor company, which had dominated the industry either side of the war. Now, however, it was in deep, self-inflicted trouble. So much so that when Henry Ford's only son Edsel and the Ford Vice-President in charge of overseas operations, Ernest C. Kanzler, reviewed the situation for Henry Ford in 1926, they wrote, 'We know we have been defeated and licked in England.'

The chief reason was Ford's refusal to replace or modify his cherished Model T. Perry, who had badgered Ford to set up shop in Britain, had always pressed him for modifications, most obviously doors and also built-in lights. He could point to the way that Ford customers often specified Manchester-built rather than imported bodies. But Ford stuck to his inflexible single model, 'any colour as long as it is black' policy. By 1919, Perry had left. The main reason he gave was that Ford had refused to build a new manufacturing plant on land which Perry had selected and bought at Southampton docks. But there was more to it than that. Ford had just emerged from vicious boardroom fights in the United States which had forced him to buy out some principal shareholders and marked him for life. Perry had relied heavily on his personal chemistry with the now pre-occupied Ford. He had not hidden his criticisms of some of Ford's assistants. Now two of them produced a report critical of him, and in the difficult atmosphere, Perry decided to resign, a decision which Ford was deeply to regret.

The immediate reaction was for the company to send American executives to run its British business. Working practices were changed to more American lines but the Americans managed to alienate many of the dealers whom Perry had carefully cultivated, forbidding them to sell other makes and sometimes shipping vehicles to them unordered, with instructions to sell them.

Their principal problem, however, was the growing obsolescence of the unmodified Model T. It was old fashioned and uncomfortable, attracted a heavy annual tax because of its horsepower and, as Kanzler pointed out, it did about ten miles less to the gallon than its competitors. At Edsel Ford's urging there had been a facelift in 1925 but by the time the Model A replaced the Model T at Manchester in 1927, Ford had become almost an also-ran in British sales.

In 1928 Ford produced only 6,224 cars and trucks compared with 12,520 in 1927 and as many as 21,815 in 1926. In the same year Austin and Morris between them had produced 100,000 cars alone.

It was a disastrous situation and in 1928 Henry Ford himself appeared in Britain to tackle it. It was a stately progress, separate audiences with the King and Queen and the Prince of Wales, lunch with Lloyd George, a search for antiques. But Ford had business imperatives too – to see how his plan for a huge new factory on swampland bought at Dagenham to the east of London were progressing, and how he could revitalize the British company which was the key to his foreign operation.

He turned to the man who had first brought the company to England. Perry was invited back to become head of a new European operation. The old company was wound up and the Ford Motor Company Ltd was set up at the end of 1928. It had responsibility too for Ford operations in Denmark, Sweden, Finland, Germany, Holland, Belgium, France, Spain and Italy.

Perry's most pressing job was to convert the nearly 600 acres of marshland at Dagenham, crisscrossed by canals and riddled with refuse pits, into the largest and most modern car plant outside the United States. It was to be capable of producing 200,000 vehicles a year. Perry was to complain that the Ford planners had badly underestimated the cost of the project. Another two million pounds had to be found to meet the expense of the vast piling operation which had to be undertaken to support the concrete rafts on which the plant was built.

The plant was almost self-contained. A jetty could take ships of up to 10,000 tons to bring in components as well as coal or ore to fuel the power station and blast furnaces. The Americans insisted on their own power although Perry protested that the country's largest power station was within sight at Barking. Beside the factory, the Ford Corporation arranged that two American firms who supplied the company in the United States should be given sites. Briggs Motor Bodies established a plant for steel body pressings, and Kelsey-Hayes was set up to produce steel wheels. Perry, who had spent some of the intervening years setting up the Slough industrial estate, would have liked other firms on the site too, but Detroit vetoed it.

Finally, on the last weekend of September 1931, special trains were organized from Manchester to bring down about 1,500 workers who wished to transfer to Dagenham together with key items of equipment which were needed for the start of the new plants. Production began on the Monday morning. The plan was that up to 20,000 people could be eventually employed. The site had been chosen in the knowledge that the London County Council was building an overspill housing estate in the area.

The creation of Dagenham, which was built like all of Henry Ford's European plants on the water's edge for ease of movement and possible escape from import dues, established the geographical spread of the industry for the next 30 years.

By the middle of the 1930s, there was Dagenham in the southeast, with farther north at Luton the growing works of the Vauxhall company which was now also American-owned. In 1925 it had been taken over by General Motors. Its President Alfred P. Sloan had stitched a farrago of American motor makers together into the world's largest motor company and then turned his sights on Europe. After talks with both Austin and Morris had come to nothing General Motors took over Vauxhall in December 1925 for two and a half million dollars, making it the company's first manufacturing plant outside the United States. It was still a small producer, making about 1,400 cars with about 1,800 people in 1925. It had just started to move away from its stylish big cars to the more popular small car market, but the move was given greater impetus by the Americans. In 1930 the Vauxhall Cadet was launched and by the end of 1934 the plant was producing about 20,000 cars with over 6,000 people and was established as one of the 'Big Six'.

In the original motor city of Coventry there was still a wide variety of manufacturers. Daimler, the first, had become a highly specialist up-market producer. Different sorts of speciality were provided by Alvis and SS Cars, later to be known as Jaguar, which had moved down from Blackpool to be nearer its suppliers. Rover was a medium size producer which had decided not to compete with Austin after the war, concentrating at first on big three and a half litre cars. By the early 1930s, after big losses and a bad reputation for quality, it was beginning to re-establish itself with a successful line of middle range cars. It had a slogan 'one of Britain's fine cars' but little to show that its name would eventually encompass all that was left of the indigenous mass-production car industry.

The big volume producers in Coventry were Singer, Standard and the new Rootes group, a reverse take-over of the manufacturers Hillman and Humber by successful motor dealers.

Standard had early departed from its name. The intention of its founder R. W. (Dick) Maudslay that it should manufacture with

as many standard parts as possible had been frustrated by the
demands of survival. Two years after it began the company was
rescued by Charles Friswell, the extrovert London motor agent
who had successfully challenged Harry Lawson's patents. He
offered to take all that Standard could make and gave the cars
great publicity. In a public relations coup, he arranged to ship 70
vehicles to India in 1911 as the official cars for the Durbar
celebrations of the coronation of King George V as Emperor of
India. Friswell made clear what kind of cars he wanted, and they
did not include standard parts.

After the war, the company boomed. It had a successful
touring car for which it was credited with the first really water-
proof hood and then a smaller car, the Standard Nine in 1927.
Maudslay died in 1934. By then his eventual successor, Captain
John Black, had become managing director.

Black was another of the motor industry characters whose
temperament would have a major effect on the industry. A tall
imperious man, he had put money into the company when he
arrived and ran it as an autocrat. His abrasive attitude to his
managers was a byword and he was eventually forced out when
he became increasingly erratic, sacking his long-serving
engineering director. For years he cut a considerable figure in
Coventry life, often followed by his butler, another imposing
man. On occasions unfamiliar guests would mistake the butler
for Black, infuriating the industrialist.

Black was described as 'extremely vain' by one of his fellow
manufacturers and they were infuriated by his attempts to have
friendly relations with the unions. Standard was one of the most
unionized companies, although pre-war that was not saying
much. The union official, Jack Jones, found him a 'dashing,
debonair man with a touch of the dynamic' who enjoyed chatting
to people on the shop floor. Secretaries at Jaguar remembered
him giving them lifts when he passed them on the rutted lane
which led to their factory.

The Rootes Group was the creation of two more of the
industry's new personalities, Billy and Reggie Rootes. Their
father, William, had set up a cycle business in Hawkhurst in Kent
in 1888 and it had expanded into what by the 1920s was the largest
motor agents business in Britain. Billy, who had started as an

apprentice at Singer in Coventry and raced their motor cycles, was the extrovert ebullient salesman. Reggie, who had trained as an accountant, looked after the day to day running of the business.

Rootes had grown rich on the expansion of the car-buying public and held a variety of franchises. They had been close to Austin, supporting the company financially in its post-war difficulties and they had had a lucrative contract for distributing big American Chevrolets in southern England. Billy Rootes had a particular interest in exports and had travelled widely abroad for Clyno.

In the mid 1920s they had taken over a coach-builder, Thrupp and Maberly, and were looking to expand their business by breaking into manufacture, which appeared to offer big profits.

In 1929 they took over the Humber and Hillman companies which were on adjoining sites in Coventry. Both had grown from cycle manufacture. In 1927 Humber, which was concentrating on larger models instead of its pre-war light cars, had swallowed Hillman which was making steady but unexciting medium range saloons. A cash crisis followed, and the Rootes Group stepped in. Rootes' 1930s progress was assisted by the success of the Hillman Minx which became a mainstay not just of the company but of suppliers like Pressed Steel in Oxford where its body was made.

Farther north, Rolls-Royce was established in Derby after its move from Manchester. Its old factory remained in the industry, taken over by a component manufacturer, Douglas Mackie. Yorkshire pride centred on Jowett at Idle near Bradford which had started making engines to replace French imports and turned to cars in 1905. Its later slogan was 'Take a good look when it passes you'.

In Birmingham there were the wide expanses of what was known as 'the Austin' at Longbridge and the Wolseley factory controlled by Morris. In Oxford, the Morris empire continued to grow, spreading to Abingdon with the MG works.

The opening of Dagenham had been accompanied by fulsome advertising which stressed the advantages of having everything on a single site – 'the best-equipped, the most self-reliant'. By contrast Morris praised the virtues of what his advertising copy called the 'sensational policy' of Morris specialization.

His publicity hymned the advantages not only of specialized models (in 1935 he had eighteen of them), but also of specialized production with different parts being made by specialist manufacturers and all brought together for assembly at one site. Yet by the mid 1930s even the arch-assembler Morris found himself making more and more of his own parts, even if it was in separate supplying companies which he had steadily bought up.

Morris had set out his views in 1924.

There is no point in producing any article yourself which you can buy from a concern specializing in the work. I only buy a concern when they tell me they cannot produce enough of the article in question for our programme . . .

It will be argued that, with our large output, we could do the thing cheaper ourselves; that we are piling up transport costs and so on. This is largely an illusion. The outside firm that makes perhaps only one important part, is probably making in even larger quantities than we should. It is interested in nothing else; therefore it can keep its governing brains on the problems connected with that unit, in a way impossible to a concern manufacturing a highly complicated article.[4]

Morris inspectors checked the raw material before it was delivered to their suppliers, guaranteeing the material, allowing them a percentage of scrap and placing long contracts; the delivered parts were tested before being transferred into the Cowley stores.

But even when he wrote those words, Morris had already bought the suppliers of three of his key elements – engines, bodies, and radiators. Since the war Morris had had his engines made by the French Hotchkiss company in a factory it had established for machine-gun manufacture in Coventry during the war. But when the business started to take off in a big way in 1922 and Morris wanted production stepped up to 500 or 600 engines a week, the company said they could only produce a maximum of 300. The French parent company refused to invest more money and suggested to Morris that he buy them out.

Morris' reaction was regarded as typical of his direct approach. He had the factory valued by a production engineer and then made an offer to Hotchkiss. But when the company talked of sending a contract when it was ready or in a month's time, Morris replied, 'Let us get this straight. There is a little office next door to me; you can go in there and within an hour you can complete everything for me to sign, or the deal is off.'

Morris put in as manager Frank Woollard, an old acquaintance, who was a pioneer and enthusiast of flow production techniques. Within a year the replanned factory with an extra shift had doubled production. In the drive for greater production Woollard followed the best American methods and by the late 1930s the factory was estimated to be as modern as any in the United States.

Woollard's and Morris' efforts, made possible by the big profits which Morris ploughed back into investment, exorcized the criticisms of British manufacturing techniques which could be made before the war. Woollard described the continuous production technique: 'regularity is the keynote . . . regularity in sales as to quantity of type; regularity in material as to quantity, quality and type; regularity in material as to quantity, quality and time; regularity in processing, workmanship and inspection.'

The approach was being continually updated at Cowley culminating in a major reorganization in 1933–34 as a reaction to falling profits. Four moving assembly lines with chassis drawn by a moving chain as parts were delivered to them by overhead conveyor were finally established and were regarded by many at the time as more advanced than Ford's new Dagenham operation.

In some cases Morris' enthusiasm outran the technically feasible. A huge automatic transfer machine introduced to make engine parts in 1923 was unmatched on either side of the Atlantic. But the rest of the production process just could not cope with its technical demands and it was not until after the Second World War that similar machines were once again introduced.

Morris had similar difficulties with his plans for all-steel bodies. His visits to America had convinced him that the future lay in that direction and he persuaded the American firm of Edward G. Budd of Philadelphia to take part in a joint venture. It established the Pressed Steel Company at a plant across the road from the Cowley works in 1927.

The enterprise was plagued with technical and commercial difficulties. Although some bodies went onto Morris Oxfords in 1927, Miles Thomas described the first attempts:

The Pressed Steel Company in 1926–27 were using raw dies, the labour was new and unpractised, the American techniques of welding and the method of attaching the cloth upholstery to the steel bodies was new in Britain.

When the first Morris Oxford bodies were pushed through to my despatch department for examination by the Morris management all hell was let loose. The panels were ripped; the aperture for the windscreen was awry and would obviously leak in the first shower of rain; the doors only fitted where they touched . . . the whole thing was an impossible product. To heighten the gloom, someone wryly said that we ought to advertise it as an all-weather body – it would let all the weather through.

'W.R.' (Morris) was like a bear with a sore head – literally. He had a habit when he was worried – and that was very frequently in those days – of scratching the hair at the back of his neck. When he was angry – and that was not infrequently either – he would unconsciously when seated cross his legs and waggle his free foot up and down jerkily. Those were the danger signs. No one asked him a question to which they wanted an affirmative answer when those signs of nervous tension were present.

Morris' worries with Pressed Steel continued when it became clear that other manufacturers would not put work into the plant to fill its capacity because of its close connection with Morris. Meanwhile, his own suppliers refused to quote against Pressed Steel because they thought the enquiries were not serious. Morris soon sold his shareholding.

At Longbridge, Austin, an engineer to his fingertips, had taken great pleasure in designing his own machinery as well as his cars. Now he modernized his plant again as soon as his financial difficulties had started to ease. Under C.R.F. Englebach the works was reshaped in 1925–26 with series production of bodies, the introduction of cellulose paint and more rational component machining and assembly.

Austin, who as early as 1904 had approached Sankey's about getting pressed steel body parts to go onto wooden frames, was as quick as Morris to see that the future lay with complete pressed steel bodies, and by 1926 they were being manufactured to his design.

The Austin Seven had proved a runaway success and by 1928 over 22,000 a year were being produced, half the firm's output. When Morris announced a new small car, the Morris Minor in 1928 and Clyno a nine horsepower model which would only cost £115 or less, the scene was set for a new battle between the manufacturers.

'Some people,' said Morris, 'think that my idea is to try to crush the Austin Seven off the market – which is absurd. But I say this – the price will not be higher than that of the Austin Seven.'[5]

At the start of 1929 Austin and the Morris business dominated the industry. The Morris empire had reached its peak with 51 per cent of British small car production – a figure never achieved since by any manufacturer, while Austin had grown to over 37 per cent. Trailing far behind was Ford at 5.7 not far ahead of Standard which had 4.9 per cent, while the newly Americanized Vauxhall produced little more than one per cent. Within four years Morris had plunged to little more than 27 per cent, just behind Austin which was down to 28·8 per cent. The big difference was made up by Ford which, with Dagenham on stream and a new small car at last designed for the English market, had risen to 18·9 per cent. But it was also accounted for by the way in which other manufacturers had tapped an obvious public demand for smaller cars with new small Vauxhalls taking 7·1 per cent, Standard 8·9 per cent and the reorganized Rootes group 9·1 per cent. Standard and Rootes had been quickest to produce the slightly better small car – the Nines and Tens.

The decline of Austin and particularly Morris was partly due to what was happening inside the industry. Ford, under Perry, was finally getting its post-war act together, while General Motors' investment in Vauxhall started to show results. On the other side, Morris' autocratic management of his business was handi-

capped by internal rows and his absence on regular annual cruises
to Australasia from 1927 onwards showed a slackening of his
once sure grip. Austin was relatively less affected though Sir
Herbert was ageing; he was 65 in 1930.

However, the prime reason for the transformation of the big
two into the 'Big Six' was an external one. In 1928 small cars of
ten horsepower and under accounted for about a quarter of the
market; five years later they were 60 per cent of all car sales. In
part this was a reflection of popular taste, an indication of where
the new motoring classes were coming from. But it was helped
on its way by the big slump which began with the Wall Street
crash of 1929. Even so Britain was the country whose car
production suffered least among the major nations from the
slump. While the United States' experience was catastrophic
with production in 1932 only a quarter of what it had been in
1929, and Germany lost half and France about a third of its
production, in Britain the effect on companies was much less
severe than the earlier recession of 1920. Between 1929 and 1931
production fell by only thirteen per cent.

At the same time there was a vast expansion in the number of
competing models being offered. Manufacturers competed with
each other less on the question of price as on the design of their
models.

By 1938 the *Economist* was contrasting the 'relatively high price
of popular British cars compared with those of standard American cars in the United States.' Headlined 'Is Motoring too dear?'
it pointed out that the 'Big Six' produced 40 different types of
engine and even larger numbers of chassis and body types. The
Big Three American producers, with vastly greater US sales,
actually had fewer models in production.

> The big British manufacturers have steadily extended their
> range of models, with a view to competing in all, or in most,
> sections of the popular market. This is a species of insurance
> against changes in popular taste but the manufacturers' losses
> on unprofitable models form a heavy first charge against the
> profits of the 'popular' classes. It was estimated last year that 26
> out of 40 models achieved sales of less than 5,000 units. And so
> small an output in the 'popular' class is uneconomic.

The big challenge to the pricing policies came from Ford, in an almost desperate measure to establish itself after its difficult first years in its new Dagenham plant which had coincided with the slump.

On October 1st, 1931 the first Ford had been driven off the Dagenham production line. It was a commercial lorry. The decision had been made to defer production of cars until the company could decide on a suitable model. A handful of Model As were turned out but Perry pressed the Ford organization for a small horsepower car to suit the British market. Without it, he argued, the impact of the horsepower tax against which he continually crusaded, would prevent the company breaking back into the mass market. Eventually he triumphed. British engineers were sent to Dearborn to help plan the car under Rowland (later Sir Rowland) Smith. Smith said he had two letters in his pocket: one with the specification; the other a letter of resignation. The design was worked out by Ford's chief American designer, Sheldrick, and the first dozen cars were built in the US Rouge factory within six months of the design being completed.

The new model, the eight horsepower Ford Y, was introduced in 1932. Ford took over the Albert Hall to exhibit and 50,000 people paid the 1s 3d (6p) to view it. By the time it was on public sale in May the car had been extensively modified to suit British conditions after road testing.

It was an almost overnight success. In 1932 the company sold 8,260 of the new car but still made a huge loss – £726,000. The following year the car was available for the full twelve months. Sales went up four and a half times and the company made a profit almost as big as the previous year's loss. In 1934 Ford's 27,000 sales were over 50 per cent of the eight horsepower market, but then sales abruptly fell off apparently following the introduction of the new Morris Eight from the re-equipped Cowley Plant, which was to become the most successful car ever sold in Britain before the Second World War.

The Ford response was worthy of Morris himself. For all the talk about being self-contained, the company bought about 65 per cent of its components from outside. So under its purchasing director, an Irishman, Patrick Hennessy, who had come from the firm's tractor plant at Cork, an overhaul of its suppliers was begun.

In Hennessy's words:

When we examined this purchasing question, it was quite obvious that the man who was buying knew far less about what he was buying than the man who was selling . . . and so from that time on, we made a practice – and I instituted this practice and system – of breaking down the cost. We would take a piece whatever it was – a connecting rod or a battery – and we would break it down with the help of our cost estimators and our time study people and by getting information from America or anywhere else we could get it. The buyers broke the thing down they were buying to material, labour overheads and the profit the man would be entitled to if he were making the thing efficiently on efficient equipment.

So when the seller came in next and asked five pounds for something, we were able to say, 'But that's complete nonsense because this thing can be made and sold at a profit at just two pounds.'

The exercise allowed Ford to cut its costs so much that the company felt able to reduce the price of the £120 Ford Eight as the sales began to fall off. In 1935 the car became the first, and according to Ford, the last, to be offered fully-equipped at £100 only. It was made possible only by the purchasing review. 'I don't think we could have done that otherwise' was Hennessy's verdict.

Even so, it took Ford along a financial tightrope. It bought market share, but it made little or no money.

None of us ever thought there was a prospect of a profit, but we hoped we might be able to do it ultimately. We eventually got the thing so that we weren't making a loss and I think we made a very small profit. And, of course, that was probably one of the great milestones in the history of the company, and it made that car a great success, and we sold a great many more than we would otherwise have sold. . . . At that time it was probably the right thing to do because we needed that stimulation in the market and that excitement and we got it. And, of course, we have since sold the spare parts to service those cars at quite a reasonable profit.

It was good for the organization because they had to battle day and night, and there was tremendous driving force behind it, to get our costs down until we came out of the red. That increased the efficiency, the thriftiness of the organization perhaps like nothing else would have done.

It was an example of what in Ford they called 'Ford spirit', a warning to the indigenous motor industry that, just as in 1911, there was a new infusion of energy and organization to challenge them.

But Ford faced more than straightforward competition. There was still a strong anti-Americanism which affected the company. Perry himself had given this as his reason for wanting to start manufacture in Britain: 'I didn't think as an Englishman that I was playing the game if I went on importing American cars.' In the First World War he had had to combat a campaign by Lord Northcliffe against buying Ford cars by pointing out that all its plants were controlled by the Ministry of Munitions. In 1929 the view of Ford as a foreign interloper, even though manufacturing in Britain, appeared to have been given blessing from the highest quarters when the Government dropped a case against Morris simply in order to allow him to compete against Ford.

Because of the highly personalized nature of the Morris business in which Morris controlled all the ordinary shares, and tended to plough profits back into the business rather than paying dividends which would be liable for supertax, Morris was sued by the Inland Revenue. The case was taken by the Attorney General himself, Sir Alfred Jowitt. Suddenly, in the middle of the proceedings, the case was dropped in the most extraordinary way. Jowitt announced in court that he had to consider whether 'the result of winning my case is going to be conducive to the national good.'

Clearly concluding that it was not, he said:

I think we must all have been impressed by the evidence showing that there was at least a possibility of serious competi-

tion between Sir William Morris and his companies and Mr
Ford and his companies with regard to a market which must
always be a more or less restricted market. Though it is
certainly not for me to take sides in that controversy between
those eminent gentlemen, at least equally it is for me to see that
they are both of them fairly armed for the fight and I can well
understand that for the purpose of that fight it is desirable that
Sir William Morris should have at his disposal very large
capital reserves.

Second, something has been said by Sir William Morris
with regard to the development of the export market. So far as
that is concerned, he has no more sincere well-wisher than I am
and I sincerely hope that he will not allow his energies to flag or
his determination to become less keen.

If that was not enough, Jowitt then strolled along the street arm
in arm with Morris.

Ford had attempted to deflect some of the opposition by
making 40 per cent of its new company shares available to British
investors, although the majority holding naturally remained
with Dearborn. In addition, as far as exports went, Perry
tirelessly pointed out at annual meetings the proportion of British
motor exports which came from the company – in 1933 for
example, over 50 per cent of parts, over 60 per cent of tractors and
about ten per cent of cars. With that he coupled persistent attacks
on the way the horsepower tax discriminated against the very
vehicles which export markets wanted:

> This country is now the only large producer of motor cars
> which persists in imposing domestic taxes which retard expan-
> sion of exports . . . it is admitted by everyone who has
> experience of the export market for British automobiles that
> this country cannot compete because, in order to secure our
> domestic market, we have to build small horsepower taxed
> cars. Foreigners, including our own colonists, do not like these
> cars and will not buy them in any considerable quantity.

What Perry did not, of course, say was that it was those very
restrictions which had encouraged Ford to manufacture in
Britain.

On paper British manufacturers had been successful in the export–import business of the 1920s and 1930s. Before the First War there had been a persistent balance of payments deficit between imports and exports. But from 1926 onwards exports consistently outpaced declining imports. They grew from an average of less than a sixth of car production to over a fifth by the end of the thirties.

It was clear that the protective wall built up by the McKenna duties were having a considerable effect. But it was not entirely straightforward. When car prices rocketed at the end of the war, as many as 19,939 cars came in during 1922 and 22,067 the following year. However when Labour repealed the duties in 1924 the floodgates appeared to open, with 42,000 vehicles imported. Morris stomped the country in protest enlisting Cowley workers too. The Labour Chancellor, Philip Snowden, called it a 'ramping, raging, lying campaign'. Morris declared it would cost a million men their jobs; the Society of Motor Manufacturers and Traders later estimated that there were little over 200,000 people in the industry at the time. Morris, however, triumphed and the Conservative Government which replaced Labour in 1925 restored the duties. When they were formally converted to tariffs under the Import Duties Act in August 1938 there was little objection even though the move was designed to allow the tariff to be raised still further against motor imports from Hitler's Germany which, it was claimed, were being heavily subsidized.

Looking behind the statistical totals, however, the British export performance was not as rosy as it looked. Almost 90 per cent of exports went to countries of the British Empire where, except in the case of South Africa, they were given an advantage by Imperial Preference. Yet even here they were far less successful than they might or should have been.

As early as 1911 *Automobile Engineer*'s correspondent in the United States was writing that:

The motor-car trade of the Empire has gone to America in the main through the greater commercial application of the Americans and through the great suitability of the American car for rough country. It has so often been repeated that high clearance, standard track, great axle strength, exceptional strength of steering and great flexibility of springs are essential features for a successful colonial car. On the other hand, never yet have I seen a Colonial motor car from a British factory which fulfilled these requirements in all respects.

Few British makers or designers realize what a car has to do day in and day out once it is away from Western Europe.

The description could have applied equally to the years between the wars and indeed in the 1950s and 1960s when a market thirsty for cars, any cars, tested and found wanting what Britain had to offer. So in the 1920s and 1930s, apart from a few small Continental markets, it was not the Rubies and the Chummies and the Minors which took their proud owners on nice little 'runs in the country' which the export markets wanted, but something a lot more substantial. That was a market already seized by the Americans and compared with their huge production runs, even the new Dagenham plant had to abandon plans to supply export markets to any extent with the big new V 8 model.

About 90 per cent of exports went to the Empire (which was taken to include Ireland) and a large proportion of that was accounted for by Australia where chassis sent out from Britain were assembled. But it was a dangerously large proportion (21 per cent in 1936) and when the market collapsed, as it was to do, it left British manufacturers seriously exposed.

Even so, as the 1950 PEP Report which considered the future of the British industry pointed out, between the wars Australia had still bought mainly from the United States as had another larger Imperial market, India. The only places where British cars did dominate were in nearby Ireland and the most British of the dominions, New Zealand.

Morris had swung into typically vigorous action to widen his foreign sales, establishing an export office in London in 1925 as well as French showrooms in Paris. In 1927 he produced the Empire Car, a roomy 15·9 horsepower car which he shipped to Australia. It was a technical disaster, and the unsold cars had to be shipped back to Britain at a loss of £100,000. It was one of Morris' greatest defeats, and one of which he was reminded on his annual voyages to Australia.

He was no more successful in his attempts to manufacture in France. Finding little appetite for the Cowley from the French, who preferred larger cars, he decided to buy the old Leon Bollée plant at Le Mans in 1924. The plan was to build a modified version of the twelve horsepower Bollée car. But the plant was antiquated and its French components often sub-standard. Morris believed that the chauvinistic French had deliberately sent him their poorer quality parts. The French public was no more accommodating. Morris had managed to sell only half the 2,500 cars he had produced by autumn 1928 and had already lost £150,000. Production came to a halt and the company was finally liquidated in 1931.

Austin too burnt his fingers abroad. He arranged in 1929 for a group of American businessmen to set up a factory in Pennsylvania to build an American version of the Seven, called the Bantam. By the middle of 1930 there was talk of definite orders for 184,117 cars. In the event 8,558 were sold that year and only 1,179 in 1931.

Austin was more successful with licensing agreements on the Continent. In 1927, a German company, Gotha Wagenfabrik, agreed to make the Seven under licence, marketing it as the 'Dixi'. The company was later taken over by BMW and about 14,000 Dixis had been sold by the end of 1930. A similar number were sold in France under the name of Rosengart. Lucien Rosengart had resigned from Peugeot in 1928 and produced a modification of the Seven which was built with imported parts. It had separate front seats and a third seat crosswise at the rear. It was a considerable adaptation and it proved popular selling 11,000 by the middle of 1930.

Continental markets were not easy for British manufacturers. In the early 1920s a guide to the industry had already noted the 'French practice to stipulate that all vehicles built for Government or municipal service shall be entirely constructed in French factories with French labour.'[6] Import duties in force on the Continent were raised to new heights as the dictatorships in Italy and Germany attempted to protect and revive their industries in the 1930s.

Ford, with its responsibility for all the corporation's continental markets found life almost impossible. In 1934 Perry was telling his shareholders:

When our company in 1928 acquired the Italian business, Ford cars were sold in Italy in considerable quantities. At that time the import duty payable on a car which retailed in the USA for less than £100 was £98. In June 1930 the duty was increased to £269.

When in 1932 we introduced our British-made car which sold on this market at a retail price of £120, the import duty was £184 and the Italian public bought hundreds of our British £120 cars at a retail price of £364. In January last, the Italian Government increased the duty to the exorbitant figure of £282.

By the following year he was reporting that 'duties upon imports, prohibitions, quotas and other restraints have multiplied in France during 1934 with the consequence that if the company is to continue its hitherto prosperous career it seems abundantly clear that Ford products will have to be made entirely in France.'

By 1938, the industry was beginning to feel the consequences of Hitler's policy in Germany, of what he called 'my irrevocable decision to make the German automobile industry independent of the security of international imports and to place it on a solid and secure basis.' Hitler had warned that 'so-called private business is either capable of solving this problem or it is not capable of existing as private business.' But by 1938 British manufacturers were estimating that his government was giving export subsidies of over 40 per cent and German imports into Britain leapt, exceeding 3,000 (mainly from Opel) in the first three months of 1938. As a result the McKenna duties were subsumed under general import tariffs allowing the Government to raise them.

For all the flurry, the balance of trade position was still strong. Imports had risen from the 1936 figure of 12,143 to 18,560 in 1937 but in 1938, they actually fell back again to only 9,180. Exports meanwhile were booming, reaching a record 78,113 in 1937. So when William Morris, now raised to the title of Viscount Nuffield, rose to his feet at his company's thirteenth annual general meeting in May 1939, he was able to report a gross profit of £1.7 million and to announce that 'I am hopeful, provided the internal tension eases, that the Company will enjoy a greatly improved year in 1939.'

By the time Morris spoke his company appeared to have regained the stability it had lost at the beginning of the decade and the industry itself had settled into a coherent pattern in which all the companies which mattered could now be numbered on the fingers of two hands.

As the *Economist* put it in late 1937, there were three main groups – 'large, small and specialist manufacturers. In the first category there are six names – Morris (including Wolseley and MG), Austin, Ford, Standard, Vauxhall and the companies under the aegis of Rootes. In the category of small manufacturers, we may include Rover, Riley, Triumph, Armstrong, Alvis, SS, Singer and Jowett. Finally the luxury manufacturers so-called include Rolls-Royce (with its subsidiary, Bentley) and Daimler (with its subsidiary, Manchester).'

Yet if the industry was established, it was also growing old. Austin and Morris, opposites in many ways, were both autocrats who found difficulty working with others. Both had failed to devise a proper succession or a system for bringing in young men which was to be a particular strength of the system which Perry was even now building into Ford. Nor could either found a dynasty. Morris was childless; Austin's only son had been killed in the First World War.

Morris was the most difficult. It is perhaps unfair to put too much weight on his remark that he believed in Government by benevolent dictatorship and his £50,000 donation to Sir Oswald Mosley's New Party. But he ran his company in the most dictatorial way, regularly falling out with almost everybody on whom he relied at a senior level. As he owned all the shares from 1924 to 1936, it was completely his company. Some acquisitions, such as Wolseley, were for many years owned by him personally and separately from Morris Motors. The problem was that, when Morris started to lose day to day interest in the business in the early 1930s, he could not let others alone to run it. Sir Miles Thomas who worked for Morris for more than twenty years, finally becoming his vice-chairman, described him as unpredictable and volatile; a man who always seemed to act intuitively on the spur of the moment.

His attention to cost was legendary. Thomas recounts Morris' reaction when he found soap left in a bowl of water in an assembly plant washroom. 'That bright-eyed tight little man fumed and swore and became tremendously hot under the collar. He cursed roundly the habits of people who did not leave washbasins in the state in which they would expect to find them. He cried to high heaven about the extravagance of leaving a piece of soap to waste.' Yet his generous settlements to men who he forced out of his business were also well-known.

Morris' main problem was human communication. He stopped attending board meetings in the 1920s, but would then disconcertingly call out managers in the middle of their own meetings which had effectively replaced them. Miles Thomas found 'Bill Morris was at his unhappy worst at a meeting. He realized that he was inarticulate, and could not clothe his ideas in well-considered words. He lost his temper easily, wriggled in his chair and on numerous occasions simply had to leave the boardroom. Of these shortcomings he was acutely aware and avoided both calling and attending round-table discussions. He was much better at explaining his thoughts and impressions face to face with one executive only. Grudgingly he let his team of managers get together and sort out the operational planning themselves in formal recorded meetings.'[7]

When asked by his biographers what qualities he most looked for in his managers, Morris' answer was 'loyalty'.

We have been told that he is sensitive to criticism; in one sense, he is, but the instances of which we have been told do not show that he reacts adversely to criticism as such, but rather that he is sensitive to criticism in personal terms, especially if brusquely expressed. If that should come from people he has chosen to work with him, it may well set up a barrier to co-operation.[8]

By the early 1930s, Thomas claims that Nuffield, who was away on his Australasian voyages for up to four months at a time, was responsible for little of the ideas of the company, and would concede privately his failure to bring in young men or arrange for proper delegation.

In 1933, typically without consulting anyone else, he brought in Leonard Lord for the major reorganization at Cowley. Lord had been a highly effective production and lay-out organizer under Woollard at Wolseley's. A tough glum Yorkshire man, as difficult as Morris, he was brought in to revamp the factory and its models, and succeeded brilliantly.

Lord, a bitter man, with a huge inferiority complex, was to have an enormous influence on the post-war course of the industry and is blamed by many for its decline. But at this time, Thomas describes him as 'a power-house of energy'.

He was proud of his new authority, almost to the point of arrogance, but in a remarkably short space of time, he made that Cowley factory into one of the most efficient instruments for assembling motor cars to be seen anywhere in Europe.

He walked roughly over the toes of anyone who got in his way. He wore a lighted cigarette constantly in a corner of his mouth, blowing off the ash without taking it from between his lips. He loved sketching ideas for fascia boards, instrument mountings and other details on pieces of scrap paper, then getting the drawing office to work out the practical designs. New Morris models swiftly began to take shape.

But Lord was not to last. After three years he was gone after a row with Morris when he suggested that he should receive a much higher salary plus a percentage of profits.

After a brief period looking after one of the Nuffield trusts, Lord took over at Longbridge with the same ruthless approach that he had shown at Cowley, and designed the Austin Eight which would compete against the Morris Eight he had just produced at Oxford.

The bitterness of the split was never to be forgotten. Thomas remembers Lord sitting in his office when 'suddenly blowing the ash off the inevitable cigarette between his lips, [he] said, "Tommy, I'm going to take that business at Cowley apart, brick by bloody brick." ' It was a useful guide but a bad omen for what was to happen after the war when Lord had succeeded Austin.

By the time the war began, Lord Austin was well into his seventies. He could look back on remarkable progress; from building his own car before the Red Flag Act to his pioneering of

standardization and rational factory lay-out. He was still designing successful cars almost 40 years after he had started and
heading the second biggest mass car maker in the country. His
life had refuted the crassly arrogant description of him by one of
the first society motorists, John Moore-Brabazon. 'His dark
clothes and a bowler hat, his brusqueness and inability to suffer
fools gladly, his directness and the patent fact that he was a
mechanic, nothing more or less.'

Austin's appearance was easy to caricature. In 1929 in a series
of interviews with Austin, the *Autocar* wrote: 'Sir Herbert has
always carried his weathercock about with him. The position of
his hat is a sure indication of which way the wind is blowing. The
bowler pushed well back towards his neck indicates that there are
storms brewing. Workmen who are familiar with these signs
trim their sails accordingly.'

Yet Austin, unlike Morris, could retain the loyalty and services
of his colleagues for long periods. On the Austin board until his
death was Englebach who had laid out the Longbridge which was
Austin's monument.

'It has become the aim of the Longbridge factory,' Austin said
in 1929, 'to justify certain additions to the slogan which we now
hear so frequently, "Buy British". There is, of course, the
addition, "Buy Best", which the wise have long taken for
granted. But the other addition is "Buy Cheapest" and that is
now an accepted fact. If a motor car is British, best and cheapest,
what more can anyone ask?" ' It was a fine aim but one which was
to prove elusive even in the uniquely favourable conditions of the
interwar years.

Now as the storm-clouds of war once again gathered, it was
time for the captains and the kings of the early industry to begin
to depart. After the clouds had burst and then cleared away, the
sun would again smile on the industry. But it would be one
which had irrevocably changed, and with Government and
unions both playing a much more active and interventionist role,
would never again see the dominance of such self-made
individuals.

Austin starts up his first Austin car at Longbridge in Birmingham in 1905.

Herbert Austin in trilby in one of his early Wolseleys.

The Argyll company spent £220,000 on their factory near Glasgow and the workers wore uniforms. It was bankrupt in two years.

By contrast this was the workshop in Cook Street, Manchester where Henry Royce built his first car.

The Specialist Cars
'Swift as the Wind, Silent as a Shadow'

There is a story that William Morris, Lord Nuffield, was once introduced to a businessman on one of his frequent foreign visits as the maker of Morris cars. The man's face remained blank and unimpressed. But when it was pointed out that Morris also made MG cars, a smile of enthusiastic recognition broke through.

So it was that, though the big manufacturers might dominate the industry and pay the wages of tens of thousands of workers, it was the smaller specialist manufacturers who grabbed the limelight. They provided the glamour and the reputation for excellence in which the British industry was often content to bask. They offered a distinctive British style, whether it was for the American college student spinning through California in his open topped MG or the Arab Sheikh in his air conditioned Rolls or the Japanese businessman in his rare imported Jaguar.

Names like Rolls-Royce, Bentley, Aston-Martin or Jaguar became better known than Austin, Morris or Standard, because of the glamour of open-topped sports cars and race-tracks or the respect for high performance success. However, they produced a fraction of the output and often depended on the big manufacturer for key parts.

Sir William Lyons, the founder of Jaguar, summed up the specialist car as 'one which offered particularly high standards of design, manufacture and performance – with an emphasis on quality and luxury, particularly if it were a saloon or convertible. These attributes appealed to the connoisseurs of motoring who were invariably prepared to pay a considerable premium for such vehicles. Generally speaking, it was produced in small quantities and many of the best-known names of pre-World War Two days were manufacturers of this type.'

The specialist cars covered a wide spectrum, stretching from those like Rolls-Royce who provided both luxury and perform-ance, to high performance cars of immense power and expense like the Bentley, down to souped-up and rebodied versions of mass manufacturers' products like MGs, to those specially put together for enthusiasts with little spare cash like Morgan. There was another distinction too; between those firms who manufac-tured all or most of their own component parts to standards which they claimed others could not match, and those who depended on other manufacturers for a chassis or an engine or a gearbox or more – and then added their distinctive specialist touch.

That was how Lyons himself began. He was one of the natural successors of the hundreds of small firms who had begun before the First World War to assemble motor cars to designs of their own making but from parts made by others and often imported.

The original companies are long gone, shut down or metamor-phosed into something different. But one survivor has remained, as if preserved in aspic throughout the century, refusing the temptation to expand and to change to mass production and providing the same kind of custom-built service in the 1980s as before the First World War.

The Morgan company of Malvern in Worcestershire grew like so many from the enthusiasm of a young man caught up by the craze for motoring. In this case it was Henry Morgan, the son of a West Country clergyman, who after a public school education became a draughtsman at the big railways works at Swindon. The first car he ever drove was a hired three and a half horsepower Benz which ran away with him down a hill. His father paid for the damage and also put up the money for him to build his first cars.

Morgan started a garage business in Malvern and developed his first car, a three wheeler, using the workshops of Malvern College where a friend's father was a master. It was based on a tubular chassis rather like a ladder with a central backbone, cross pieces supporting the engine and the two side tubes doubling as exhaust pipes. The engine was a seven horsepower Peugeot which he had originally intended to use for a motorcycle. The basic design remained for nearly 30 years. In one of those recurring personal connections which make the early motor industry seem like one extended family, part of the design was drawn out by John Black who was later to become chairman of Standard.

The car was exhibited at the 1910 motor-cycle show but it was its success in races and hill climbs which rapidly established it. Morgan raced it himself at every opportunity and demand for the car soon outran supply. With £3,000 from his father, he set up a factory and by the time war broke out, production had reached about 1,000 a year and the company's profits were £10,450. The company grew on a wave of enthusiasm for light cars – sales of the new *Cyclecar* magazine launched in 1912 were an extraordinary 100,000. Its reputation was boosted when the country's greatest First World War air ace, Captain Albert Ball, VC, bought, and was photographed in, a Morgan. By 1921, nearly 2,500 were sold.

The car was sold on grounds of cheapness – 'the perfect answer to the cost problem, selling for nineteen years on its reputation for economy; if you can afford a motor-cycle and sidecar, you can afford the greater comfort of the Morgan' – but also on its sportiness. In 1930 it was advertised that out of fourteen Morgans entered for the Land's End trial, eleven had won gold medals and two silver. The car was 'fast' and 'comfortable' and motoring charges were low.

The company usually provided three basic models – a two seater standard, a four seater, and a more sporting version which justified a favourite slogan: 'The private owner can win in a Morgan.'

By the middle of the 1930s, however, with increasing affluence sales dropped – 659 in 1934, only 286 in the following year. But in 1936 Morgan had produced its first four wheeler, the basis for further success. After the Second World War it produced about 400 a year until demand dwindled in the 1960s. It was saved temporarily by exports to the United States and then it became almost a collector's item, as larger sports car firms turned to more modern designs, and demand revived. By the 1980s there were four-year waiting lists for British customers.

Throughout its career Morgan maintained the same formula – buying in engines and gearboxes but building its own bodies, chassis and suspension, often with customers specifying particu-

lar modifications and coming to the factory to inspect. Its parts
came from the big manufacturers; Ford Eight, and then Standard
Vanguard engines from Sir John Black, powered the first four
wheelers; by the 1980s they came from Ford or Landrover.

This was usual practice for most of the celebrated small
production sports car companies which boomed during the inter-
war years. Companies like Frazer-Nash or Lea-Francis bought
proprietary engines and based their appeal on the performance
they could wring out of the engine, along with their special
bodywork and perhaps some unique feature such as the Frazer-
Nash transmission. Others like the Jensen brothers took whole
chassis from manufacturers.

Companies which insisted on making all their own parts were
in a different league – celebrated, expensive, and often destined
for a short life.

The most famous name to emerge in the inter-war years to
challenge the reputation of companies like Rolls-Royce and
Napier in blazing a trail across Europe was that of Bentley.

Like Henry Royce, and a number of the early car makers,
W.O. Bentley had been an engineering apprentice in the big
railway workshops – in this case in Doncaster. By the time the
First World War broke out, he was an agent for a French motor
company, DFP, in London. There he made a breakthrough,
developing an aluminium piston, which gave great advantages in
weight, and which, when war broke out, took him into the Royal
Naval Air Service where he was set to develop aluminium pistons
for aero-engines. To his astonishment his engines were highly
successful, a fact confirmed to him by the pilots he met in his
visits to squadrons in France. When the war ended, he started to
make cars together with F.T. Burgess, a designer he had met
during production of his aero-engines.

Bentley's cars owed much to Continental thinking. In some
ways they were racing cars adapted for the road, nicknamed by
the Italian car maker Ettore Bugatti as 'le camion le plus vite' – the
fastest lorry. Bentley himself said, 'I wanted a car that could be
driven hard without minding,' a car, as he put it, 'with long legs'.
Many of the British designs in his view were all right – but only
'for local trips'. The cars he admired were the 1912 Peugeot and
the 1914 Grand Prix Mercedes.

On the race track, the Bentleys were spectacularly successful. They won the Le Mans race four years running from 1927 to 1930, and on the open road they were hardly less impressive – perhaps the most potent symbol still of the vintage years of motoring. But financially they were a disaster.

Bentley found himself forced to contract out almost all the manufacture. It meant he had little control over costs and was at the mercy of his two main suppliers. Henry Royce observing Bentley's rise from the seclusion of the Sussex countryside wrote, in 1925, 'Regarding the Bentley, the makers are evidently out to capture some of our trade . . . it would appear more costly than ours to produce for equal silence.'

Bentley himself wrote:

> We had to design almost every individual component from universal joints to gearboxes, from back axles to distributors. All I can remember that we were able to obtain from proprietary firms were the Rudge wire wheels, the electrics and the steering wheel.
>
> In the end we solved our production problems mainly through a firm at Twickenham which had been at a complete loss for orders. They did about 80 per cent of the car while another firm took on the back axle, the gearbox gears and the bevel gear for the engine. By this time in 1922 we had become not manufacturers of motor cars as we had intended, but assemblers and testers.[1]

By 1924 the firm was turning out 322 cars in a year, but it lost over £56,000. It was liquidated and reorganized and continued both to make over 300 cars a year and, almost always, to make a loss. It had been rescued by one of the enthusiastic Bentley drivers, Wolf Barnato, the son of a rich diamond magnate. He put in £143,000 and insisted on management changes. Even so, over 30 per cent of Bentley's cost remained indirect – on sales, administration, service – and racing.

In 1931, with the company set to lose over £84,000, the managing director, J.K. Carruth, wrote to Rolls-Royce suggesting a working arrangement between the two companies. Bentley's main trouble in the past, he suggested, had been 'the delivery of new models to the public before adequate tests have been made.'[2] More threateningly he pointed out that Bentley had 100 chassis in stock which were likely to come onto the market at cut-prices.

Rolls-Royce heeded the warning but refused the bait.

So on the 21st October 1931, the receiver appointed to Bentley Motors made a conditional agreement to sell to the Napier company for £84,000. It would have brought Rolls-Royce's greatest rival back into the car business. However, a rival bid quickly materialized, and the Bentley company was sold instead to British Equitable Trust for £125,175. It was simply a front. The Trust was acting for Rolls-Royce, which had anticipated an auction if its name got out, and now absorbed its rival.

The last new Bentley had appeared in 1931, a four litre six cylinder car which was a failure. The Bentley eventually became little more than badge engineering for Rolls-Royce – a slightly different badge on a standard model. But in the 1980s there was talk once again of reviving Bentley as a separate, more sporty, model.

Rolls-Royce itself had opted to go in the opposite direction. After the First World War, it decided not to go back into racing but to sell the cars on the smoothness of their engineering. The ethos was summed up in an internal memo in 1922 which complained that 'there was creeping in from all sides a desire to increase speed and power at the expense of silkiness.'

With its reputation enhanced by the war, the company's production expanded from over 2,000 in 1920 to a peak of 3,347 in 1928. In 1922 a smaller version, the 'Twenty', was added to the Silver Ghost, and the Ghost itself was then replaced by the Phantom.

But the company was increasingly worried by its poor profits. In the early 1920s it was only making about £160,000 a year and 40 per cent of that was coming from the aero-engine business which was less than a quarter of its turnover. As car production fell back in the 1930s almost to the levels of the immediate post-war period, the management became increasingly concerned about the quality and cost of its cars. It was distracted by an attempt to start Rolls-Royce manufacture in the United States at Springfield, Massachusetts. The plant was closed when it became clear that Americans preferred the English-made variety.

By 1933 Ernest Hives, who later as Lord Hives was to run the company, was writing, 'The reputation of Rolls-Royce was built up on silence and smoothness. There are a number of cars which are most silent and have less vibration and better performance.'

The company increasingly turned its eyes to what was happening on the other side of the Atlantic in the big American companies. A director, Sir Ernest Sidgreaves, reported after one US tour that 'not only are we not progressing, but we are definitely going back, in other words we are being surpassed by the Americans in particular respect to those features on which our name and reputation have been built up.' Hives, who became general works manager in 1936, was alarmed that 'in spite of us charging fabulous prices, there remains very little profit.' He set about reconsidering Rolls' proud determination to make all its own parts, and bought radiators from an outside firm. A comparison of costs revealed an alarming situation. Shock absorbers which cost nearly £8 for the company to make could be bought for £3; the exhaust system, which cost nearly £13, could be bought for £1 if an American type was used. The difference between buying dynamos and starters or making them themselves was the price of a chassis.

Hives wrote crisply that the company 'had dropped so far behind with major components such as frames, springing, engines, steering, brakes etc. that where we can get help outside we have got to take advantage of it.'

The argument within Rolls-Royce did not reach a conclusion until after the company transferred its energies into its aero-engines with the approach of the Second World War. But it had its effect later when the company reverted post-war to its old Claude Johnson policy of concentrating on a single model.

The mass manufacturers looked on the specialist cars with a mixture of emotions. While they could see their appeal, they were a diversion from the serious and profit-conscious business of mass production – one which must not be allowed to get in the way.

The attitude was seen at its clearest in William Morris, who became, almost by accident, the maker of what was probably the most successful sports car – the MG. Morris had produced what were called sports models of both his first cars. But they had standard engines and chassis and as his official biographers wrote: 'he was not going to have the subsequent requirements of the enthusiasts leading Cowley on to making modifications in routines which would interfere with their costs for the wider market.'

Morris' involvement with real sports cars came almost through the back door. As he expanded into manufacturing he had kept his old Morris Garages business as part of his private property, employing managers to run it. In 1922 Cecil Kimber became general manager and started to compete in sports car competitions using a special version of the Oxford with an aluminium body and a modified engine. Kimber was a determined enthusiast who had worked for various motor engineering companies before coming to Oxford, and with his rally success he started to offer specials for sale. Although they used chassis, radiators and engines from the standard Morris line, the engines were hotted up and special bodies and other components fitted. The letters MG simply stood for Morris Garages.

Demand grew quickly; from twenty produced in 1925, numbers rose to 400 in 1927 and 1,800 in 1930. At first they were made in a mews, and the cars were pushed out into the street in the morning to make room for construction to take place. In the early days men could work from six in the morning until ten at night.

In frequent pain from an old motorcycle injury, which left one leg two inches shorter than the other, Kimber was a martinet who worked his work force hard, and loved his cars. He insisted on sumptuous catalogues and told the artist responsible, Harold Connolly, the basis of his designs – 'that a sports car should always look fast even when it is standing still.'

When manufacture moved to Edmund Road in Cowley in 1928, Kimber began to build cars that were more than just modifications of the Morris range. The trend continued when MG set up a factory in Abingdon in 1930. The early 1930s saw a string of rally successes, but the cars were abruptly withdrawn from racing by Morris and his new production supremo, Leonard Lord, in 1935.

Morris sold MG to Morris Motors and it became a part of Lord's organization. Lord visited Abingdon, and inspected the factory. He looked at the racing shop and said, 'Well, that bloody lot can go for a start.' A more considered explanation is given in Morris' biography. Pointing out the costs of racing and the way cars were increasingly being modified to take part, it says: 'Morris absolutely refused to allow the production model of the MG to be modified to suit these developments, nor did he wish the MG management to produce special racing models for official entries. He did not want people to be able to say, "Of course these are not the cars they sell." '[3]

Kimber was upset at the changes but soldiered on until he was sacked over a dispute over Second World War aircraft work in 1941. Ironically, and tragically for a man who loved fast cars, he died in a slow-motion accident on a train when the carriage he was travelling in rolled backwards and was derailed in 1945. A few days before his death, he had talked to John Black about designing sports cars for Triumph. He wrote to a friend, 'I feel somewhat pessimistic about the future of the real enthusiast's car. Sunbeam-Talbot, Riley and now MG have been or will be wrecked by the soul-deadening hand of big business interests and recently I have been staying with John Black who had just bought Triumph, and what he proposes to do with that old name makes me want to weep.'[4]

For all Kimber's pessimism, MGs remained an enthusiast's car into the 1980s, a mainstay of the company's exports. The factory became the biggest employer around Abingdon. As Ken Pabst, one of the 700 workers made redundant in 1980 when it closed, said, after twenty years in the works, 'I think you had all the pride in what you were doing. It was a small factory It was a little bit of a kick to work in it. MGs had this reputation. Nearly every day you had some sort of celebrity coming round on tours. To start with, you felt that you were producing something that everybody wanted.'

For men like Pabst, the option of working in a big mass production plant like Cowley was one to be rejected – the specialist car makers, however mundane their skills, felt them-selves a bit special too.

The company which perhaps most of all managed to combine that special pride and quality with a shift into mass production was what is now called Jaguar.

Jaguar started in an even smaller way than companies like

Morgan, with the production of motor-cycle side-cars. Again it was a young man's enthusiasm. William Lyons was not yet 21 when one William Walmsley moved into his road in Blackpool and started to build what he called Swallow Sidecars next to his house.

Lyons who had worked briefly for Crossley Motors in Manchester and was employed by a local dealer, bought a sidecar from Walmsley and then persuaded him to set up a joint business in 1922. They put up £1,000 and Lyons' share was guaranteed by his parents who went to the bank with him as he was not yet 21.

William Lyons was to be one of the most complete of the great figures of the British motor industry – a brilliant conceptual designer who would whittle away at a piece of wood to provide the shape he wanted, but was also involved with every detail of his factory organization from the intricacies of wage rates to the exact positioning of instruments on a dashboard. Years after his death, the company's cars still bore his recognizable imprint.

He gave the impression to one of his early secretarial staff of never having been a young man – a contrast to the more 'bluff and hearty' Walmsley. Another of his first workers described him as 'a very dedicated businessman, economic and frugal – the business came first, unlike his partner, who was more interested in what he could get out of it.'

In spite of the flamboyance of his cars, Lyons remained studiously unassuming in keeping with the frugality he valued. He was formal, if not cold, addressing long-serving workers as Mr or Mrs, but he was as single minded and tough with employers and Governments as he could be with workers. There was no design team to speak of; it remained Lyons, and even small decisions on his cars could not be taken if he was away. That was as much the case at the end as it was at the modest start.

The firm employed what Lyons described as 'three men and a boy' on the empty two floors of a building which was producing electrical equipment. It was not until five years later that Lyons turned his thoughts to making cars. Like many other enthusiasts he had been impressed with the Austin Seven, which was frequently rebuilt and adapted for racing in competition with cars like the MG. Lyons' view was that:

the conception of this car had a strong appeal except that the body was a very stark affair, albeit very practical. . . I believed that it would also appeal to a lot of people if it had a more luxurious and attractive body. We therefore bought one of these and produced the first Austin Swallow, an open sports two-seater, and, in the following year, a saloon model; both had their own special radiator cowling and looked very different from the ordinary Austin.

Lyons travelled to London and won an order for 500 from the rising dealer firm of Henley's. The numbers were far greater than the firm had planned for. As the workshop struggled to turn out two cars a day, Lyons received a call from a Blackpool station complaining that his hundreds of waiting chassis were jamming the station. The company had already moved into larger premises, but now Lyons knew he had to make a bigger jump. Most of his supplies came from the Midlands as did some of the skilled labour he could not find in Blackpool. So he decided to move to Coventry.

He found a disused shell factory which had been empty since the war. It was a series of narrow compartments each separated from the rest in order to minimize the effects of explosion. It was in poor condition. Contractors asked to repair it quoted a figure which exceeded Swallow's assets.

Lyons acted in typically decisive fashion. He employed labourers to do the job himself and moved in even though it would soon be winter. The electrical cable which supplied power to the factory was almost immediately stolen and another had to be bought and laid. To get increased production new methods were employed; instead of one bodymaker being responsible for the framing of a complete body, parts were machined in jigs and then fitted together like a jigsaw. Lyons withstood a bodymakers' revolt at the new methods and got his 50 bodies a week by Christmas.

The conditions were appalling. Connie Teather had been a secretary at the Blackpool factory and came down to Coventry a few weeks after the move. She recalls:

The factory was very damp. All the walls were running with

water. There was no central heating. There was just a big
boiler in the cellar. The windows were small oblong slits high
up on the wall. Everything was made on the premises.
Everything.

When I got there on the Monday morning they had coke
braziers to keep the men warm because the doors of the factory
were permanently open. They were very hard conditions – a
lot of people came and went.

In the office we had wooden trestles covered with brown
lino and lino on the floor, but for the first fortnight we had
orange boxes.

It was very exciting. We didn't fancy going into an office
that was full of decorum. It was very exciting for young people
and we caught the enthusiasm of Sir William. We had to be in a
hurry.

That enthusiasm kept people working in the factory to nine or
ten at night – and Lyons did not pay overtime.

He won through because of that enthusiasm coupled with a
tight control of his costs. He made a careful time study of each
operation and provided a book of vouchers for each car. When a
workman completed an operation, he tore off a voucher, signed
it and gave it to the foreman for authorization. At the end of the
week the vouchers were totted up to calculate the pay.

It was typical of Lyons' thorough approach; he never slackened
control of his company. Years later he was to be found negotiating intricate details of piecework deals with union officials while
salesmen from the component companies complained that minor
decisions about an instrument for a car's fascia panel could not be
made if Lyons was away.

The Lyons system was challenged immediately he arrived in
Coventry. In the first week new workers taken on in Coventry
objected to the payment system and staged a demonstration by
storming into the stores and tipping parts all over the floor.
Lyons stood his ground, telling them 'like it or leave.' Only a
few left.

His next step was to produce a more original car. Although he
had used other chassis besides the Austin, building Morris, Swift,
Wolseley and even Fiat Swallows, he wrote, 'I badly wanted to

produce a chassis which did not inhibit body design to such a degree.'

In 1930 we designed a chassis frame which would accommodate the Standard sixteen or twenty horsepower engines suspension and transmission. Rubery Owen made it for us and R.W. Maudslay (of Standard) agreed to supply the complete chassis using this special frame.

This hybrid was to be called the SS1, a name which was agreed upon after long argument with Maudslay and Black, which resulted from my determination to establish a marque of our own. There was much speculation as to whether SS stood for Standard Swallow or Swallow Special – it was never resolved.

With the success of the SS1 the company's ambition grew. Lyons believed the way was clear to make a complete car of his own. He set to work to design a new body and called in an engineer, Harry Weslake, to design a new cylinder head for a Standard's successful six-cylinder engine. He persuaded John Black at Standard to put in the new plant to make the engine, which SS could not afford. The car was launched at the end of 1935. SS's nickname, 'the cad's car', did not stop sales.

Lyons wanted a brand new name for it and asked his publicity staff to provide a list of animals, fish and birds. He recalls:

I immediately pounced on Jaguar for it had an exciting sound to me and brought back some memories of the stories told to me towards the end of the 1914–1918 war by an old school friend . . . who had joined the Royal Flying Corps . . . He used to tell me of his work as a mechanic on the Armstrong-Siddeley 'Jaguar' engine.

The advertising declared 'The car of the future has appeared – swift as the wind, silent as a shadow come the new SS Jaguars.'

Its introduction to the company's distributors was dramatic. Lyons unveiled it at the Mayfair Hotel, and then asked the audience to write down their estimate of the car's selling price on cards which were handed out. 'With two scrutineers from the gathering as supervisors, a comptometer operator calculated the average of all the prices handed in. This came to £765, so when I announced that the actual price was £395, it created quite a lot of excitement and added much enthusiasm for the car.'

The competition was surprised too. At Rolls-Royce they compared the appropriate Jaguar at £450 with the £950 Bentley. Even after allowing for the Bentley's better engine, they estimated that 70 per cent of the difference could be accounted for only by the use of 'good manufacturing techniques backed up by sound purchasing of fabricated parts.'

The company's sales rose from 1,720 in 1935 to 2,469 in 1936 and 3,554 in 1937. There was a temporary fall in 1938 as SS cars switched over to an all metal body, but in 1939 a record 5,378 cars were sold.

Lyons' ambition to manufacture all the key ingredients of his cars himself was brought closer by the time the war ended. Standard decided to concentrate production on a single new model and a new engine and offered SS cars the opportunity to buy the machinery which had built their engine. Lyons, who had been worried that rival firms might get the use of what was largely his design, seized his opportunity.

After the War, the company's name was rapidly changed to Jaguar to avoid any possible confusion with Hitler's SS storm-troopers. Its expansion became one of the successes of the post-war years, starting with the brilliant XK range.

Jaguar was the one specialist car maker to make the transition to becoming a large, if not quite a mass manufacturer, and yet to maintain its image and its engineering excellence. In the 1950s its cars emulated Bentley and won the Le Mans race five times.

It was an achievement that W.O. Bentley himself recognized. He wrote:

> Lyons can be said to have achieved, while pursuing roughly similar aims as we pursued, the final success that for various reasons eluded us.
>
> The cars have always retained their character and their individual feel and he has never been tempted into producing too many of them.[5]

Lyons put it rather more prosaically:

Into this select group [of specialist cars] we injected the Jaguar models – different in design and appearance and with a good performance but produced in relatively large volumes in order to make the price realistic. I believe that in those now far-off days we started a whole new approach to specialist cars.

7

The Component Makers
'Motoralities and Monopolies'

The huge expansion and consolidation of the motor industry between the wars spread far beyond the confines of the motor car manufacturers' plants. It stretched its tentacles far and wide, into all kinds of companies, small and large, within engineering and outside it. With even Ford, the big manufacturer most anxious to integrate its whole operation, still buying 65 per cent of its requirements from outside firms, a whole host of companies reaped the benefit. They ranged from the large, like Briggs Bodies and Kelsey-Hayes, specially introduced by Ford from America to provide its bodies and wheels, or Pressed Steel, bodymakers to the world, to the small jobbing companies who might fit in their pressing of valve caps for the motor industry beside making copper parts for the railway industry or patent wrenches for the general engineering trade, so that it was questionable whether they could be said to be part of the motor trade at all.

When statisticians came to count the number of people employed in the industry, it was easy to reach different conclusions about who was to be counted. The only general agreement was that there were more people employed in jobs dependent on the car manufacturers than the total number who actually worked in their factories – a fact emphasized by people in the component companies who called the likes of Morris and Austin not motor manufacturers but, more accurately, assemblers.

Although each manufacturer might, and did, call on hundreds of different suppliers – the majority of their purchases came from a small number of big suppliers. In some cases, like the tyre company Dunlop or the Black Country ironfounders or the big Birmingham electrical company of Joseph Lucas, they were companies which had existed before the motor car was invented. Many of them grew with it, but from the standpoint of the 1980s it must be said that those who ultimately prospered most were the companies who used the profits they made from motors to spread the risk and diversify into other industries.

The increasing strength of these component companies was recognized by the *Economist* in its 1935 motor industry supplement. It declared:

The motor industry as a whole is moving towards increasing specialization and standardization. The manufacturer is more and more becoming an assembler of parts provided by specialists in different lines.

Tyres, sparking plugs, batteries, electric lighting and starting equipment, clocks, speedometers and gauges, carburettors and radiators, glass, bodies and upholstery – all these are products of specialist manufacture. They provide the mainstay of important firms, which, although not actually motor manufacturers, are almost as dependent on the motor industry as the car manufacturers themselves.

Listing such firms as Dunlop, Lucas, Triplex Glass, Pressed Steel, Briggs Motor Bodies, S. Smith and Son and ICI, it observed, 'The predominance of a few large companies is noticeable in the case of most motor accessories.'

Both the first two companies listed by the *Economist* pre-dated the motor industry, though from their impressive headquarters in Birmingham – in the case of Dunlop its 'fort' – they seemed to symbolize the power and strength of the motor connection and the way it swept up new inventions to speed it on its way.

The invention of the pneumatic tyre had first helped inflate the cycling boom of the 1890s out of which so many motor manufacturers had sprung; then, imperfect as it still was, it accelerated the spread of the motor car. In Britain its potential for profit was quickly recognized by Harry Lawson and others in their quest for quick returns.

The Dunlop company was based on the invention of a pneumatic tyre by a Belfast vet called John Boyd Dunlop in 1888. It was a domestic contraption intended to make the tricycle of his ten year old son run better and more comfortably on the harsh city streets. Using rubber sheeting, canvas and rubber solution, components which he had used in his practice, Dunlop constructed a pneumatic tyre of rubbered canvas which enclosed a rubber tube and fitted it round a home-made wooden disc. He then bowled it along his yard in competition with a solid tyred wheel. The solid wheel eventually toppled and fell; the new invention ran the length of the yard and bounded back off closed doors. Dunlop first fitted the device to his son's tricycle and then registered a patent, No. 10,607 on July 23rd, 1888. A local bicycle maker soon began to construct both wheels and bicycles to carry pneumatic tyres, and in 1889 the Dunlop patents were bought out by the Vice-Chairman of the Irish Cyclists Association, Harvey du Cros. He formed the Pneumatic Tyre and Booth's Cycle Agency Ltd in Dublin with a capital of £25,000. Dunlop received £3,000 worth of shares and £300.

He had not, as it turned out, been the first to patent the pneumatic tyre. His invention was challenged by the re-discovery of an earlier patent by a Scotsman, R.W. Thomson, who had invented an 'aerial wheel' as early as 1845, fitting it to a horsedrawn brougham and carrying out experiments in Regents Park in London. The Dunlop company's lead was consolidated by buying two more patents, which related to the crucial problem of early tyres – fixing them to the wheel. They cost over £200,000 but established the company. The tyres were so eagerly sought after that du Cros, with Ernest Hooley and Harry Lawson, decided to float Dunlop to the public with a capital of three million pounds. Their chief market was still the cycle trade – the first car to appear with pneumatic tyres was a French Peugeot in 1895 – before the Red Flag Act had even been repealed in Britain. It was entered by the brothers Michelin for the Paris to Bordeaux race, but was no instant success, coming in ninth. The quality of rubber available found difficulty in standing up to the bad roads, and solid tyres remained a favourite for motor cars and a necessity for heavily loaded commercial vehicles until the end of the century and beyond. It was not until the First World War that Dunlop developed new textile with its cords running in the same direction which could be coated with rubber to make an effective tyre which could stand up to heavy loads.

The problems of the early pneumatic tyre were set out by S.F. Edge, himself a Dunlop sales agent, in his description of the Thousand Miles Trial of 1900 which established both the importance of the pneumatic tyre and the urgent need to improve it. He wrote:

> The life of the average pneumatic tyre did not exceed one thousand miles and luck was needed to cover that distance on a set of tyres.
>
> There were no such things as spare or detachable wheels. When a puncture occurred, which happened very often, due both to the quality of the tyres and the numbers of horse shoes and nails found on the roads, it was almost impossible for one man, unassisted, to remove a cover, and still as difficult to refit it again. Each cover was held on by numbers of so-termed security bolts which easily nipped the tube and punctured it again during the process of refitting. Valves varied and it was not uncommon, unless one was very careful, to be stranded with a pump connection which would not fit the particular valve.[1]

Edge won the 1902 Gordon-Bennett race, in which all a car's parts must come from the driver's country, on a Napier fitted with Dunlop tyres but only after the car had been designed as Edge put it 'round the capabilities of the tyres.' The previous year he had had to scratch from the race when he took his Napier over to France with Dunlop tyres, and quickly found that 'no tyres made in this country were the slightest use for such a car as they simply came to pieces within a few miles and left the rims.' Edge fitted French tyres and entered another race instead.

Dunlop had only produced its first motor tyre in 1900 and bought a company making motor wheels in 1906. But it was Michelin tyres, brought in from abroad, which were the first to be used by British motorists – and British tyre measurements were therefore set in millimetres. The first separate import figures for tyres in 1913 show £2·5 million worth coming in, and only £708,000 worth exported.

Dunlop expanded hugely during and after the First World War, buying a cotton mill in Lancashire in 1916 and starting to build Fort Dunlop on 300 acres in Birmingham; after the war the growth continued with more rubber estates and a steel mill being purchased. But like many motor manufacturers at the time, it over-reached itself. The company lost the huge sum of £8 million in 1921 and was reorganized, diversifying widely, buying the Macintosh company in 1925, going into aircraft wheels and equipment and establishing factories throughout the world.

After the First World War Dunlop found itself facing competition not only from the Continental producers like Michelin, but increasingly from the big American companies. Eventually it was the Government which provided protection. In 1926 the McKenna duties were extended to cover tyres, and the result was a spectacular mushrooming of foreign-owned factories in Britain. The American Goodyear company set up in Wolverhampton in 1927. Michelin which had set up a sales office in London in 1905 built its first factory at Stoke-on-Trent in 1927. In 1928 Firestone began in London as did the India Tyre and Rubber Company, which was later taken over by Dunlop. In 1929 the Italian firm Pirelli set up.

World production of rubber rose to keep pace with the increase in motor manufacture round the world. Between 1911 and 1929, it grew by about 44,000 tons a year until the slump cut American motor production by three-quarters. From then on there was a world surplus of tyre production and Dunlop axed hundreds of workers, but the companies based in Britain still managed to export, if at a reduced rate. In 1939, 3,764,364 tyres were exported with a value of £2·9 million. That compared with 4·2 million tyres in 1920.

So the tyre industry exhibited much the same pattern as motor manufacture itself; the original imports of superior foreign products continued even after British manufacture was established, with the British makers then having to rely on protection to keep them out. So too with the key component – engines.

From Frederick Simms onwards, British manufacturers had been keen to import foreign engines. Beside Daimler, French de Dion engines had been an early and reliable staple for both big companies like Humber and small entrepreneurs anxious to get into the motor business; Peugeot and Asters were among others imported, and Aster engines were made under licence at Wembley from 1899.

A number of well-known firms started by producing replacement British engines to take over from imports. One of them was Jowett, which made its first engine in 1901, and did not go on to full scale car manufacture until four years later.

Another was White and Poppe, founded in Coventry in 1900 to make engines for motor cycles, but by 1906 it was providing engines for fifteen makes of car as well as carburettors. Both Singer and Morris began with their engines, and by the start of the First World War the firm was turning out something like 2,000 engines a year.

Existing manufacturers of other types of engine like Crossley in Manchester and Willans and Robinson in Rugby turned to making petrol engines. But after the First World War, the increasing demand and profits of aero-engine manufacture were a seductive counter attraction. Firms like Napier and Rolls-Royce concentrated their production there, and limited petrol engine manufacture to their own vehicles. Morris' difficulty in finding competitive tenders for his engines, going to the United States, itself pointed up some of the shortcomings of the industry. When the commercial vehicle maker, Dennis, absorbed White and Poppe after the First World War, it is thought to have speeded the demise of a number of small car-makers who found themselves unable to get suitable engines elsewhere.

The old coachbuilders who had been in the trade long before the internal combustion engine benefitted from some of the trade the new industry brought. At the upper end of the market firms like Mulliners and Park Ward continued to provide a service for the likes of Daimler and Rolls-Royce. Morris used an Oxford coach-builder, Raworth, for his early bodies, later taking the company over. But they were soon overtaken in the mass production field by the new technology of the metal body which was initially built on a wooden frame.

Here Austin was an early pioneer. He was a friend of the Sankey brothers, John and George, whose father Joseph had established a company at Bilston in the Black Country in 1854 to make stamped metal goods and pressings. They were quick to see the potential of the new industry, and by 1904 he was asking them to use their expertise to make metal body shells which could be mounted on wooden frames. They were soon supplying

Argyll in Scotland, as well as Daimler, Humber, Rover and Star who were nearby in the Midlands. Within two years, Sankey's innovation had been noted in the United States and they were shipping untrimmed and unpainted bodies across to Edward E. Cary Inc. of New York.

The firm made a second technical leap a year or two later with the patenting of a method of making all-steel wheels devised by its works manager, Wingfield Burton. They made two halves for an artillery wheel shape which were then welded together. To exploit the invention the firm bought a factory at Wellington in Shropshire where they became the country's biggest wheel manufacturer, and in due course employed a third of the labour in the area. The first cost estimates for the two-seater Morris Cowley in June 1915 specified 'set of 5 Sankey steel wheels – £2.10s.'

Sankey's was just one of the companies whose fortunes prospered with the huge expansion of the firms they supplied, and Morris in particular. Their spread of products included clutch plate pressings, fans and brackets and chassis frames. After the First World War, they were part of the long rationalization of the components industry, being taken over by the company who had supplied much of their steel, Joseph Lysaght. This in turn disappeared into Guest, Keen and Nettlefold, which, as the GKN group, was to be the dominant engineering component maker.

Another company which was to become a major influence on the motor industry's fortunes (also later part of GKN) was founded by Edward J. Hardy in Coventry in the 1890s. This was an example, not so much like Sankey's of an existing business extending its range to accommodate the new motor industry but of a new trade created by the motor revolution.

Hardy had started by selling cycle parts in the 1890s, but switched to making car components in 1903. In 1914 he patented a universal joint which he called the Hardy Patent Flexible coupling. It provided one of the first reliable transmissions from engine and gearbox to the axle, so eliminating belt or chain drives. The war boosted his sales and he then went to the United States to license the invention. There he came into contact with American manufacturers and arranged to bring back two American products, a self-lubricating bearing and the Spicer coupling, manufacturing them in Britain.

Hardy formed the Hardy Spicer company which employed 45 people in 1927 to turn out 240 propeller shafts a week. Taking American experience to heart, he stuck to a rigid standardization policy which helped his prices. The shaft became almost standard equipment for British cars. Within seven years over 3,000 were produced a week and the workforce had multiplied ten times. By 1939 nearly a thousand people were employed; by 1955 over 2,300.

The company had also acquired rights to the constant velocity joint designed by A.H. Rzeppa, which it developed post-Second World War to provide the key component which made possible a generation of front wheel drive cars, starting with the Mini, and which brought in millions in overseas royalties for its parent company. Component makers like Hardy Spicer were often more innovative than the assemblers they supplied.

While the British assemblers had few lessons for their American counterparts, taking lessons from them instead, their suppliers not infrequently had expertise which the Americans appreciated.

A colourful demonstration of this came in 1927 when Henry Ford was involved in a car accident. The firm of Triplex, which had developed non-splintering safety glass, immediately sent a telegram by Western Union addressed to him at the Detroit General Hospital, Michigan. 'Regret to hear of your accident,' it read, 'Trust you have not been cut by broken glass. Fit Triplex and be safe. Triplex, London.' It was a brash and a cheeky initiative which paid off. The firm's sales director was invited to Ford and Triplex subsequently had a factory set up in New Jersey to supply the Ford Motor Company with its products.

Safety glass had been an early British invention. It had been patented in 1905 by a Swindon solicitor, John Crewe Wood, who saw that if a plastic laminate such as celluloid could be sandwiched between two pieces of glass it would prevent them shattering. He was before his time. There were too few cars, and his adhesive proved unsatisfactory. It was left instead to a Frenchman, Edouard Benedictus, to patent a safety glass in 1909 which he had discovered by accident – dropping a glass bottle which had contained nitrocellulose and finding it did not break. His trade mark was three large Xs – hence TripleX. The company quickly offered British patents and approached the well-established glass firm of Pilkington's with which it was to have a spasmodic relationship for many years before finally taking it over in 1965. Pilkington's turned down the patent because it thought it too expensive and because of questions over the existing Wood patent. Instead, in 1912 George Marius Delpech, a pioneer motorist and aviator from Kent, bought the rights and set up a factory in Willesden importing his glass from Bohemia and Belgium.

The company benefitted from wartime orders for goggles, but still managed to go into receivership in 1921. It was quickly rescued and trade multiplied with motor sales and what came to be called the 'splinterless boom'. The breakthrough came in 1927 when Austin decided to fit Triplex safety glass windscreens as standard items – an order for 1·4 million square feet. Triplex built a second Willesden factory and bought an old factory at King's Norton in Birmingham which it rapidly expanded. The order set alarm bells ringing on all sides.

Pilkington's had by now become closely involved with Henry Ford's initially unsuccessful efforts to establish his own glass-making plant for windscreens using plate glass. In 1922 the two companies agreed to exchange all their 'experience, knowledge and inventions, both present and future, whether patented or not.' Between 1922 and 1924 Pilkington's had also received orders to ship over 2,000,000 square feet of plate glass to Detroit – at one stage six per cent of its total plate glass production.

Now with Triplex's advance it became thoroughly alarmed seeing the home market for automobile plate glass rapidly disappearing. At the end of 1925 Pilkington's board noted that Triplex had 'apparently engaged themselves to buy glass from Czechoslovakia and we have no intention of being kept out of what may be a growing trade.' It therefore approached the company for a trial order of 5,000 square feet of thin plate glass.

Pilkington's bought shares in Triplex and the Austin deal, which gave Austin special terms, was rapidly followed by another between Triplex and Pilkington's under which Triplex agreed to take at least three quarters of its plate glass from

Pilkington's, but at a special price – fifteen per cent below that quoted by Pilkington's to any other safety glass manufacturer.

While Pilkington's debated whether they should take over Triplex, another competitor moved sharply. The combative William Morris worried that Austin had stolen a march and the company would discriminate against Morris Motors. So he secretly built up the biggest share holding in the company and installed a nominee director, Graham Cunningham, who had become managing director by the end of 1929. Meanwhile he drove his usual hard bargain – taking his first batch of Triplex glass at a price on which Triplex made a loss.

Once assured of supply, Morris steadily sold out his shares in the 1930s, while Pilkington's increased its involvement, forming a joint company Triplex (Northern) in its home town of St Helens. It put pressure on its partner by obtaining patents for a French process of tempering glass which it then manufactured, selling it on to Triplex as Triplex Toughened.

Both companies benefitted from new Government regulations in 1932 which made safety glass standard, and motor industry sales were the main source of Pilkington's increased sales of plate glass in the 1930s as its other markets stagnated.

The Triplex saga illustrated the complex and uneasy symbiosis between assembler and component maker. The manufacturer looked to ensure his source of supply but also to dictate his price, and the component maker was keen to win large orders but wary of domination, if not outright take-over, if he became too dependent on the big companies. The tension was seen at its keenest in what increasingly became the key part of the car – its electrical equipment.

Before the First World War, electrics had been a very minor part of the vehicle with not even headlamps fitted as standard at first. The main requirement was for electric ignition systems but only once a relatively reliable form had been found. Some early vehicles had a trembler coil operated by a battery; later the magneto and the sparkplug became the key components. But between the wars one electrical gadget after another became standard equipment – first lighting, then starters and dynamos in the 1920s, and windscreen wipers, trafficator indicators and (for some) car heaters in the 1930s.

When Morris costed his first Cowley in 1915, he was one of the first to provide lights as standard. The total price of electrical components came to about ten per cent – most of it on lighting; by the 1950s the average cost of all electrical components was reckoned to be about ten per cent of bought out components, while in the 1980s it was estimated that as much as 40 per cent of the cost of a vehicle would soon be taken up by electronics.

For electrical power again Britain at first relied on transatlantic know-how. The Chloride Company was established in Britain in 1891 to produce batteries for Britain and its Empire using American patents. At first they were mainly for static use, for industrial and domestic lighting and power, but soon they became a power source for submarines and early motor vehicles. By the time the First World War broke out, Chloride was the principal supplier of motor batteries, a position it consolidated after the war by taking over numerous smaller competitors and winning key contracts with Ford and Vauxhall.

But its success paled before its increasingly giant competitor, Joseph Lucas, the Birmingham electrical company which by the middle of the 1930s was employing over 10,000 people and making annual profits of well over £200,000, bigger than those of many of the motor manufacturers themselves. Building on its success with fast growing Morris Motors, Lucas came to dominate the business, buying up its fiercest competitors and making deals with others.

The founder of the firm, Joseph Lucas, had started his business by hawking paraffin from a three wheeled basket skip round the streets of Birmingham. By the 1870s he had become a traditional small Birmingham manufacturer making metal goods like shovels and oil cans as well as becoming a more up-market lamp and oil dealer. He started production of a successful ship's lamp, called the 'Tom Bowling' after a well-known sea shanty, and in 1878 he produced a cycle lamp to be slung from the axle of a penny farthing. It was called the 'King of the Road', and sold well.

Joseph Lucas and his son Harry were quick to spot the potential of the faltering beginnings of the motor industry. At their 1902 shareholders' meeting, a month before he died, the old man announced that the company would enter the motor business with a range of what his son had christened 'motoralities'.

'We have every reason to believe that we shall have a fair share of the motoralities business as it develops and it is our duty to follow that business as closely as possible as it runs in the same groove as the cycle trade and we do not want to follow anything outside our own business.'[2]

The company's catalogue included, after its more important 'cyclealities', a list of its first motor products; petrol burning headlights, horns, pumps and various lubricators. The diversification rescued the company from falling profits as the cycle craze flattened out. From 1904 profits climbed, boosted in 1907 by the law requiring all cars to carry lights. By 1909 the company was offering a set of electric side and tail-lamps and by 1912 a dynamo lighting system.

Lucas products were not at first outstanding enough to impress William Morris. He went elsewhere to equip his first car, the Oxford, but for the 1915 Cowley, his accounts list 'set of 5 "Lucas" lamps, dynamo etc. £10.10s., fitting 7s. 6d.'

Morris was to claim later that his order had established Lucas fortunes, though the component company was inclined to suggest that its innovation of 'sets' of equipment made things easy for the manufacturer. Either way the big volumes bought by Morris as he grew rapidly after the war helped the massive expansion of Lucas. In 1921 it sold Morris over £94,000 worth of equipment; by 1925 that had risen tenfold to £907,860, with Morris taking well over half its hugely increased motor industry production.

Just how much the Lucas business depended on the Morris order, as well as individual personal contacts, was demonstrated by the near-panic which gripped the company in 1922 when Peter Bennett, the irascible joint managing director, sacked the director who dealt with Morris, Charles Breedon, after a row.

Frank Thacker, a salesman newly arrived from Rolls-Royce where he had worked as a designer at Henry Royce's Sussex home, was called in to see Bennett and Oliver Lucas, the other joint managing director. He recalls:

It was arranged that my first call should be to Morris Motors which they felt very concerned about, as Charles Breedon was very friendly with W.R. Morris, and would have put his side of the break-up over to him.

The next morning it was arranged that I went over to King Street for last minute sessions and their best wishes, and I was to get in touch with them as soon as I got back. They both came down to see me off. Outside the front entrance was a very large Daimler four-seater car. As I had previously never driven anything larger than a cycle car, and that for only five miles, you can imagine my feelings. So with my heart in my mouth and putting over what I hoped was a casual air, I climbed – literally – into the driving seat and pulled the chain which operated the starter. I put it into gear and started off, with the two gaffers waving me off.

W.R. Morris had his office at Cowley in an old building which I think had been a college. He was pleasant enough with me and I had no difficulty in talking to him. He expressed his sympathy for me at joining Lucas and warned me that I was working for a bigger humbug than Horatio Bottomley!

I explained that I should be the Lucas representative dealing with Morris Motors and he stated that this was quite agreeable to him. I drove back to Birmingham and arrived safely at the works.

The two joint M.D.s were eager to learn how I had got on and asked me particularly to report verbatim what W.R.M. had said to me. I'm afraid I was very naive at the time, and so I told them exactly – word for word. It was received in rather stony silence!

The next day I saw them again to discover how I was to carry on visiting the rest of the trade. No mean task this, as at this time there were about forty firms, all endeavouring to cash in on this newly developing industry.

So Lucas succeeded in keeping in with Morris, and then forced themselves on their reluctant neighbour Austin in 1926 by taking over its two main competitors, C.A. Vandervell and Rotax.

The company's interest in the motor industry had been hugely enhanced by its acquisition of its magneto business in the First World War. After the war, it launched into an almost non-stop programme of takeover – in 1924 it bought Brolt, a supplier both to commercial vehicle makers but also to Beardmore and Jowett cars; in 1925 it took EIC which already produced magnetos for motor bicycles and was about to start making them for cars, and in 1926 it bought C.A. Vandervell. Vandervell had started making batteries and dynamos even before Lucas and controlled the commercial market. He also had the Austin contract for most electrical items. Lucas took over the company in conjunction with Rotax, a keen competitor on the car side, but within a few months it bought out Rotax too, so establishing a virtual monopoly. Vandervell was re-organized to supply commercial vehicles, while Rotax supplied the aircraft industry.

Austin had bought entirely from Vandervell. He was furious to be faced with a monopoly supplier but was eventually pacified by being offered electrical sets at a price Lucas claimed Vandervell could not have offered.

A Lucas board minute of August 25th, 1926 gleefully reported: 'We have successfully arranged for the whole of next year's business with the Austin Co. for all their models. This is very gratifying as it will be remembered that this was the one place where there was a possibility of our having difficulty due to their attitude over amalgamations.'

Many years later the company was to tell the Monopolies Commission that 'Austins were the most resistant and most awkward about it. Their bitterest enemies in those days, Morris, were entirely in the Lucas camp, and Austins did not welcome it at all. Sir Herbert Austin was a very bitter man about it.'

But it was not until 1963 that the Commission was called to look into the stranglehold which Lucas had established. Another five companies were bought up in the next four years, and a string of restrictive deals struck with competitors at home and abroad.

When in 1928 the formidable German company Bosch warned Lucas that it had had a dozen offers to set up in Britain, Lucas responded by buying off Bosch in a deal in which the German company agreed to keep out of the British car market but were allowed to buy half of the CAV business, which was renamed CAV-Bosch. At the same time Lucas negotiated to pay Dane-geld to a big American company, Autolite, which was a large supplier of Ford in the United States, to keep them out.

The Lucas Board were told that:

If Autolite came to England to manufacture for Ford only, which is what they were prepared to do – and we lost half our Ford business to them, it would cost us about two or three times as much as we are paying them under the agreement.

It will be realized therefore that the bargain we have made is quite a good one on these grounds only, but when the effect which their presence would have on Vauxhall to commence with and the all–British group as time went on is understood, it will be seen that the Ford position is only one side of the question, and their presence here would force down the Ford prices on which the above calculations are based.

In the event, Lucas paid Autolite $50,000 a year to use its expertise and both companies agreed to keep out of each other's countries. As it turned out, Lucas made few technical innovations during the inter-war years but was able instead to rely on American products and production engineering and to draw on the technical excellence of Bosch. As the company itself said proudly, 'From this agreement we had complete access to Bosch's technical knowledge and experience.'

It was an extraordinary restraint of trade; another example of the protected and insular nature of the British industry, which was compounded by a demarcation deal with its major remaining British competitor, S. Smith and Son.

Smith's had started as clockmakers, founded in 1851 by Samuel Smith at Newington Causeway in London. The business expanded into the West End and opened a motor accessory department in 1904, making what it called 'motor watches' and never forgetting the sale of the first car speedometer that year to King Edward VII for his Mercedes. It bought the Goldenlyte headlamp company in 1908 and the car lighting and starting business of Trier and Martin in 1913. During the war it made aircraft instruments and developed the altimeter fitted to the Vickers Vimy bomber which made the first crossing of the Atlantic. Smith's also manufactured the KLG sparkplugs which had been developed by Kenelm Lee Guinness, a pre-war racing driver, buying up his company after the war and going on to make a deal with the Swiss company Jaeger to make its speedometers.

The company lost money in the 1920s, but by 1927 was making profits again. Its production of magnetos, lighting, and ignition systems provided some competition to Lucas, as Smith's held contracts to supply equipment to a number of smaller car makers.

In 1930 the two companies made a deal. Smith's sold to Lucas all the assets of its Lighting, Starting and Ignition Department and the whole of its shares in ML Magneto. The two companies then drew up lists of products they made which the other agreed not to manufacture for the next fifteen years. Lucas reserved starting, lighting and ignition equipment, ammeters, batteries, lamps, electric horns and *electric* windscreen wipers. Smith's kept spark-plugs, clocks and watches, speedometers, petrol meters, gauges, dashboard thermometers and *mechanical* windscreen wipers.

At the same time Smith's made a lucrative arrangement with the ever-present Bosch which enabled them to use German patents on ceramic plug manufacture in return for selling a ten per cent stake in KLG.

So when the *Economist* came to sum up the fortunes of what it called the 'accessory manufacturers' at the end of 1935, and looked at the profits trend of four companies, Lucas, Smith's, Triplex and the radiator suppliers Serck Radiators, it concluded that:

> while it shows the influence of rising output upon profits, these have not been 'highly-geared'.
>
> Although the motorist has come to require a fuller dashboard of instruments, the number of companies originally catering for the demand was too large to permit substantial profit margins, and even now after a number of bubble companies, particularly in the safety glass industry, have been weeded out, conditions are still competitive. However the emergence of Triplex as the premier producer has been marked by an increase of profits during the last six years by over eight times.
>
> The instrument and lighting equipment makers show stability rather than rapid progress.

Tough bargaining from the assemblers and the big component companies' ruthless way with competitors meant that during bad times the smaller companies had suffered. 'The depression has seen the leading manufacturers in each department establishing themselves more firmly than ever before at the head of their trades,' said the *Economist* in October 1934. As for the smaller concerns, 'losses have been frequent and liquidations not altogether absent.'

But for large and small component makers alike the relationship with the assemblers remained perpetually difficult. Although the near monopoly conditions and protectionism kept prices higher than they might have been with foreign competition, particularly compared with the generally lower prices that prevailed in the United States, they still remained vulnerable to the squeeze exerted by the purchasing power of the big companies. At the same time the continuing refusal of assemblers to standardize, producing instead a huge range of models all slightly different, denied component makers the economies of scale that would have helped their profits and reduced prices to the motorist. It was the same old problem that had been obvious before the First World War when Rubery Owen in the Black Country had first adopted the American method of cold pressing of frames only to find itself deprived of the big American savings in production because its customers refused to standardize and would often insist that their patterns should not be supplied to other companies.

Therefore, although both assemblers and component makers benefitted in the short term from the huge protection afforded by the McKenna duties, both suffered long-term from the development of the idiosyncratic British vehicles.

The component makers who eventually did best were those who raised their sights beyond the short-term prosperity of the motor industry and used their opportunities and their profits to invest elsewhere in other industries or abroad. The most obvious diversification was into the aircraft industry whose steady growth received an enormous boost from rearmament in the late 1930s. Amongst them, two of the best-known names, Smith's and Lucas, had early started to develop their aircraft interests, and unimaginable as it may have seemed in the late 1930s, they were to come to supersede their motor industry commitments altogether when another war was over.

An early motor publicity stunt. Ford's agent in Scotland drives a Model T to the summit of Ben Nevis and back in 1910.

Ford's first assembly plant in Britain at Trafford Park in Manchester.

William Morris at the wheel of his 1913 Oxford.

Morris production continued for part of the First World War. This was the most modern part of the factory in 1915.

8

The Workers
'The Highest Paid Labour Known to the Factory Industry'

Just as the motor car was both symbol and agent of industrial and social change in the twentieth century, so the workers who produced it became too a distinctively modern species. They were different from their counterparts in many traditional industries, themselves a symbol of changing attitudes, becoming involved and at times even seeming to direct events on the social and political stage. They came to be variously and exaggeratedly regarded; as objects of envy for their high wages or as deserving of sympathy for the conditions of work on the relentless production line; as the arch-materialists interested only in what the pay-packet could buy or as the recruiting ground for politically motivated revolutionary change; as wreckers or as the backbone of the economy.

The workers came from all over the place, from everywhere and nowhere; from the old carriage builders or the ranks of the cycle makers and the light engineering workers; from farm workers anxious for a more secure livelihood; from the unemployed in the mines and the textile mills who uprooted themselves to live in the new industrial towns.

The huge plants they worked in were a new phenomenon – they were employing thousands of workers in the mid-1930s when there were little more than 500 factories in the whole country which employed more than a thousand people. Their size brought new patterns and problems for both management and men. They were seen as the ultimate expression of what came to be called 'economies of scale', or as the worst examples of de-humanizing industrialization; as universities of trade unionism or simply as warmer and more protected places to work than those outside. For many years annual lay-offs during the summer were regular occurrences; the high wages were supposed to compensate for the weeks without work. In bad times people queued for jobs; in better circumstances there was often a huge turnover and people swapped from machine lines to milk rounds and back again depending on the pay or the weather.

By 1907 the Society of Motor Manufacturers and Traders estimated that there were already 34,000 people employed in the industry, a figure that had risen to over 200,000 by 1924. The Ministry of Labour which counted those employed both in constructing and repairing vehicles estimated the numbers to be over half a million by 1939 and over 650,000 in 1947. The peak was reached in 1970 when 513,000 were employed in manufacture alone.

The industry was not like anything which had gone before. It required a mixture of skills, and no skills at all. It employed the craft of the old carriage builders though their special skills were diluted by the demands for steel in bodywork; it needed the precise craftsmanship of the skilled engineer for the key engine parts and the preparation of the machine tools. Yet many engineering workers had to learn unfamiliar production skills and green labour from the fields or the mines was often regarded by management as equally suitable to operate the repetitive processes of the assembly lines.

The argument about what was called dilution of skilled labour, of how much skill was really needed for particular operations, was a constant and unresolved argument throughout the industry's history. It was sharpened up by the multiplicity of trades unions which fossilized the divides between trades, and then overlaid them with bitter arguments about money and differentials. Dilution was an issue in both the First World War and the Second; the value of skilled men was still the issue 60 years on in 1977 when the toolmakers' strike at what had by then become British Leyland nearly sank the company altogether. The argument about the relative value of sweat and skill in a worker's pay-packet shuttle-cocked to and fro throughout the industry's history. It reached perhaps the heights of absurdity by the middle of the 1970s when in one company some factories paid skilled men more than semi-skilled line workers, while others in the same group paid line workers significantly more than the skilled engineering workers.

These arguments were already there in embryo when Frederick Lanchester set up his first factory in the 1890s in a galvanized shed. 'In those days,' he said later, 'when a bodybuilder was asked to work to drawings, gauges and templates, he gave a sullen look such as one might expect from a Royal Academician if asked to colour an engineering drawing.'[1]

Lanchester, with his brother George as Chief Assistant, employed eight men. His wages bill showed that the most highly paid was a man called Hopton who was described as an all-round mechanic and toolmaker. He got 34s a week (£1.70). The lowest paid was the apprentice Albert Lee who received 5s a week (25p), while the worst paid adult was the labourer who received 18s a week (90p). Wages made up half Lanchester's costs. But even if the best-paid Mr Hopton had wanted to buy one of the cars he made, he would have had to have saved his wages entire, for several years. But by the standards of the time, this was still good money . . . above the going rate. Average wages did not reach that figure until more than a decade later.

From the beginning, the new industry paid over the odds and became a target for workers from other industries to emulate or to desert for. It was a particular worry to the engineering employers and their associations which had an abrasive relationship with the car firms which dipped in and out of membership. Engineering was in the front line of industrial strife and challenge by the end of the nineteenth century and employers and unions both attempted to organize themselves to protect and advance their interests. In the early years the motor companies managed to stay fairly aloof. Although the moulders' strike immediately after the First World War hit some of them, particularly Austin and firms with older traditions and histories like Napier, they worked on through the 1926 General Strike. Unions were not officially recognized in key plants like Ford's at Manchester and Dagenham until pressure from the Ministry of Labour under the trade union leader Ernest Bevin during the Second World War. It was part of a deliberate policy of paying high wages as well as a measure of the unions' comparative weakness.

The motor makers, bosses and workers, saw themselves as a

new industry, setting new patterns. They consciously set themselves apart from the old engineering industry, although as the years went by and their numbers increased, they became more and more bound up with it.

The high wages being paid by the emerging industry were a source of concern to other Midlands employers as early as 1906 when the Birmingham and District Association of the Engineering Employers Federation attacked the cycle and motor industries for wages 'far in excess of the district engineering rates'. It blamed them for helping to create unrest in the engineering industry. By 1914, Austin had applied for membership of the Association. But the company was still only allowed in 'subject to assurances that they would gradually bring their rates into conformity with district rates.' It was not to be. By 1927, it was estimated that motor earnings were 27 per cent above those in general engineering.

The new Ford plant in Manchester, the first assembly plant in Britain, prided itself on its high wages. Writing in 'Ford Times' in 1914 the company described its employees as 'the highest paid labour known to factory industry'. It also set out details of what it called a 'profit-sharing plan' which actually involved discretionary benefits. It meant, 'for all adult males and all under the age of 22 who are the bread winners of the family, a minimum income of £3 a week for 48 hours. It means clean, healthy factory conditions and a comparatively high standard of comfort in the home'.

Ford made a point of the 'keen pleasure' it took in alleviating the tragedies of boys who lost their fathers, paying them full rates to help the family. With the kind of sententious homily of which Henry Ford was fond, it declared 'To the lad, we have been able to say, "Tommy, boy, you have to play a man's part for your mother; and because we are calling upon you to play a man's part, we will give you a man's money to play it with."'

The scheme did not long survive the application of American management after Perry's departure in 1919, but by and large the big companies were in advance of general industrial practice in conditions and fringe benefits, such as paid holidays, until the time of greater Government control and involvement at the time of the Second World War.

Certainly there was no doubt about the attraction of working at Ford before and just after the First World War. The first employment manager at its Manchester plant, Mr Johns, described how he would take his labour from men who hung around the gates of the plant. 'Every morning I could pick what I wanted. From toolmakers down to someone for sweeping floors. Any amount. All sorts of trades.'

Jack Rogers, who joined the machine shop at the end of his apprenticeship in 1919, described the scene. 'There was a small office on the outer wall of the works and casual labour used to hang around this office outside and there was a small picket window. When vacancies occurred, someone would come to this window and say, "We're hiring men now, come round."'

The system continued until 1922 when a new employment manager, Mr Rigg, took over, and changed things. 'Occasionally the people who were running the job [before him] would put up their hands and indicate ten and before they knew where they were, there were about a couple of hundred inside the yard.' Rigg started to recruit instead through the Employment Exchange, interviewing away from the plant, and within three months the queues were gone. The reason for them however remained. Ford's well paid jobs. Another early Ford worker, John Holden, who started as a sixteen-year-old clerk in the First World War got £1 a week. It surprised him: 'I would not have expected more than 10s (50p) a week.'

Jack Rogers estimated that the one shilling and ninepence (8¾p) an hour which he could earn after three months' probation in 1919 was already double the 10d or 11d which was the rate of pay for a skilled tradesman generally.

Another feature which appealed to him was the way that the factory was free of the demarcations which prevailed in unionized firms in other industries. Ford insisted that a worker must be willing to be transferred to different jobs. 'He might be a driller. But he would be expected, if the need arose, to go over to a milling machine or become a press operator; he might even be sent to the assembly line.'

The system allowed Ford to make use of unskilled workers. On each section there was 'a skilled man who could set all the machines up and therefore the operator himself was able to

function although he had not very often any previous experience
. . . He would not have been allowed to do so at one of those
union factories. If a man were not a driller, he would not have
been allowed to drill. By so doing, certain of those operators
developed a flair for that particular kind of work and in time
attained considerable efficiency. So much so that they themselves
then sometimes became the machine setters-up.'

Ford with its transatlanatic influence provided the most radical
example of changing industrial habits. But the home-bred British
companies also set new standards and patterns. One significant
difference however between Ford and most of the Midland-based
British companies was in their attitude to piecework – the system
of payment where a price is fixed for the number of pieces turned
out, or operations performed, and the worker is paid strictly by
results. Henry Ford was implacably opposed to it and so traditionally Ford was more rigorous in keeping the production line
up to speed instead of leaving it to worker's incentives to keep the
numbers up.

Austin, in some ways the most traditional of the manufacturers, had reorganized on a planned piecework system in 1926.
Under the scheme an average production worker was timed and
paid over the odds if the job was done quicker with special merit
bonuses paid to the extra-efficient. Workers could double the
standard union rate.

The Ford factory in Trafford Park in Manchester was able to
draw on a wide area of mature industrial experience for its labour
force. Difficulties in other industries and events such as the post-
First World War moulders' strike only increased the queues at its
door. But Morris' big expansion at Cowley, and to a lesser extent
the mushrooming growth of Coventry had to tap sources of
labour with little or no industrial tradition.

The early exaggerated reports of the start of the motor industry
in Coventry talked of workers camping out because of the lack of
housing as the city expanded. The *Coventry Times* reported on
September 16, 1896 that 'hundreds of work people will be
required and for these accommodation is urgently needed.
Unless local builders immediately supply this want, it is more
than likely that the several companies will build model dwellings
for their own workmen.' It was an over-statement but the

expansion was still huge. Workers were drawn in from the countryside around as well as from the fading watchmaking and textile industries of the town, and they came from farther afield too. The number of extra people employed in the Midlands metal trades before the First World War was double as many as were sucked off the land. The new workers came from as far afield as Northamptonshire and even London. After the war, they travelled even farther.

Between the wars the population of Coventry doubled while Oxford's increased by nearly half. The numbers of the new workers were swelled by those from areas hardest hit by the slump. Miners in particular from south Wales and the north-east brought with them as well a traditional commitment to trade unionism which the motor industry had conspicuously lacked.

In Oxford the biggest single source of new labour for the car industry was from farm-workers. A study of the background of car workers between the wars showed that over a third of Oxford car workers had come from rural or non-industrial backgrounds, while over ten per cent were from mining families. By comparison, in Coventry only nine per cent had come from the land and between a half and two-thirds from engineering of some kind.[2] Morris' huge expansion at Cowley between the wars meant that by 1939 motor vehicle manufacture was far and away the biggest source of employment in the city of Oxford, with wages to be earned which were over double those available to farm-labourers in the villages around.

Like Ford's, Morris' high wages policy was deliberate. 'A low wage is the most expensive method of producing. A moderately high wage gives a man an interest in life. Men are only going to work if they are going to earn more comforts, hobbies and amusements,' he wrote. But he also found high wages a way of keeping out unions and their demarcations. 'I never allow trade unions to interfere with me,' he told a local newspaper in 1927.

With his concentration on assembling parts made in other people's factories, Morris was particularly reluctant to employ many skilled workers. One member of the Amalgamated Engineering Union who was taken on at Cowley in 1921 reported to his local committee that 'the firm seemed to prefer semi-skilled labour and sub-divided operations in the assembly shops so that men who were quite unskilled could learn their portion in a day or two.'[3]

This approach was vital to the early manufacturers. It helped to avoid paying the traditional skilled men's rates. That minimized the number of people in the trades represented by the craft unions who had the greatest industrial coherence and strength from their traditional fight to maintain their standards and privileges. It was not until other unions, notably the Transport and General Workers, were able to organize the semi and unskilled workers in the industry that the car workers were able to exert the kind of pressures on management which their would-be leaders in the trade unions had long wanted. Between the wars this was rare, and it was management who dictated the pace of events. Sir Charles Bartlett, the head of Vauxhall, who played in the works cricket team, was a rarity among autocrats, who usually confined themselves to sponsoring company sports days like Standard or annual outings like Jaguar.

John Holden, who started at Ford's Manchester plant in the First World War, described the ethos. 'You had to work hard, you had to keep the factory very clean – cleanliness was very very important. You were expected to work hard all the time you were there, not be late, not ask for any favours and you didn't expect any, but you were always well-treated. One of the bad things about it is that because of the motor trade being seasonal, you were liable to be stood off for three or four days.' It was the car worker's persistent complaint.

After the departure of Perry from Ford at the end of the war, the new American managers enthusiastically applied the principles of what was called 'Fordliness' to the British operation. It meant tighter control with shorter meal breaks and tougher discipline. Offenders could be first fined and then dismissed.

The Ford devotion to cleanliness was made manifest by the way the plant was shut down on Friday afternoons for the whole work force to give it a thorough clean. When manual workers changed into their working clothes at the factory at the start of their shift, they were provided with a hook on a wooden batten to hang their clothes and when the shift began, the batten was raised up to the ceiling and out of reach.

Smoking – a pet aversion of Henry Ford – was forbidden in the plant. 'A Woodbine during the day may cost you a week's pay' was one slogan. It was not to be permitted until the Second World War. Other plants also were concerned about smoking – Morris allowed it, Austin did not, until Lord, a heavy smoker himself, changed the rules at Longbridge.

One unique example of Ford's crusade for moral uprightness, however, was maintained wholesale by the new post-First World War American managers no longer hidden behind the euphemism of profit-sharing. This was what became the standard practice of paying check visits to employee's homes to investigate their private lives.

Jack Rogers remembers that the visits took place during a worker's three-month probationary period, after which, if approved, his pay would be increased and he would be established.

> The requirements were first of all satisfaction at work and secondly a standard of behaviour must be achieved in the ordinary social system. An official of the company, who I think was called the Welfare Man, had been appointed and his duty was to visit the house of the individual concerned and ensure that the person was a respectable member of society. Drinking to excess or undesirable associations or failure to maintain his wife and family at a standard commensurate with his salary or wage would mean that he hadn't made the grade.

One visit would be enough unless the inspector did not like what he found. In that case,

> a man could be warned that he had not measured up to what the Ford Motor Company considered to be a right standard, and if he changed his ways, then, of course, a further visit would ensure that such behaviour had been corrected.

Rogers described the attitude of workers to the scheme as rather mixed.

> There was not altogether a feeling of resentment. I think the high rate of pay they were getting made them realize that they had to offer something in return.

It was a practice which did not survive the end of American managers but it was the most distinctively transatlantic feature of the Ford operation, a reminder of how much Detroit could pull the strings when it wished.

A much more radical and fundamental challenge to traditional British industrial practice, however, came from Ford in 1926 when it proposed to cut working hours from 48 to 40 a week, restricting production to five days a week, without cutting wages. In the context of the national industrial strife of 1926 where the demands for longer hours and pay cuts from the heavy industries were met by the union slogan, 'not a penny off the pay, not a minute on the day,' it was extraordinary.

Ford had already been running into difficulties as the Model T aged, and the *Manchester Guardian* commented: 'In the circumstances it would scarcely have been surprising had there been a set-back in labour conditions at Trafford Park, instead of this new advance.'

The plan, introduced to cut overheads and increase efficiency, was a remarkable success. Workers were encouraged to submit ideas for time-saving; and as five day a week output moved up to equal five and a half day production, they received staged increases culminating in a £6.12s a week minimum rate which was higher than before. After a few months, pay and production were both up, and costs down. Ford continued with its arrangements until the Second World War, and then only lengthened its hours under protest after insistent government pressure. It was a sharp contrast to its competitors, unpopular with the engineering employers' associations, and an indication of the different approach which kept Ford on the whole out of British manufacturers associations.

At the other extreme from Ford's carefully planned and co-ordinated environment was the experience of workers who went for jobs to the small and growing workshops of the new companies, often in places without the kind of industrial tradition which permeated Trafford Park.

Jack Beardsley was working for an engineering firm in Blackpool in 1928 when he was laid off. After two or three weeks he heard of a vacancy to do metalwork and make brackets in a small company, called Swallow Sidecars, which was just beginning to build cars on the Morris Twelve chassis.

He found about 25 people working in the small factory and was employed to alter the springs and chassis as well as making hood frames. There were a few other specialists: bodybuilders and a trimmer who made the hoods. But there were no general labourers and everyone was expected to help out as necessary. The workers were almost self-employed. 'We were all on piece work. We got a price per article we made. The old man said I should be able to make a shilling an hour. I soon got round that.'

Beardsley was soon on the move. In 1929 the firm moved to Coventry where it was to become famous as Jaguar. It took over an ammunition factory disused since the war which had no electricity or heating. The approach road was so rutted that suppliers objected to risking their vehicles down it, and the electric cable run down the lane to supply power was soon stolen. Secretaries worked on orange boxes and then on trestle tables covered with linoleum while the cars were built on trestles. Heating was by improvised braziers made from oil drums. When a skilled craftsman was hired from a Coventry factory, he could not start work until a bench was built for him.

Beardsley remembers 'the coldest winter I have ever known' as a time when 'everybody was happy and glad to be working.' The company's founder, William Lyons, refused to employ contractors, and the work force did all the conversion of the factory themselves. Both manual and office staff worked till eight or nine at night, and no overtime was paid.

When the firm recruited it only engaged skilled men in a few specialized trades – bodybuilders and a peculiar Coventry trade – wing fitters and bonnet fitters whose job it was to trim the bonnet lids after they were put on. Semi-skilled men came from as far as south Wales and Scotland and turnover was high. 'They used to roam about from factory to factory – they could work in four factories in a year if one offered a little more money.'

Beardsley remembers it always being busy except for the period between Whitsun and the autumn Motor Show, the sharp and bitter memory shared by thousands of car workers. 'The motor industry was dead until the show. This happened in all the motor industry. We used to employ the skilled men to do development work and factory reconditioning and do the tracks.'

The effect of the Motor Show was make or break. For Jaguar it was always make, but when companies had less success with their new models, the work force felt the effect. It was standard practice for hundreds of workers to be laid off in the slack period; how many were taken back would depend on the success of the cars they had built.

It was an important recruiting point for the unions who struggled throughout the 1920s and '30s to organize the growing semi-skilled labour force. It was an argument used to justify paying high wages to production line workers – as the skilled men, who were often on fixed rates, were generally protected from regular lay-off.

Harry Urwin, who had worked in the machine tool industry in Coventry before becoming a Transport and General Workers official said: 'Everybody watched the Motor Show in October. If a model was successful then you were in employment. Large numbers were already laid off; they only kept the key people developing the new model.

'While wages were relatively high, you were very fortunate if you got regular employment. For a third of the year you got overtime; for about a third, a flat rate, for the other third short-time. The only continuity was for people like pattern makers and coppersmiths, prefabricating the next model.'

The unions were on the whole unsuccessful in organizing car-workers between the wars. Unions representing skilled men, the AEU and the NUVB, largely ignored the growing numbers of non-skilled and semi-skilled workers, although belatedly changing their rules to accommodate them. In the Midlands, the Workers' Union had some small success among the semi-skilled which increased when it amalgamated with the Transport and General Workers Union. Yet the formidable trade union leader Jack Jones says that when he became District Organizer in 1939 for Coventry, one of the most industrialized cities in the country with a population of a quarter of a million, 'total membership had slumped to 2,000 or so. The membership of the Amalgamated Engineering Union was not much better. The overwhelming majority of workers in the area belonged to no union at all.'[4]

The industry's strike record was good. It was less strike-prone than comparable industries like engineering – averaging only about four strikes a year in the interwar years, and then often ineffective disputes. In the mid-1920s, it ranked fourteenth in the number of strikes per worker, behind industries like tailoring or shoemaking: ten years later it was eighteenth.

One of the first strikes in the industry affected Ford before the First World War, when men at its body-making plant, which had formerly been a shop-fitting works, came out. They sent pickets throughout Trafford Park, but the carpenters, a key element, refused to come out and the strike collapsed.

The huge expansion at Longbridge during the First World War production of munitions inevitably brought strains and in 1918, over 10,000 – half the work force – came out over accusations of victimization against the chairman of the Works Committee. The firm caved in and the man was reinstated.

Austin barely survived the effects of the 1919 moulders' strike. Napier's attempts to bring out a new post-war car were so much delayed by it that the car failed and the firm gave up car production to make aero-engines instead.

Longbridge continued to have a trickle of disputes. Many were without reference to the unions, and Austin's technique was to use the NUVB in particular as a kind of policeman to get workers back, refusing to negotiate except with the union, even though most workers did not belong to it, or necessarily pay its officials any attention. After a dispute over piece rates in 1923, the union journal noted that Austin 'gracefully gave way and promised not to offend in future.' It was glad to be called in, observing in the journal that the plant needed the 'most watchful care' in protecting labour for skilled men. In the 1926 general strike the union actually told its Austin members to remain at work.

Another strike over the re-organization of the works and introduction of new production methods in 1929 saw apparently key concessions made by the Austin management. Over half the 9,000 work force, led by a recently arrived south Wales miner, had voted for a 'stay-in' in protest. Austin acted decisively, closing down the plant and refusing to negotiate except with union officials. But most of the workers, who were non-union, refused to go back. Negotiations which followed produced a new concept which would cast a long shadow – mutuality. It meant that changes in rates had to be mutually agreed. Austin also agreed to recognize shop stewards of the NUVB and provide a room in which they could hold a weekly meeting. But by the middle of the 1930s as more unskilled workers came in (among them women who were much more heavily represented in Birmingham factories than in the country as a whole) the shop steward organization faded away again.

In Oxford, in spite of encouragement from socialists and communists at the University, efforts to unionize the Morris plant at Cowley were much less successful. Morris' high wage policy, coupled with the sacking of activists during lay-offs, prevented the unions becoming established. The N U V B branch actually lapsed in 1921 and after attempts to revive it, its secretary wrote to the union head office in 1927 'to point out the futility of any attempt at organization in this district.'

The unions had more success at the neighbouring plant of Pressed Steel established by the Americans at Morris' invitation. Conditions here were worse than at the Morris plant across the road. The work was both dirtier and more dangerous, and earnings sometimes suffered by comparison with the Morris plant. Both were on piece work, but Pressed Steel did not pay a guaranteed basic (known as a bonus) as well.

In July 1934 a strike began over the low level of piecework rates. After a fortnight the dispute ended with management agreeing to join the local Engineering and Allied Employers Federation which meant recognizing the unions. It was a major and unexpected breakthrough as trade union recognition had not been an original demand. In spite of recent efforts by the T G W U to recruit in the factory, most of those involved in the strike were not union members. The strike committee was composed largely of immigrants from south Wales, a substantial proportion of them being ex-miners. They were prevailed on to insist that the unions be brought in, in part by the Communist Party activists, but the ambivalent attitude to the unions continued. Two years later one of the strike leaders, now a union shop steward, was asked why he had not kept his men at work during an unofficial dispute. His answer was that he was not a paid union official and was 'working for the men and not the union.'[5]

Ford's harmonious labour relations deteriorated after the move to the larger Dagenham factory where the 1,500 or so workers it brought down from Manchester were augmented by another 2,500 drawn from a variety of sources, primarily the new housing estates of the East End of London, but also with a significant influx from Ireland.

The move, in 1931, was followed by a three day strike in March the following year when Ford's disastrous showing in the market, which was affected also by the slump, led the company to impose wage cuts. It was particularly bitter for the loyal Manchester work force who were finding their difficulties in settling in marshy Dagenham, compounded by the higher cost of living in London. The wage cuts were modified for the two lower grades as a result of the strike, but they stayed in force.

Just as the rise of the Cowley plants had excited the ambitions and enthusiasms of the Oxford University socialists to try their hand at industrial organization, so the move of Ford to London under the noses of the trade union hierarchy led to a stepping up of pressure for unionization.

Vic Feather of the TUC's organization department became a frequent speaker at union meetings and met Perry to try to get recognition. But his efforts were not to succeed until the centralized control and direction of labour which came with the Second World War pushed employers into much more formal arrangements.

Between the wars, the *Economist*'s view of reasons for the industry's lack of union organization (expressed in 1926) generally held true – it was 'a young industry, able to start with a clear sheet, free from the innate prejudice of a chequered past.'

The novelty which impressed those fresh to the industry, whether would-be organizers and agitators, or workmen looking for a job, was perhaps most of all the impact of the production line, the inexorable forward movement which dictated the speed at which men worked.

Vic Feather's report to the TUC as if discovering a new world said: 'So far as conveyors are concerned, men actually on the production side, where the work is very strenuous, had to work hard. But if you go round into other departments such as the toolroom, electrical maintenance or repair you can say very truly that they are not driven any harder than in any other shop.

'The belt,' he said, 'sees to it that there is not much chance to slack.' The same report spoke of a situation where 'men are told that if a man is holding him up, to "push him out" and the atmosphere is so tense that men are willing to strike their mates down.'

Workers at Ford were paid on fixed rates, at that stage at two shillings (10p) an hour; their speed of work very much depended on the line. It was strict Henry Ford policy. As Perry pointed out in a pamphlet: 'By observation he discovered that big wages were the very best investment which could be made, that any ordinary decent man could and would do more work in eight hours than ten or twelve hours . . . He is a great disbeliever in all forms of what I would call "artificial wages". For example, piece-work.'

But in the Midlands' car factories, piece work was regarded as the key to production by both managements and workers. It affected attitudes to production lines. Many south Wales miners arriving at the Oxford factories found themselves making more money and having more material possessions than ever before. Other, often older men, found working on the line difficult or impossible. One man who left and found work instead as a builder's labourer, described it. 'It was the man against the machine, and the machine always wins; the faster the machine, the faster we had to work.'[6]

But others were eager to work flat-out and earn more. Tom Ward, who worked at the Standard plant in Coventry spoke of men unhappy when the line did not speed up.

The track would start at perhaps time and a quarter. And it would go up to time and a half, £3 a week. Speed it up as you get used to it; double time. And when it got to double time, they'd stop. No more. No faster. And what we used to do, we'd pick a body up and jump the pegs and we could make about £5 a week. It was always good money in the motor trade if you could do the job. But if you were slow, you were in some trouble.[7]

The new motor plants could be forbidding places particularly after the introduction of all metal bodies and full-scale production lines in the 1930s.

Glyn Davies was 21 when he travelled from Pembrokeshire on the west coast of Wales to Luton in the south-east of England to stay with a cousin, a former miner from Merthyr Tydfil, who was working at Vauxhall.

The town was buzzing with migrants from every part of the country. Quite a number had come from the north-east. One man I knew said he had walked all the way from Newcastle.

Davies found work in the parts department, but two years later in 1938 after a merger of departments, transferred into the press shop.

It was hard and the first day I went there I nearly packed it in. I had to wear a leather apron and great big leather gloves. I was given a grinding wheel. It was my job to tidy up the edges. I was standing there and then I saw a chap beside me was up to his elbow in blood. He had lost his hand in the press. He was running round maddened with pain and people were running after him.

Locals could also find conditions a surprise. Bill Roche started at Pressed Steel in Cowley in 1937. He lived nearby and his father had been a printer at the University Press, the biggest industrial employer in the city before the motor industry arrived. He remembers that migrants like the Welsh were not welcomed.

The local people were not happy about outsiders coming in. There was even talk – though I don't think it can have been true – that they had agreed to take a penny an hour less. There was a feeling that if there were people waiting outside the gate management could get away with more.

Roche's father died when he was twelve and at fourteen he looked for a job.

The plant was the one place where there was reasonable money. In a way it was a prize to be employed there. I remember taking home as much as £2 a week in those days. It was better money than the assembly plant and because Pressed Steel had a variety of work, you didn't have the lay-offs. At the assembly plant they had a large labour force and there used to be three or four month lay-offs. There weren't many jobs going.

When he went to work at the plant Roche described it as 'frightening'.

It was black, dirty, so different. One of the first things was to have a medical. I remember going to the first aid post for it and seeing the casualties coming in; people who had cut themselves and one man with a shoe off and blood pouring.

Most people had a horror of being told to work on the assembly line. That would not have been a happy day. But there was a lot of self-selection on the unpleasant jobs. Men and women would put up with piece-work. They knew the job; they were working the machines all the day and the thought of going onto something else was a nightmare.

Productivity was not a word heard much in the 1920s and 1930s. But the improvements in factory engineering and design meant that it steadily improved throughout the inter-war period, though it lagged far behind the performance of the American companies. They had longer production runs because they produced both more cars and fewer models.

Before the First World War Ford was the only manufacturer which managed to produce more than one car per employee per year. With increasingly organized production facilities, after the war the general output of vehicles per operative rapidly increased, doubling from 1·45 to 2·86 by 1935 according to the PEP report into the industry published in the early 1950s. Morris motors was producing three times the number of vehicles in 1935 as it had in 1924 with roughly the same number of people.

But the British performance blanched before that of the American industry, which was more than three times better – with 8·76 cars being produced per operative in 1935.

The progress of the industry in the inter-war years had been against a background of persistent large-scale unemployment, which meant that it was never short of the unskilled labour on which it came to depend. It gave managements the ability to dictate to their work forces, although their behaviour was often directed by a wish to do well by their employees if only to keep the unions from challenging that authority.

The impact of the Second World War would diminish that

authority for ever. First the government would play a far more active role in labour relations than it had ever done, delivering to the unions the greater status and the recognition they wanted. When that was combined with a swing not just to full employment but to actual shortage of labour the balance of power, firmly with management throughout the first half century of the industry's existence would be substantially altered. But in 1939 even union leaders could scarcely have dreamt of what was to come.

9

The Second World War
'Blackout, Blitz and Bureaucracy'

The Second World War did not spring unannounced and unexpected on the motor industry as had the war in 1914. This time there was no panic Ministry descent on factories to commandeer any movable vehicle as there had been at Daimler in 1914. For more than three years the industry had been planning and preparing for war, ever since the 1936 Defence Statement had handed it a key role in the building up of Britain's air power.

The industry took a huge pride in its wartime achievements. Its production of vehicles – which reached 160,522 in its peak year of 1942 – well surpassed Germany's best year's production of 119,725 though it was less than the number of vehicles imported from North America in that year. When the Society of Motor Manufacturers and Traders celebrated the jubilee of the industry in 1946, its commemorative volume was entitled 'Vital to the life of the Nation':

> In her vital hour of need it was a veritable godsend to Britain, and to the whole of the free world, to have an industry of such great war potentiality ready to hand. And in fine fettle too, its destinies guided by efficient, capable brains and its factories manned by competent craftsmen skilled in many and diverse trades . . .
>
> It is perfectly true to say that every firm in the motor industry – and in those allied to it – gave service that was indispensable to the war effort. Whatever was required of them was delivered with celerity and efficiency; however difficult the problem, it was solved.

Not all those words stood up to close inspection. There were grave difficulties not easily or quickly resolved about the supply of skilled workers; British aircraft production, to which much of the motor industry turned, never reached the levels of the heavily bombed German industry. But in the roseate after-glow of victory in 1946 there was room for justifiable pride in the industry's contribution to victory in the most desperate war the world had known. What was not and could not have been appreciated in 1946 was how much that war had changed the prospects for the industry.

Above all Government involvement had steadily seeped through almost every one of its arteries. The industry's production targets had been set; its labour directed and allocated, its wage rates and conditions scrutinized and marshalled; its supplies ladled out; its future pored over and planned by a Cabinet committee. It would never again escape from the shadow of Whitehall. On the shop floor the war-time move to corporatism meant management was to be locked into a negotiating embrace with the unions which could all too easily turn into an arm-lock.

The first Government move to enlist the motor industry into a crash rearmament programme came with an announcement in the Defence White Paper of March 1936 that the Government would give financial guarantees to manufacturers who extended their plants to undertake rearmament work. By May the Minister for the Co-ordination of Defence, Sir Thomas Inskip, could announce that seven manufacturers had agreed on a 'cut and dried programme' and that urgently needed machine tools were being brought in from the United States, France and, ironically, from Germany.

This was the start of what was called the 'shadow factory' scheme. The factories were owned and paid for by the government, but managed by the motor industry – seen as an example of an efficient producer. The plan provided for an initial payment of up to £50,000 a year with a further management fee based on units produced – £225 per aircraft and £75 per engine.

Lord Austin agreed to become chairman of the industry shadow scheme. The plants were to produce parts, but in the event of war would make whole aircraft or engines. The seven factories were to be managed by Austin, Daimler, Rootes, Rover, Standard, Wolseley and Singer, supplementing the fifteen or so companies already making airframes and the four – all with some motor industry connection – Rolls-Royce, Bristol, Armstrong-Siddeley and Napier – who made engines.

But before the scheme was off the ground there was a flicker of the new abrasive relations into which industry and Government would enter as one of what the *Economist* styled the 'potentates' of the industry kicked against the pricks of Government say-so.

William Morris, Lord Nuffield, withdrew Wolseley from the scheme, his letter crossing the Ministry's letter of appointment. He argued that a new factory was not needed; that he already made aero-engines at Wolseley and they would do perfectly well; the Government's scheme was technically and strategically unsound, and each factory should make separate engines. The Ministry countered that Wolseley's Scorpio engine was too low-powered for the RAF and pointed out that the motor manufacturers had unanimously agreed the deal, and that they had included a representative from Wolseley.

Morris sulked and closed down Wolseley aero-engines. When the Air Ministry decided it wanted some Scorpios, after all, the plant was already shut. Eventually, Morris was persuaded to build and operate a factory to make Spitfire fighter aircraft in 1938. It was basically the same shadow scheme, but to save face, Morris, according to his deputy, Oliver Boden, insisted that 'there should be the minimum amount of interference from the Air Ministry to enable the position to be tackled in a somewhat different way to the present shadow scheme of the Ministry.' A huge site was bought at Castle Bromwich near Birmingham and construction began.

Morris' participation, however, did not last. There were problems about designs, changes of mind over the amount of Spitfires and bombers to be produced and parts from Castle Bromwich were diverted to the key Spitfire factory at Southampton.

At the height of the Battle of Britain in 1940 the representatives of Vickers, the Spitfire makers, and Morris clashed. The root cause was the desperate struggle to provide as many aircraft as possible to the air force. Morris had planned the factory so that almost everything could be mass-produced. But while it paid off in the long run, it delayed initial production at a crucial point in the war.

More seriously, the daily combat experience of the R A F led to a string of modifications to improve the Spitfire's performance in battle. This caused obvious difficulties for a factory gearing jigs and presses for long mass-production runs.

The climax came on May 17th, 1940. Miles Thomas, who had succeeded Boden as Morris' Vice-Chairman, listened to the telephone conversation between Nuffield and Lord Beaverbrook, the Minister of Aircraft Production. He heard Nuffield 'making it abundantly clear that in his opinion the Minister could either have Spitfires or modifications, but he could not have both.

'The moment of truth had arrived. Sarcastically, certain that he was putting the ace of trumps on the table, Nuffield shouted, "Maybe you would like me to give up control of the Spitfire factory."

'In a flash came the reply, "Nuffield, that's very generous of you, I accept!" There was a click in the earpiece, the line went dead . . . Nuffield's face was ashen. For a long time he did not say anything.'

Thomas saw it as 'the turning point in Nuffield's personal career. In that same year, he relinquished the position of Director General of Maintenance of the Royal Air Force. He had begun to sulk in his tent.'[1]

It was a symbolic moment. The autocratic founding fathers of the industry were being forced to give way to the new realities of Government direction and control. The motor industry had become too important to be left to the motor manufacturers. For Austin, a decade older than Morris, his Chairmanship of the shadow factory scheme came to a more natural end. He died on May 23rd, 1941.

The shadow factories were a success. As newly laid-out plants they had the advantage over the older aircraft factories and had fewer problems over craftsmen's resistance to the use of unskilled labour. But even apart from Nuffield's row, it was still not all good news. The development of the jet engine was removed from Rover in 1943 because of what was described as 'the chaotic condition of the production organization assembled at Rover's shadow factory.'[2]

Eventually, the shadow factories operated by the motor

industry were to turn out about twelve per cent of the aircraft and aircraft parts made in Britain during the war.

Meanwhile the motor plants proper produced an extraordinary range of war material. Car production virtually stopped. From 1940 to 1944 just over 16,000 cars were produced according to SMMT figures, although taking into account cars for military and government purposes the number seems to have been considerably higher. In the five years between August 1940 and June 1945, Austin, the most prolific producer during the war because of special arrangements bitterly resented by Morris to supply official cars, turned out about 38,000 cars, the equivalent of about eight months' pre-war production.

Otherwise Longbridge's efforts were bent, as in the First World War, to ammunition and aircraft parts, alongside more traditional motor products such as suspensions for tanks and industrial and lifeboat engines, and such jobbing work as the production of two and a half million steel helmets and 600,000 jerrycans.

The Cowley plant even returned to the foundation of Morris' fortune in the 1914–18 period – the production of mine sinkers. But it was only a tiny part of an effort which again heavily concentrated on the aircraft industry. One Cowley speciality became the repair of damaged aircraft. Under an arrangement with Nuffield before the war, Morris became the sole private firm engaged in the work, and after war broke out Nuffield headed the RAF's Civilian Repair Organization, holding for a short time the title of Director General of Maintenance, RAF. During three crucial months in the Battle of Britain, Cowley put 150 seriously damaged machines back into service. The plant went on to build training aircraft and engines for Beaufighters and Lancaster bombers as well as a range of ammunition, glider parts and torpedoes.

Another Nuffield subsidiary, Nuffield Mechanizations in Coventry, designed and built some of the first British cruiser tanks which were intended to be faster moving and lighter than more traditional versions. Morris himself was closely involved in the design but the Crusader proved famously unreliable in the Western Desert, with engines which broke down and cracked and a demand for maintenance which meant that a quarter were out of action at any one time. Nuffield engineers had to be sent to Egypt to design modifications.

The two American subsidiaries, Ford and Vauxhall, had not been drawn into the shadow factory scheme, even though they were both stepping up production. It was presumably because, given Henry Ford's pacifist attitudes in 1914 and America's current isolationism, there was doubt about their commitment. But Perry at Ford, who had played an important role in First World War production, was alarmed to find that there was little thought of what Dagenham could contribute to the war effort.

The chilling realization broke at Ford that as the plant was positioned so obviously in the path of German bomber squadrons on their route to London, the Government did not expect it to survive very long. The shadow factories were being established much farther away from the range of German bases.

The only contracts Ford had received at the start of the war were for 3,000 extra tractors, engines for barrage balloon winches, and, later, engines to operate specialized equipment which allowed aircraft to detonate magnetic mines.

The factory, with RAF advice, went ahead with efforts to camouflage itself, and on October 22nd, six weeks after the outbreak of war, Perry received an invitation from an Assistant Chief of the Air Staff to construct and manage a shadow factory for the production of Rolls-Royce Merlin engines. A site was found in Perry's favourite north-west, at Urmston, close to the Trafford Park location of the original Ford factory and in spite of bombs during construction, the factory started production in May 1941.

When the blitz came, Dagenham suffered much less than some of the Midland factories and its potential was put to use. Ford made a huge amount of vehicles for military use during the war – over 144,000 wheeled vehicles, with another 41,700 for civilian use, 136,000 tractors and nearly 14,000 tracked Bren gun carriers – one of the key infantry vehicles. It also turned out 93,000 engines and reconditioned 157,000.

The temper of the times was summed up in a booklet produced by Vauxhall to celebrate its war performance, which included the production of nearly a quarter of a million trucks for the armed forces and the successful Churchill tank, as well as ammunition and other small items. In a foreword, Sir Charles Bartlett, its chairman, wrote:

> We worked hard and long, often under very considerable difficulties, but so did most other firms. We had to contend with black-out, blitz and bureaucracy; but so did most other firms. We had to see our skilled men taken from us, and to try to train green labour to do work of which we ourselves had had no pre-war experience; but so did most other firms.
>
> At the same time, however – and this is an important point which is not always made clear – it cannot be too strongly emphasized that we were paid for the work we did; and so were all other firms. Few people made big profits but we were all allowed to pay our work-people reasonable wages, and to earn a reasonable return upon the capital employed.
>
> Our turnover throughout the war has hovered around £22 million per year . . . very nearly half a million pounds a week, most of it spent on wages and materials. And that figure does not include special war equipment such as tank materials, armour plate, guns, fittings and a host of other things which we handled, but the value of which was not included in our turnover figures.
>
> Who paid us? Who provided £40 a minute, 24 hours a day, seven days a week, throughout six years of War? You did.

The First World War had been a very profitable time for the car companies. The Second World War was less so. The big companies made money but their profits after tax were down on average by a third or more. Ford, which had made £626,000 in 1939, made about £400,000 each year during the war returning to profits of over £600,000 in 1946. Vauxhall which had made over a million pounds in 1939, made only about £400,000 a year during the war rising to £597,000 in 1945 and £817,000 in 1946. Austin, less profitable on its larger production, saw profits fall from £344,720 in 1939 to £232,480 in 1940. Figures for the rest of the war were similar apart from 1942 when it was up to the pre-war level. But in 1946 net profits more than doubled to £625,369.

The companies and their workers paid another harsher price too. They became a target for German bombs. One of the first to be hit was Vauxhall at Luton. On Friday, August 30th, 1940, 39 people were killed when an afternoon raid dropped over 50 bombs. It caused considerable damage particularly to the heat treating department, but no machine tools were damaged and the factory was back in production by the following Thursday.

Ford, belatedly camouflaged at Dagenham, was the target for incendiaries and high explosives, but ironically suffered less than the Midlands. The first bombs fell in September 1940 but did little damage, but on October 16th, 1940 a parachute mine destroyed part of the radiator plant causing some deaths and halving radiator production for two days. In April 1941, men controlling the boiler plant pulled away incendiaries by hand.

Much more serious was the damage inflicted on Coventry on the night of 14th November 1940. Seventy per cent of one Daimler works was destroyed, Humber, Singer and parts of the Nuffield companies were also badly damaged. Six hundred people were killed in the city and a thousand injured. Water, gas and electricity supplies were disrupted and food had to be brought in from outside. It was a savage blow against the city which had been the centre of the industry, and which as war production stepped up, was once again seeing people flooding in for work in its factories, just as in 1896, or 1914 or in the Depression years.

During the Second World War, the numbers employed in the engineering industry rose from 1,466,100 in 1939 to 2,959,700 in 1943, the peak year. There was a dramatic growth in the number of women workers. While they had always been employed in substantial numbers in the Midlands, some firms had had a ban on the recruitment of women in production work. These included Vauxhall and Ford, both of which now took them on for the first time. By the end of the war Ford was employing over 2,000 women.

In engineering as a whole, the proportion of women rose sharply. In 1939, just under ten per cent of engineering workers were women – 144,900 out of 1,466,100, but by 1943 when the numbers in the industry had doubled to almost 3,000,000, the number of women was up seven times – to over a million. Although their numbers dropped as the war went on, they were to be an established part of the workforce after the war, although

there were still restrictions. Until the 1970s for example, Ford at
Dagenham refused to have women on the production-line.

The war also brought a great influx of unskilled workers –
raising once more the problems of dilution of skilled men's jobs.
The government had anticipated the difficulties; it was already
having to meet them in shadow factories.

As the official wartime report of the Ministry of Labour and
National Service put it:

> Expansion to the extent desired could not be achieved unless
> arrangements were made for the 'breaking down' of engineer-
> ing processes in order to economize in the use of skilled men
> and to employ to the maximum extent upgraded workers and
> persons trained to carry out a narrow range of skilled
> operations.
>
> In August 1939, therefore, an agreement was reached
> between the Engineering and Allied Employers' National
> Federation and the Amalgamated Engineering Union under
> which certain relaxations were made in existing trade customs
> to allow less skilled classes of male workers to be employed on
> work normally performed by skilled men.

The importance of the deal and similar provisions which
applied during the war, said the Ministry, 'cannot be
overstressed.'

Behind the officialese, things were not so smooth – in
Coventry in February 1940 registered dilution (recruitment of
unskilled workers for skilled work) actually came to a halt.
Prospective 'dilutees' who had been earning large sums on piece
rates were reluctant to change to the skilled rates which were paid
on a time basis. The gap between the two had narrowed so much
that in some cases the unskilled received more pay. Employers
were often unwilling to take men from other industries and
retrain them, while skilled men had left some of the factories
most at risk from air-raids to go elsewhere.

It took Winston Churchill's appointment of the trade union
leader Ernest Bevin as Minister of Labour to tackle the problem.
But the changes he made changed the industry for good.

The foundation of the Bevin arrangement, which gave his
Ministry the power to direct labour, was the 1940 Emergency

Powers (Defence) Bill. It went through Parliament in May 1940. Under this, the Government had complete control over people and factories. It could direct managements on how to run their plants and, in the case of factories controlled by the Government and producing vital supplies, it could impose a 100 per cent tax on excess profits.

The Ministry of Labour's powers over movement of labour spread extraordinarily widely. Ford, with 3,000 workers lost to the forces, was inevitably short of labour. It built on a southern Irish connection which had begun with its tractor plant in Cork and continued with recruitment to its Dagenham foundry of particular Irish groups. It cemented the connection with a recruiting campaign which brought hundreds of Irish over particularly for the unpleasant foundry work. Their fares were paid by the Ministry of Labour as too was a concession of two cheap return tickets a year back to Cork.

On his appointment to the Ministry, Bevin had moved swiftly to bang heads together in the engineering industry. The general unions had agreed that where no suitable male labour was available, women could be employed, but there were still difficulties. He quickly got employers and unions to make an agreement to extend the use of female labour, and wrote personally to their leaders to deal over the increasing problem of the toolrooms, the key centres of skill in the factories, for which men were showing a great reluctance to be recruited because they could earn more on production lines. 'I regard it essential that this problem should be dealt with immediately' wrote Bevin

The problem had been complicated by the way employers, particularly in Coventry, had enticed labour into the shadow factories. By inflating piece rates they had sucked in men from other plants and weakened the position of skilled men paid on a time basis. The answer, reached within days of the Bevin letter, was a national agreement that skilled men in the toolroom should be paid not less than the average of skilled production workers in the same plant.

But in Coventry this was still not enough. So the two sides struck the Coventry toolroom agreement – a momentous deal which would echo down the car industry's industrial relations nightmares, famous to the unions, infamous to the employers.

Under the deal the skilled men in the toolroom would get the average earnings of skilled production men not just in their plant but throughout the district. The object was to prevent labour moving from one factory to another. Its effect was to force up pay in one factory after another so inflating the average and starting the spiral again. It was a major weapon in the unions' bid to increase wages, particularly in what they regarded as the smaller and more backward firms.

The unions benefitted even more from a piece of Bevin legislation which was passed on July 18th, 1940. Order No. 1305, Conditions of Employment and National Arbitration was tabled under the Emergency Powers Act. It prohibited lock-outs by employers as well as strikes by workers unless they had been reported to the Minister and 21 days had elapsed without Government action. Management was now to be scrutinized by Government.

Momentously it also bound employers to recognize terms and conditions of employment which had been agreed between employers and unions in that trade or district – whether or not they themselves recognized the unions. It was enough that the agreement had been reached between 'substantial proportions of the employers and workers employed in the trade or industry in the district.' If there was any question, the unions could report the situation to the Minister and he had the power to refer it to Arbitration. It effectively handed power to the unions even in plants where the management had refused to do business with them.

Jack Jones in Coventry had no doubt about the impact of the Government orders.

They had a profound effect upon the lives of people in industry. I made it my business to master the various clauses in the Orders and pass the information in understandable terms to the shop stewards and branches, so that they would be aware of the advantages and disadvantages of the new legislation. Restrictions on the right to strike were offset by increased use of conciliation officers and Ministry of Labour prosecution of employers who were not applying the 'recognized terms and conditions'. For the first time trade unionism began to operate in the smaller engineering firms.

I recall one foundry casting company where the management literally refused to talk to me. I brought in the conciliation officer, but again they stubbornly refused to acknowledge my presence. I had no alternative but to submit my case to arbitration and won . . . The firm had to pay up. In most cases, however, firms conceded the 'recognized terms and conditions' without reference to arbitration, the mere existence of the Order did the trick.[3]

As a result of the Essential Work Order, firms' ability to hire and fire was restricted.

Managements were forced to think twice before penalizing workers. Firms employed personnel officers and labour officers as a necessary precaution. The enormous growth in these professional areas is undoubtedly due to the wartime orders and the use of them by people like myself.

Union involvement at both national and local level in committees to improve production and productivity also increased their standing and their power.

For managers like Sir Charles Bartlett at Vauxhall, it did not require a major shift in their thinking. But, at the other end of the scale, for men like Mr Hunt, the general manager of the Coventry Singer plant, or William Lyons, the autocratic genius of Jaguar, it was a sea-change which marked a break with the past which was almost incomprehensible.

The temper of union–management relations, the distrust and dislike on both sides even in an apparently joint war-time effort, is again given graphic illustration by Jack Jones:

Shortly after the blitz, the General Manager of Singer Motors, a pompous, rotund gentleman sporting a gold watch-chain across his expansive stomach, invited me to see the effect of the bombing on his factory. We had met at a conference and his invitation was given on the spur of the moment, for we had not a lot in common.

The place was in a mess. Whole areas of the factory were covered by tarpaulins to keep out the rain and the wind and the only heating in the shops was provided by coke-burning open braziers. Yet he still kept up the pretence of a directors' dining room, a small room set apart in broken-down surroundings but with a white tablecloth on the table. We had sausage, chips and beans and I listened to his tale of woe.

A day or so afterwards I presented the case for three of his employees at the Local Appeal Board and established that they had been wrongfully suspended for three days. A little later our shop steward came to see me. 'Mr Hunt [the general manager] played hell with me,' he said. 'He told me he gave you a free lunch and then you went and opposed the company and won the case for these three men. He won't have anything to do with you again.'

Jones found himself arguing piece work rates in intricate detail with William Lyons of Jaguar, another employer who was unhappy about recognizing unions. He had refused to negotiate with the Sheetmetal Workers Union; like many manufacturers he had dismissed union activists, and paid one TGWU steward to stay at home even during the war.

Unions clashed with managements in factories over such matters as collections during working time for the Red Army, a popular cause for left-wingers who were campaigning for the opening of a second front.

How successful the new measures were in reducing strike activity depended on how you looked at it. The official Ministry of Labour figures for stoppages in engineering during the war calculated them to be only 35 per cent of what they had been in the 1914–18 war and only 58 per cent of the average in the years 1927 to 1938. But as union recognition spread there was no particular reduction in the numbers of days lost from stoppages; indeed they seemed to increase. In engineering in 1940, a markedly peaceful year for industry if nowhere else, there had been a low 79,000 days lost. In 1941 it rose to 318,000 and the figures in subsequent years were 283,000; 437,000; 600,000 and then 317,000.

It is difficult to exaggerate the bitterness which some employers felt about the unions and the way they were obliged to deal with them. At an engineering employers' meeting with the unions in Birmingham not long after the war, the works manager of Austin at the time stormed out of one meeting telling the union leaders, 'you are enemies of our company; you are enemies of our country; you are enemies of God. Good-day.' It was a sentiment which managements to a greater or lesser extent shared.

Jack Beardsley, who became a works superintendent at Jaguar, looks back bleakly. 'We didn't know anything about unions until 1943, but then we had to be affiliated. We had troubles then, stoppages.'

But even management could not blame the unions, loyally playing their part in productivity committees, for all the very apparent wartime difficulties of production. When Jaguar was asked to make oil tanks for the Spitfire, Beardsley remembers going to a factory at Kidderminster, which was already doing the job, to inspect production methods. 'The men wouldn't let us in. They all hammered on their benches. They didn't want to let us see how they were doing it. So we went away and made it on our own.'

The effect of the Government measures and the climate of working together for victory established the unions as never before. The Government had insisted that they were recognized in the shadow factories, but now recognition began to come in the parent companies. By the time Allied troops started to advance into Europe the citadels of the motor employers had started to fall.

Vauxhall signed an agreement to negotiate with the AEU and the NUVB in 1942, turning its consultative committee into an elected Managerial Advisory Committee. The biggest capture of all was Ford. It had already signed agreements covering its Urmston shadow factory in 1941 and 1942 providing that 'the company has the right to manage its own establishments and the Trade Union has the right to exercise its functions', but in 1944 it agreed, through the TUC, rather than individual unions, to sign a deal. But it was not until after the war in 1946, that a detailed procedure agreement was conceded.

At the same time, as the national mood shifted from stubborn resistance to Nazi Germany to hopes of victory, the new machinery of Government control and regulation began to turn its attention to the fate of British industry when peace came.

The Ministry of Reconstruction under Lord Woolton set about devising a strategy for post-war recovery. When Ministers came to calculate the vast cost of the war and the destruction of Britain's currency reserves, the recovery programme put the need for an unprecedented export drive as its key priority. Government papers assessing the country's interwar performance came to the conclusion that traditional exports had declined; Britain's position had only been maintained because of the contribution of the new industries and motor manufacturing in particular.

The documents prepared for the War Cabinet's Reconstruction Committee declared that 'the motor car industry was rapidly expanding before the war and can be regarded as one of the most prosperous and successful of our industries.' But once again it drew attention to the proliferation of models, and the lack of standardization which, it suggested, would pose difficulties in competing against the Americans.

> The motor car industry has developed under conditions tending to give it a monopoly in the home market which has been mainly on low-powered cars of a wide variety of different models. It has thus had no strong incentive to produce high-powered cars; still less to embark on large-scale mass production, reduction of the number of models and standardization of components and accessories, all of which are needed if costs are to be lowered far enough to enable us to compete fully in the world market.
>
> Manufacturers at present show little sign that they intend after the war to produce one or two models on a large scale, in the expectation that demand will materialize great enough to absorb them. Nor does it seem that they propose to treat the export market as more than an accessory to the assured home market.

The committee found little enthusiasm among manufacturers for producing a high-powered 'export' car and even flirted with the possibility of a joint scheme between a number of companies to produce such a vehicle. But it had little confidence in it. Unless Government intervened, it said, there was little prospect of large-scale manufacture of types likely to produce the substantial increase in exports the Government sought. At the Ministry of Aircraft production, Sir Stafford Cripps' special advisor, Sir Roy

Fedden, was even given a design brief to plan a new car which would compete at home and abroad against American vehicles. But the vehicle, rear-engined, was never taken seriously by the manufacturers. . . . Yet the report to the committee concluded limply: 'It is by no means certain that an initiative designed to alter this state of affairs would succeed if undertaken.'

The Cabinet's ministerial sub-committee on Industrial Problems considered the motor industry at its meeting on April 5th, 1945. It was a formidable line-up. Apart from Woolton, there was Bevin, Hugh Dalton, then President of the Board of Trade; the Chancellor of the Exchequer, Sir John Anderson, as well as a future Chancellor, Sir Stafford Cripps. The committee also discussed a paper from the Paymaster General, Lord Cherwell, which stressed the motor industry's own concerns, particularly its evergreen dissatisfaction with the level of taxation. Both the level and, to a lesser degree, the structure of the taxation, he argued, were 'serious obstacles to the necessary development of exports.' But the discussion was cut short by Anderson who, sticking to his Treasury brief, declared that 'no change in motor taxation involving loss of revenue could be contemplated.' Cherwell's intervention was unsuccessful, but it had put down a marker, which Labour ministers were to pick up in the post-war years when Dalton, as Chancellor, finally removed the horse-power tax.

For the moment, the meeting was inconclusive, although civil servants were sent to arrange discussions with manufacturers about standardization. What was much more significant was the change in the mood which the whole examination represented. The industry, which had seen exports as no more than an accessory to its assured home market, was now, like the rest of the economy, to be directed into export. Supplies of steel and other materials were to be allocated to it only on the basis of its export plans.

More crucial still, export was now clearly identified as one of the keys to economic recovery. As such its performance would first be monitored, then scrutinized and finally interfered with as being of the greatest importance to the nation. Whether in war or peace it was to remain the government's view that the motor industry was now too important to be left solely to the motor manufacturers.

10

The Forties and Fifties
'The Devil Drives'

In February 1948, in the motor city of Birmingham, the Labour Government's Minister of Supply, George Strauss, announced that the Government would only allocate steel to motor firms which exported three-quarters of their output. 'Materials must go to the firms who can export and do. And that means that those who do not, cannot have them. Needs must when the Devil drives. And if that results in some firms having to close down, well, it is always regrettable when an organization which has created a tradition, loyalties and reputation has to disappear.' It was a hard, cold message, a chilling demonstration of the extent of outside dictation which continued after the war.

The *Autocar* which had earlier printed a special message from Mr Strauss emphasizing 'that the magnificent efforts of the motor industry are fully appreciated,' described it as the 'sword of Damocles falling'.

Not this time the lifting of wartime controls to be followed by a huge boom in home sales . . . instead a continuation of both control and shortage. Apart from the problems with steel, the National Arbitration Order regulating industrial relations continued until 1951, while regional policy soon forced companies wishing to expand to move to new works far away from their existing sites; the Government interfered in wage bargaining, while the shortage of power and coal supplies led to firms having to close factories for periods in the late 1940s. New words like wage inflation and wildcat strike became familiar, while waiting lists for cars stretched to nine months.

Yet, for all of that, the 1940s and early 1950s were years of enormous success for the industry. The numbers of cars produced showed a dramatic climb interrupted only by the effect of

Korean War steel shortages in 1951 and 1952. From 219,000 in 1946 they reached a million in 1958, three times the pre-war best. Exports boomed as never before as the world thirsted for cars of any sort. Small British saloons were even sold in America and in 1950 Britain became the world's biggest exporter, surpassing even the United States. On the back of this expansion, profits and wages rose and the number of people employed swelled.

There was tremendous excitement in the industry, a huge drive to turn out as many cars as possible, typified by the reaction of a sales representative of a big component company. 'We had such a job to make as many as the motor companies were demanding that on Friday the reps used to pick up the rejects off the assembly line and whizz them back to their own factory for reworking over the weekend to have them back on Monday.'

By the end of the 1950s British design was triumphing – producing one of the most original British cars – a genuine world-beater in the Mini, a climax to a period in which British vehicles had spread round the world as never before. It should have been a springboard for sustained success. But the legacy of the 1940s and '50s is one of defeat snatched from the jaws of victory; of the canker of decline concealed among the fruits of progress. The boom put off the difficult decisions; easy profits were not turned into sufficient new investment; assured sales meant that costs of labour and production were not kept to a necessary discipline; the drive for production sacrificed the British reputation of quality; the triumphant British progress hid the modern strengths of the re-emerging Continental manufacturers; the transformation from British Empire to Commonwealth signalled the ending of the Imperial Preference which had assured so many easy export sales.

By 1954 British exports were levelling off while French and German were climbing sharply. As old Imperial pretensions were brutally cut down to size by the Suez fiasco of 1956, both West Germany's production and exports passed Great Britain's. Meanwhile, with no great flurry of Western interest, the Nissan Motor Company of Japan had purchased its first designs from the British Motor Corporation and in 1955 the first post-war car designed in Japan, by Toyota, made its appearance.

To use a phrase which was to become popular later, the British companies found difficulty in 'managing change'. By contrast the American-owned Ford, which was able to draw on a wider experience and vision, began to forge ahead.

Once again strong personalities had much to do with it. Nuffield, Lord and Sir John Black of Standard Motors all worked out their character in the performance of their companies.

Nuffield had grown increasingly erratic. His hypochondria had reached the stage where he regularly tested samples of his own water, heating specimens in a test-tube in the office. On one famous occasion he spilt the contents over a Defence contract worth millions, obliterating key parts of it. More seriously he insisted on over-riding people below him, even though he was not in day-to-day control of the operation.

The most telling decision was Nuffield's insistence that Morris should continue to manufacture its successful pre-war small cars and not bring out a remarkable new model which had been developed by a team including its designer, Alec Issigonis. This was the Mosquito, later to be known as the Minor. The car had a monocoque steel body into which the chassis was incorporated, and the more rounded styling which was in favour. At the last minute the car had been widened by the simple method of sawing it in half with the two sides moved apart for several inches until Issigonis called halt.

Nuffield's deputy, Miles Thomas, believed he had a winner and wanted to switch production as soon as existing supplies for the pre-war cars were used up. Morris, declaring the new car looked like 'a poached egg', pointed to the thousands of orders for the old cars. The Minor had to wait until 1948 to be launched on a progress which led to sales of over a million.

The Minor was exactly the sort of vehicle the British public, with its liking for small cars, could take to. Compared with, say, the Volkswagen, a direct competitor designed earlier, its performance was unexciting and ponderous. But its pleasingly symmetrical shape and its lack of fuss made it a favourite for years. Even in the 1980s, companies could carry on a comfortable existence by meeting the demand for reconditioning the car and a particularly successful variant, its wooden beamed station-wagon. It became the stand-by of those who wanted something dependable and manageable, which would not frighten them

with unduly sharp performance. The country parson, the
woman school-teacher, the old age pensioner, treasured their
Minors for years, while it became one of the first police Panda
cars for local patrolling, a fitting replacement for the steady tread
or ponderous pedalling of the local bobby.

The Minor is still the fifth best-selling British-made car of all
time, while its designer did even better, creating three out of the
top five.

Alec Issigonis had not even seen his first car until after his
twelfth birthday at the end of the First World War. Born in
territory disputed between Greeks and Turks, in Smyrna, he
came as a refugee to Britain in 1922 as his parents had British
nationality. By 1934 he had joined the design team at Humber
after working and studying in engineering. It was an ironic move
that a man who was to devote his life to the cause of the small car
should start as a designer of limousines.

By turns charming and arrogant, regarded by those who
worked for him as often domineering, Issigonis' passion was to
squeeze the maximum interior space out of as small a frame as
possible. It made him the most influential designer of his day,
completely dedicated, never marrying, drawing out his concepts
regardless of where he was, on the concrete floors of workshops
or café tablecloths alike.

About the Minor he was typically uncompromising, saying, 'I
put together the car I thought Morris should make.' Years later
he would say of his most famous creation, the Mini, 'You can't
tell one car from another – the only one that stands out is the
Mini.'

He liked to refer to himself as 'an ironmonger', a reproof for
those who wanted to bother him with what he saw as the
academic atmospheres of market research and theoretical concepts. Scornful of the niceties of trim or even interior comforts,
which he saw as distractions for the driver, he stuck out for a
functional approach to a degree which became ludicrous at times,
even defending uncomfortable seating on the basis that it helped
keep the driver awake. 'If it works, don't change a thing' was one
of his principles and the long life of his cars showed that
companies were often glad to follow his advice however difficult
a customer they found him.

By contrast to Morris, at Austin's Lord had rapid modernization plans. A million pounds had been authorized by the board for investment in April 1945. Lord had planned to be first back into peacetime production with cars which were an improvement on his pre-war models and he also wanted a much bigger factory. His new assembly plant was completed in 1951 along with the office complex which became known as the Kremlin. His first new car, the A40 Devon and Dorset models, emerged in 1947. In the *Autocar* of November 28th, 1947, opposite the page carrying George Strauss' declaration of support for the motor industry, the company's advertisement trumpeted, 'America acclaims the new Austins'. Lord had left for America on what was billed as the 'biggest drive for exports ever made by a British car manufacturer' with crates containing the new cars.

Sir John Black of Standard was quickly away with a new car. He had sketched out himself the curves of the Standard Vanguard, which appropriately shared the name with the last British battleship, which was being built at the time. Its impressively ponderous appearance was enhanced by the fact that Black insisted to its designers that the length of its wheelbase must be sacrosanct, and so the body seemed to swell as room was found for its necessary ingredients. As export markets clamoured for cars, it was rushed abroad without proper road testing. But it still sold over a quarter of a million, and was assembled in numerous plants abroad.

Ford took a different approach. Like Morris it persisted with its pre-war small cars. Apart from the introduction of the big V8 Pilot in 1948 the first new car did not appear until 1950 with the introduction of the Consul – originally intended as a small car replacement. But Ford accompanied its old model policy with the conscious intention of aiming to make its vehicles the cheapest on the market and not raising prices unless forced to do so. This enabled production to be maximized and the best advantage taken of the standardization and interchangeability of parts between models which was one of Ford's strengths. Perry set out his view in February 1947. 'Higher wages and higher standards of living for all depend on lower costs and lower selling prices through increasingly large scale production.' It was an almost banal statement, but one which Ford pursued with greater dedication than its rivals. Ford's popular car was the cheapest on the market – about twenty per cent below competitors.

In practice Ford prices followed the general movement of other manufacturers. It was its ability to expand production and achieve economics of scale, helped by assistance in American sales from its parent company, which led to success. Throughout the 1940s its share of the market rose and every year its profits surpassed those of its rivals.

Manufacturing for all companies was carried out under difficulties. A continuing legacy of the war was a 33·25 per cent purchase tax, and while the old horsepower tax was done away with in 1946 (with long-term results for engine sizes), other measures such as the rationing and taxation of petrol pressed more immediately and heavily.

Government restrictions on factory building, during the housing drive, restricted expansion. Firms found difficulty in getting cars out for sale under the combined impact of Government dictation on the numbers to be made and shortages of materials to supply them. The shortage of coal in the nightmare winter of 1946–7 led to widespread power cuts, and some large plants like Longbridge had to shut down completely. Immediately after the war the Board of Trade had decided on a 50/50 home and export market split, but in 1947 the export share was sharply raised to 75 per cent.

Production rose steadily: from 219,162 in 1946, with over 84,000 going for export; to 267,000 in 1947, half for export; then to 334,815 in 1948, two-thirds exported. But it was not until 1949's output of 412,290 that the record pre-war production was surpassed. The half million milestone was passed the following year. But then the figure of 522,515 became a peak as steel restrictions, imposed in the rush to re-arm during the Korean war, once more cut back on what the car makers could turn out. Indeed the PEP report on motor vehicles in 1950 calculated that companies were only making use of about 65 per cent of their capacity, which had been swollen by post-war expansion.

The two continuing threads which run through the immediate post-war years were the success of the American companies, principally Ford, and the decline of the Morris Empire. In 1947, Morris, who had made a third of the cars on sale before the war, turned out only about 50,000 cars of the 287,000 produced in Britain. Austin made over 62,000 and Ford was catching up fast with over 44,000.

The talk of a merger between Morris and Austin increased; its ultimate achievement taken for granted. An unsuccessful attempt was made in 1948, but the only result was what was hailed as the 'Nuffield–Austin agreement; a combination of giants'.

The *Autocar* announced that: 'Lord Nuffield and Mr L.P. Lord have recently had a series of talks which have resulted in an arrangement whereby there is to be constant interchange of information on production methods, costs, purchases, design, research, patents and all the items which would be likely to result in manufacturing economics.'

The old problems of standardization, which had bothered Lanchester and Austin in the early years of the century, had remained. In 1947 Oliver Lucas of the components firm invited a group of journalists to Birmingham to press the case for a reduction in the types of vehicle made or a larger degree of standardization of parts. He laid out on his factory benches 68 different models of distributors, 133 head lamp types and 98 windscreen wiper variations. Even the *Autocar* declared it as 'manufacturing absurdity' and 'individualism gone mad'.

The Lucas demonstration had some effect. A committee of manufacturers to encourage standardization produced results by the early 1950s with the numbers of dynamos, for example, being reduced to three.

But given the resentment between Lord and Nuffield, their deal never had a chance. It collapsed the following year; the announcement also declaring that 'no merger is contemplated'.

It was not until the end of 1951 that Morris bowed to what by now seemed inevitable and the link-up between the two biggest British-owned manufacturers was finally agreed – a merger to be poisoned by individual bitternesses.

Lord's unforgiving nature, his determination to take Cowley apart 'brick by brick', had scarcely been diminished by his success in overtaking Morris during and immediately after the war. He was widely recognized as the best production man in the industry. Colleagues praised the way he handled negotiations over the supply of steel. Yet he remained a surly and increasingly difficult colleague, and more tellingly his obsession with Morris started to impair the commercial thoroughness.

Joe Edwards was production director at Longbridge. He remembers producing careful costings for Lord for the new models. 'I would say, "This is the ex-works price; there are all the papers supporting it." He would say, "That it, Joe? What's Bill Morris' price on the Oxford, and what's it on the Cowley? Well let's put it ten pounds under that." That's it. Finished. And that at a time when we could sell every thing we made.'

The merger took place in 1952 with Nuffield becoming President of the company (an honorary title), and Lord Chairman. It had produced the fourth largest motor company in the world, only exceeded by the three North American giants.

Yet the union was barely consummated. The partners continued largely to go their separate ways, retaining the same liaisons with their different groups of dealers, their individual names, liveries, and models, and much of the old rivalry. Colleagues say the division was deliberately fostered by Lord – telling the Longbridge men after the merger that the Cowley people were no good and they should have nothing to do with them, and making similar noises at Cowley.

R.F. Hanks, who had been managing director of Morris and became Lord's vice-chairman, said bluntly, 'We have been in competition with Austins for a long time, and we shall remain in competition.'[1]

Nonetheless a study was carried out on standardizing the key components, notably engines, axles and gearboxes. One result was a decision to change the Minor engine. The car had had a pre-war sidevalve engine. But Lord thought that the overhead valve engine, produced for its Longbridge rival the A30, performed better and proposed to use it instead. It threatened redundancies among workers at the Coventry engines plant which had provided the engines for Cowley.

It was one of the first post-war cases of redundancy in the industry and a union delegation, including the T G W U official Harry Urwin, went to see Lord. The unions found Lord sympathetic, insisting that the merger would ensure continuing employment.

Then in a curiously prophetic incident he took the men round the factory in an attempt to win their confidence. In a machine shop he picked up a connecting rod which, he explained, needed five machine operations. He told the unions that he had to buy five separate machines from the manufacturers Alfred Herbert to make them, when what he really wanted was a single machine to do the entire operation. 'All I want is machines specially made – transfer machines. In Germany they are producing that sort of thing. I can spend thousands of pounds but I can't supply the men to Alfred Herbert to make that kind of tool. This won't last long. Either they'll go bloody bust or we'll go bloody bust.' Twenty years later, as a member of the Industrial Development Advisory Board and the Ryder committee, Urwin watched both companies go down.

The problems which the merger had failed to address were to continue throughout the whole string of post-war link-ups between the indigenous British producers. There was a huge range of cars, inadequately standardized and competing against each other; there were too many dealers cutting each other's throats and a mass of plants and agreements denying rationalization.

Some of those involved now argue that BMC was too big to manage. That was not the case. But it was too big for the kind of methods which had been employed by the idiosyncratic individualists who had built the industry up between the wars. As the rapidly emerging Ford was proving at Dagenham, clearly thought out management responsibilities and structures, with proper financial planning and training were essential.

Gerald Palmer was a distinguished designer who was responsible for such celebrated cars as the Jowett Javelin and the Riley Pathfinder. By the early 1950s he was technical director at Morris before leaving to join Vauxhall. At Morris he found accounting procedures almost non-existent for design. 'I never saw any costing figures during the design stage. You just had to use your initiative to make the thing as cheap as you could. One never saw any detailed costing or how the final selling price was arrived at. Directors' meetings under Lord's chairmanship were very formal; they used to assess profit on the end of the month figures.' By contrast, at Vauxhall 'there was cost-accounting in every department. Everything was minutely costed down to a penny.'

Design and training were other essentials which had not properly developed within the company. Palmer's view, from a man committed to design, remains that throughout British industry not enough attention was paid to good design. 'Styling is a combination of fashion and technique. British industry was slow to appreciate this and at Morris before the war, styling wasn't even talked of. After the war, there was some styling but all cars were designed from the inside out.'

Lord, who had designed the successful pre-war Austins and Morris Eight, would draw designs on the back of an envelope and present it to designers to make. Austin did have a chief stylist. Dick Burzi, a South American, came from Lancia before the war. He had a difficult time of it. Lord would sometimes tear up work he did not like and throw it on the floor.

Lord's inferiority complex was never more evident than when Prince Philip, Duke of Edinburgh, came to visit Longbridge. After he arrived, Lord excused himself and left it to others to take him round the works. A difficult lunch followed in which Lord lectured the Prince that he should use an Austin Champ jeep instead of a Land Rover. Then he suddenly invited him to see the new designs and took him down to the studios.

Edwards remembers: 'The Prince looked at them and then said to Len Lord, "They're no good. You will never sell them." The upshot was that the following day the Italian designer Farina flew into Birmingham and went away with a big contract. It included the 1100.'

Attitudes to apprentice training were similarly hand to mouth. While Ford had its own training school even before the war, Lord's view of apprentices was that they were lucky to be allowed in. As Edwards puts it: 'We had a place up on the old firing ground in an old tin hut with about four milling machines about 50 years old and a driller. That was their approach.'

By contrast, Ford had not only better arrangements for apprentices, but also a graduate training scheme which was revived after the war and which produced some key managers, including at least two future chairmen.

One of these was Sam Toy. A wartime RAF pilot, he was one of the first post-war graduate intake. He spent eighteen months in various departments including time as a machine operator before joining the export department in a group which he described as 'young tigers'.

Toy's experience was an example of the much broader based and more thorough Ford approach. In 1953 it had had its own merger, taking over Briggs Bodies when the American Briggs Company showed willingness to sell to ensure its supplies. Briggs was completely integrated into the Ford operation to become the Dagenham Body Plant while its old Southampton works became the centre for van production.

Ford's share increased steadily, while the fundamental weaknesses of BMC's position took some time to work out. But there were assured profits for all manufacturers.

Between 1947 and 1955 trading profits of the motor companies multiplied four times, although the sharp increase in inflation reduced the impact. Profits per vehicle between 1947 and 1953 went up by about 70 per cent. But cars still became relatively cheaper to buy for the customer. Between 1947 and 1955 new car prices went up by only about 30 per cent compared with a rise in average retail prices of about 50 per cent.

This left plenty of resources for the companies to re-equip their plants. But they made varied use of them. Overall they re-invested a bigger proportion in the business than they had done before the war, although their investment per worker still remained well behind American standards. Ford put back most and Morris, before the merger, least. Ford retained nearly £60 million in the business from 1947 to 1956. During the same period, the less profitable BMC companies put back £43 million. Vauxhall went in for the biggest expansion. In 1948 it spent £14 million on a new production plant for its Luton operations which included both cars and lorries. In 1954 it shifted lorry production to Dunstable and a £36 million scheme produced new car production facilities at Luton. Vauxhall sales expanded from 30,000 in 1947 (below its pre-war best) to over 75,000 in 1955.

British manufacturers also looked for the opportunity to bring in more automated production facilities. After the failure of Morris' attempt with automatic transfer machines in the 1920s, American companies in the United States had finally made them work after the war, and British manufacturers began to introduce them in the 1950s. When Austin introduced an automatic transfer machine for cylinder-blocks it was estimated to save 85 per cent of labour costs and machine costs per output were 30 per cent lower. But ominously Austin was only able to find a single British company, James Archdale, to develop the machine with it.

Ford's Dagenham automated block line, introduced in 1951, was regarded in the company as more modern than anything in its American factories. In 1956 it was Standard's turn to introduce automatic transfer machines for producing both cars and the Ferguson tractors it made under contract.

With the huge demand for cars at home it was difficult to lose, while abroad exports boomed. As Ford's export division mushroomed from about a dozen to 300 people in a couple of years, Sam Toy became export supply manager at 28 years of age. He recalls:

Cars were in such short supply that with the pound changing rapidly – going down from four dollars to $2·80 overnight – you could sell whatever you could make anywhere in the world. In 1948 and 1949 we were selling thousands of cars in the United States, even pre-war designed eight and ten horse-power cars. They were selling like hot cakes. Ford had not got a post-war car in the States until the forty niner came along, but then they didn't want to know.

He looks back now at those times as the 'fun years' with no-one over 35 in the department. By contrast the British companies from the Midlands had older, more staid export operations, but still initially successful.

Although Morris took a lower proportion of exports than before the war, the Austin assault on America initially showed some happy returns. Almost all the new A40s were exported. At first of 30,000 produced up to the middle of 1948, only 1,000 were sold in Britain; the rest were exported as 11,000 followed Lord's promotion route to the United States. In 1948, 60 per cent of Austin's production and 70 per cent of Ford's went for export.

However, in 1949, with new American cars available, the transatlantic bubble burst. Lord had targeted the American market, but it was a disastrous misjudgement. From June to

August 1948, 7,000 Austins were shipped to America; a year later the figure had fallen to only 460. Worse still, another 1,200 cars were sent back in bad condition because they had been stored too long.

For Ford, filling a temporary gap with its cheaply produced pre-war cars from Dagenham, the closing up of the American market was a difficulty, but for Austin it was a disaster. A special car, the A90 Atlantic Convertible, had been designed with the United States in mind and was taken to Indianapolis for a continuous week's running, smashing all kinds of records. A big advertising promotion followed but the car flopped even when its price was reduced by a quarter. In Lord's words, 'We went to Indianapolis to prove what the British car could stand up to and I think we proved it. Now the question is what benefit have we got in sales in America? I am afraid the answer is none. The response to the A90 has been disappointing.' Production of the convertible ceased in 1951 though a version struggled on until 1952. Its failure led directly to the biggest strike the motor industry had so far known – a twelve week stoppage at Longbridge after everybody working on the A90 production line, and later others who struck in support, were sacked at a week's notice by Joe Edwards, backed by Lord.

Another export misery, though for different reasons, was the Standard Vanguard. Rushed out to meet post-war demand, it was soon to be pushed into export markets without being properly tested. The result was a series of horrific failures on the rough pavé of Continental roads which helped to bring British cars a reputation for unreliability for which they would suffer for decades.

The Vanguard had been designed at the end of the war, and was Standard's flagship. The company was amused but unworried when the Chancellor, Sir Stafford Cripps, inspected it at the factory and pronounced it a failure because it was impossible to sit in the back seat with a top hat on. But when it went abroad for export its deficiencies became clear.

Years later Alick Dick, who became Standard's managing director, was frank about the problems:

The Vanguard was, of course, supposed to take care of world

conditions. But none of our engineers, and none of our senior sales force had really been round the world to see what the conditions were. So we were only surmising from what we had been told by dealers that we had appointed.

Immediately after the war the American cars had lost the export market because they were too long and low and they were being designed for the big motorways and expressways that they had. And so we were designing cars to replace those, and the roads were largely dust and potholes and corrugations.

I know we sold 10,000 Vanguards to Brazil and we had never seen anyone in Brazil at all. Actually the man who took them was a Hungarian and he gave away 5,000 of them in bribes in order to get the licences. He still made a good profit on the other 5,000. That's the sort of conditions we were up against.

Dick himself visited South Africa, a big potential market for British cars. Arriving in Cape Town, he said:

I saw a Vanguard, much to my great delight. I was even more pleased when it was driven by a particularly attractive girl. So I thought that I would go up and speak to her. It was outside the dealer's showrooms.

When I got near I could hear her voice of complaint, and I saw her go round the back of the car and open the boot. She'd driven from Johannesburg to Cape Town over dust roads and corrugations. And in the back was her mink coat, on the floor and it had got dust on it, and then it had rained, and it was set in the mud. So I went back to my hotel and had a drink.[2]

The company had problems in Europe as well. It sent its Scottish representative, the only man in its service department with a passport, to try to sort them out. He found the cars had been unable to cope with the Continental pave roads. 'The fractures in the chassis had to be seen to be believed. The shock absorbers were weak after a very few thousand miles. The Belgians put a stiffer oil in and that just made the shock absorbers go solid when they hit a bump. It used to fracture the bolts holding the shock absorber to the chassis and it used to come up and over and straight through the wing.'[3]

There were long lasting consequences for the reputation of British cars. People like Dick argued that the Continental companies, unable to resume mass production immediately after the war, benefitted enormously from the British mistakes. They had more time to develop their cars; they learnt what mistakes not to make, and they took over some of the British dealers.

The Government's command to export had led to the British industry shipping out vehicles that were quite unsuitable, while the restriction of steel which enforced it encouraged less careful checks on quality. As one manufacturer put it: 'When a production manager was left with not just a load of scrap but something which was the equivalent of actual cars, it was amazing how good scrap panels looked.'

Yet such was the thirst for cars that exports continued to climb even when the American market was closed off. Ford, like other companies, turned to Australia, the country where something like a third to a half of exports had gone before the war. By the early 1950s nearly a third of Ford's exports were going to Australia, but in 1952 import restrictions were imposed and as Sir Stanford Cooper, Ford's Vice-Chairman at the time, put it, 'Sales went down with a bump.' At about the same time Sir James Cleminson remembers being in Australia to visit the manufacturing plant of his own (non-motor) company. In a hotel he met Lord Nuffield, on one of his annual voyages to Australia. He remembers Nuffield's surprise that Cleminson should manufacture in Australia, assuring him that Morris motors would always be able to ship goods in from England.

But times were changing. Australia's experience of aircraft manufacture during the war had led it to look for ways of continuing and expanding manufacturing. General Motors and Ford established manufacturing plants. Morris had to follow suit, although he still shipped parts from Britain.

Elsewhere the French and German companies became increasingly powerful rivals. By 1956 German exports were to surpass British due to the enormous success of the Volkswagen 'Beetle'.

The 1950 PEP report had cautioned about British export prospects, pointing out that the 1948 results had been achieved when 'there was a sellers' market within the USA as well as a general shortage of dollars outside it and when the German economy was still almost prostrate.' But it was still dismissive of the Volkswagen which became the sensation of post-war car sales. Estimating the price of the car at about £700, it judged that it 'would not be competitive with British small cars since the Volkswagen is by British standards uncomfortable and noisy.' It was a classic example of British insularity, and conviction that British must be best.

But the report was only following the judgments of the British and American technical team which had looked carefully at the German industry and been impressed with its production methods, if not by its product, and also by a group of British manufacturers who had inspected German factories to see what they wanted to strip out for their own benefit. They took away machine tools but rejected the plans and the jigs for what seemed to them essentially an old-fashioned pre-war car.

Harry Urwin, visiting the Volkswagen plant at Wolfsburg in the early 1950s heard the story from the German side. 'They told us that the British manufacturers had turned it down with contempt. It was pre-war and not what the public wanted. But the Germans said to us, "The people of the world are not looking for fancy cars, they are looking for a means of transport that will stand up and will not fold up on the autobahn like some of your cars." '

With growing competition and the Korean war steel restrictions the strong rise in exports flattened out. Export figures were just under 400,000 in 1950 and it was not until 1957 that they exceeded that figure, although production had increased by 60 per cent. By then, steel restrictions had been lifted and the companies had turned, with some relief, to home sales. Although there were cogent reasons to try to meet a much greater proportion of the pent up demand, in effect the British industry, in the absence of Government direction, was abandoning export markets to others.

As yet, however, it was inconceivable that there should be any major invasion of the British market from outside. Not until after 1958 did imported cars regularly start to exceed 10,000 a year – less than two per cent of the market. Looking ahead, the PEP report, apparently incisive, had allowed the question of imports only half a page.

The Korean war difficulties were temporary and seen to be so. At home, the glad, confident progress continued until the credit squeeze of 1955 and the Suez trauma of 1956. The general blow to national self-confidence was shared by the motor industry, and it was hit by painful practical consequences too, namely: restriction of exports as the Suez canal was closed, denial of markets as a political protest, and at home petrol rationing following the imposition in 1955 of restrictions on hire purchase which had had an immediate and deadly impact on sales.

Since the replacement of the Labour Government by Conservatives in 1951, the industry had seen a lifting of some of the controls under which it had chafed since the beginning of the war. But now the industry's political friends started on a course which many in the industry now blame for its decline – its frequent and often arbitrary use as a way to regulate the economy. They squeezed credit by making it more difficult to buy cars through HP restrictions or higher purchase tax and let the car makers adjust.

George Turnbull, who was in charge of car production at Standard from 1956, and later became managing director of the British Leyland car division and then chief executive of Peugeot–Talbot in Britain, blames the Government attitude for the industry's ultimate decline. He says:

> In those days it was just a little fiscal regulator. If the economy was overheated, put some more purchase tax on motor cars.
>
> The Government was totally oblivious and if I was ever going to apportion blame for the parlous state the British motor industry got into, you have got to put it at the door of the Government. I don't care which complexion or which colour. The reality is that they didn't handle the industry in a sensitive way. It was the main primer for so many service industries; it was the main employer of labour; it was the biggest manufacturing industry by a mile and they treated it with derision. There's no other word for it.
>
> From one day from virtually full employment, I had got to sack three thousand men which I did with great reluctance. It drove more and more men into militant unions for protection.

The first restrictions on hire purchase were introduced in February 1952, requiring a minimum deposit of 33·33 per cent and repayment over eighteen months. Demand for cars was such that sales still leapt. The restrictions were abolished in July 1954 ony to come back at a lower level (fifteen per cent and 24 months) the following February and then to be tightened (33·33 per cent) four months later in July. In February 1956, the deposit was increased to 50 per cent of a new car's value and sales went down by twenty per cent.

Over the years the industry remained a first resort for governments wanting to regulate the economy. Between 1952 and 1973, the regulations for cars were changed twenty times – on average once a year. In one period of little more than two years from June 1965 to November 1967, they were altered no fewer than seven times.

At its worst, the frequent changes made a nonsense of the industry's attempts to plan; at best it presented it with great difficulties. The concern of the Society of Motor Manufacturers and Traders was such that it produced a graph which often directly correlated the rise and fall in the industry's fortunes with the effect of credit restrictions. These 'stop–go' policies shook the industry to its foundations, creating fissures never completely repaired. They had an immediate effect on labour relations – a problem which was almost synonymous with the industry in the 1960s and '70s, but had not yet emerged as such a major source of concern.

The traditional methods of manufacturers to deal with recession and commercial failure had been to lay off workers temporarily or for good. But with the increase in unionization, and a general public culture which stressed the need for more consideration for working people, the old ways were increasingly resented. Even the Engineering Employers Federation, traditional hard-line foe of the engineering unions, had attempted to persuade Joe Edwards in 1953 not to lay off his workers when the Austin A90 had failed to sell.

Now in the recession of 1956 most manufacturers made workers redundant. At Standard, it was as many as 3,500 and there was a fifteen day strike as a result. At BMC one in eight were made redundant and again there was a strike. Just as the industry resented being treated as the government's plaything in an arbitrary way, so workers increasingly reacted against redundancies which were in contrast to the general conditions of full employment which still prevailed in other industries. The number of days lost through strikes over redundancy rose from a tenth before the war to over a quarter afterwards, and it was noted that the recessions in the industry post-war began to coincide with an increase in days lost through strikes. But the impact was much more far-reaching – the resentment and uncertainty encouraged mistrust of a management and a willingness to rely increasingly on the unions, even though motor industry wages remained comparatively high.

David Buckle was a shop steward at the Pressed Steel Plant at Cowley in 1956. Up to then, he says:

> Many stewards were caught up with the immediate post-war feeling of we must get this factory back to producing cars; nothing must stand in the way of that.
>
> I date the change in attitudes to the time when Labour and Conservative Governments, both of them, began to use the industry as an economic regulator. It wasn't uncommon for us to be working quite excessive overtime including Saturday one week. And then quite suddenly you would arrive at work on the Monday morning and the foreman would say, 'The bottom's fallen out of the market, there's no work for a fortnight.' We would be shut out on guaranteed week payment.
>
> We knew the fact that the government was using the industry as an economic regulator was the cause and so we began to protest vigorously about the job insecurity, but also to disbelieve the schedules that management were putting out – the number of cars being produced a week – and we used to try to do a bit of regulation on the numbers ourselves. What we said was, 'What's the point of us going hell for leather for two or three months with all the overtime and then find we are shut out for a fortnight with very little pay?' It was the first stirrings of trade unions through shop stewards like myself trying to influence management policies on schedules.

Car industry earnings had been very high. Engineering wages which had been fifth among the sixteen major industries in 1938 had jumped to second by 1940, a position they retained after the war. Car workers did even better. Between 1948 and 1964 male motor workers increased their pay by over 160 per cent compared with 140 per cent in engineering as a whole.

Indeed the Motor Manufacturers' willingness to pay extra to keep production going infuriated the engineering employers in general, and the officials of the Engineering Employers Federation in particular. At the end of the war there was a huge row with Standard which resulted in its departure from the Federation. Sir John Black of Standard, then the most unionized of the Coventry factories, made an agreement with Jack Jones to maintain the high rates of piecework which had prevailed during the special circumstances of the war. It was a unilateral deal out of keeping with the general employers' intention of reducing piecework earnings. The Rootes group had announced a return to traditional rates and had then been faced with a go-slow in its three factories. It backed down after its threat of redundancies had been answered by an all-out strike by sheet metal workers.

By contrast Black insisted on striking a deal on his own with Jones. When the engineering employers argued with him, he refused to budge and announced that 'our lads are giving the production'. Going from the meeting to Jones' office, he told him, 'I am not having those bloody fools dictate to me. I gave my word to you and I'll keep it. It's up to you to help me now.'[4]

In the years that followed, Standard, one of the less profitable companies, struck a series of deals, pioneering a reduction in the working week to five days and an elaborate productivity deal which divided workers into large gangs and paid production bonuses.

Other employers blamed Black for the wage inflation in Coventry and the attitude of production at any cost. There seemed a strange contrast between a man who was so autocratic with his managers and so matey with the unions, spending time chatting on the production lines. But his attitude was widely shared. As the engineering employers saw them, 'motor manufacturers tended to be freebooters. Their attitude was that if anyone was to go short of labour, it would not be them. And they would often give way to a sudden unofficial demand from a group of workers rather than risk loss of production. They knew that when they had labour troubles their competitors were quick to take advantage of it.'[5]

While inflation began to preoccupy the Government, with Labour Prime Minister Clement Attlee issuing a 1948 White Paper arguing for no increase in incomes without increasing production, wages continued to climb.

While maximizing production was the imperative, the attitude might be defended. In 1955 British productivity could still stand comparison with Continental plants. They produced 4·2 cars per employee per year compared with 3·9 in Germany and 3·6 in France.

But as difficulties crowded in, and Governments started to worry about inflation, a series of rows broke out between the motor employers and their colleagues in engineering. A summit meeting in 1958 brought accusations that the motor industry had paid increases far greater than elsewhere, while the industry complained that the Federation had given away too much on basic rates. Sir William Lyons of Jaguar said they were tired of being criticized and insisted they always faced difficulties on setting piece rates when changing models. Alick Dick of Standard said that given the increase in both capital spending and productivity, better earnings were to be expected.

The motor manufacturers in turn grew increasingly worried about unofficial strikes and wanted the Federation, their formal link with the national union leadership, to take action. They suggested informing unions that shop stewards who took unofficial action would be sacked.

Further rows broke out over what was seen as the car manufacturers' peremptory attitude to sackings and lay-offs. Faced with the downturn in 1956 Edwards of BMC decided to sack 12,000 people with a week's pay in lieu of notice. The Federation urged him to reconsider and warned of trouble not just from the men but also from Parliament and the press if he went ahead. Edwards ignored them, rode out a strike and a storm of public criticism, and in the end the redundancies stuck. But the firm agreed to consult in future and to provide some payment for those with long service.

It was an indication both of how much the old ways still prevailed, and how much they were now under challenge. Lord,

who was increasingly concerned about labour problems, suggested to Edwards that he should take over labour relations full-
time. Edwards saw it as demotion, resigned and after receiving a
number of offers went to head Pressed Steel. There he turned it
from loss to profit after further redundancies. He instituted the
sort of apprentice and graduate training that he had felt BMC
lacked. Later he was to claim that his action in sacking 15,000
people in a year had led directly to the government's redundancy
payments act.

The increasingly confrontational atmosphere stored up trouble
for the future. However, the extent of the peril remained largely
hidden below the surface as the industry, gathering speed after
what seemed the temporary doldrums of 1956, steamed ahead
through the late 1950s. It was swept along by the surge in
prosperity which allowed Harold Macmillan to win a swamping
election victory in 1959 with the slogan 'You've never had it so
good.'

The numbers of cars in use in Britain doubled between 1952
and 1959. After 1956 production rose rapidly. It was up by 50 per
cent within two years and British car production exceeded a
million for the first time. Hire Purchase restrictions had once
more been removed.

The big companies cashed in. In 1953 both Ford and BMC had
bought up body suppliers. Ford took Briggs and BMC bought
Fisher and Ludlow in Castle Bromwich. Their control of body
builders who had also supplied other companies squeezed the
remaining independent producers. Jowett of Bradford, whose
post-war Javelin had had its body produced by Briggs, was
forced out of business. Ford refused to continue to make the
body, and with other financial problems that sealed Jowett's fate.

BMC's take-over of Fisher and Ludlow in turn caused difficulties for Standard. It had no body-making facilities of its own
and when it moved to step up car production to replace tractor
production and introduce a new model, it ran up against Len
Lord. He refused to invest in a larger plant because it would
benefit his rival. 'I don't see why the hell I should put money into
your company,' he told Standard's Managing Director, Alick
Dick. Dick then arranged for three separate companies to make
the body which was fitted together with difficulty at Coventry.

It was Ford which gained most as the independents declined, with Singer too disappearing. It joined the Rootes group in 1955. Ford's share of the market had risen from just over fourteen per cent at the end of the war to over nineteen per cent in 1950 without introducing any new models. So when its Consul and Zephyr medium cars came out in 1950 with substantial American design help, and were followed by new Anglias and Prefects in 1953, the company share rose from 21 to 27 per cent in a year.

By contrast BMC, which had held a 43·4 per cent share of the market in 1946 through its separate companies, had declined to less than 39 per cent by 1955. On its larger production, it made smaller profits. While Ford's profits multiplied three times in three years to £33·9 million in 1959, BMC's went from £8·3 million in 1956–7 to £26·9 million in 1959–60. But by the end of the decade Ford's rise was under challenge from revolutionary new models from the home-based industry.

The year 1959 marks one of the peaks of the British motor industry; one of the last summits before rise turned into fall. As Harold Macmillan planned his 'never had it so good' election, so the last tarmac metres of Britain's M1 Motorway were rolled out across Northamptonshire. It did not actually reach to either Birmingham or London which it was supposed to link. But with its novelty and its symbolism as well as its lack of speed limits, ardent motorists rushed to drive to the end of it, to celebrate, and to drive back again.

At the same time Ford was taking the wraps off its new Anglia, the first Ford to be designed entirely by the British company. Its rakish body, with a reverse sloped rear window, housed the new Kent engine which was to become a key factor in the company's triumphs of the 1960s. It was the first British Ford to provide four forward gears, and the first to sell over a million.

Standard, which had taken over the Triumph Company in 1945 launched its new Triumph Herald at the Albert Hall. There was a singing chorus, a comedian – Bob Monkhouse – and the car was assembled on the stage. It was again a breakthrough in design. The brainchild of an Italian designer, Giovanni Michelotti, who had worked with the Farina brothers, the *Times* described the Herald as 'more than an interesting new model with many ingenious features; it is the company's considered answer to the intensifying struggle between British and Continental firms in the world market for small cars.'

Standard claimed to have looked afresh at the type of small car now required, taking into account safety, ease of handling and servicing. It had 'a turning circle smaller than a London taxi, a body designed in separate sections that can be replaced quickly and not a single grease-gun point.' It also had some of the first safety features including a collapsible steering column. It was a remarkable car. One of the group of component makers who saw one of the first models remembers, 'We all thought it was revolutionary. We had never seen anything like it.'

The car made a virtue out of Standard's difficulties with bodymakers. The seven different units made in three factories, spread between Liverpool and Birmingham, were bolted on to the chassis. But while public demonstrations by a team of apprentices could assemble the car in three and a half minutes, things were less simple in the factory. The parts often did not fit together, and the car was well known for letting in water at the joints. Nonetheless, it still sold.

But the radical lines of the Herald had to give way for innovation to the new BMC package. It was a product of the difficulties of 1956. Petrol rationing and shortages had put a premium on low-consumption small cars and British manufacturers were horrified to find people importing German bubblecars, with room for only one or two people, to beat the shortage. It did not help that the miniature cars carried the names of the very aircraft which had attempted to invade England during the Battle of Britain, like Heinkel and Messerschmidt.

At BMC Lord summoned Alec Issigonis to make a competitor. He told him, 'You can do what you like, but it has got to have an existing engine.' The result was the BMC Mini; the prototype was produced within sixteen months and the car launched in 1959. Its small wheels, hydrolastic suspension and the way it used the same oil for engine and gearbox were all innovations. But Issigonis' major triumph was to mount the engine across the car driving it through the front wheels with the help of constant velocity joints developed by the Birmingham firm of Hardy Spicer. It was this breakthrough which was to revolutionize small car design.

The Mini was the greatest triumph of British design since the days of Lanchester, and its influence was to spread through first the BMC range and then throughout Europe. By the 1970s virtually every small car had a transverse engine, and many larger ones front-wheel drive. It was hailed as an extraordinary car and though the public took a little while to catch on, it soon became a popular success taking in one month an extraordinary nineteen per cent of the total car market.

The Mini struck a national chord, a symbol of the rebirth of British design. Issigonis' old principle of functional, no frills design chimed with the spirit of the 1960s which was to sweep away the fripperies and the evasions which cluttered both conventions and designs. The mood of the day was to hide as little as possible, as the car's name-sake, the mini-skirt, laid bare.

And so the no-nonsense Mini became an essential possession for the star-touched and famous, the pop-stars, or designers or businessmen who wanted to stress their ordinariness and lack of pretension, however much they might darken the windows of the car for their privacy while decorating the bodywork with psychedelic patterns to draw attention to themselves.

Rather like the old Austin Seven before the war (after which one model was consciously named) it became a national institution, something to joke about (How many elephants can you get in a Mini? Answer – four, two in the front, two in the back) yet also a car to respect for its unexpected power.

The way the Mini-Cooper, powered by a high-powered engine, won victories in Monte Carlo rallies showed there was more to the car than just clever use of space, and the sight of its unassuming shape steaming past more high-powered saloons on the new motorways satisfied both the pretence of being unassuming and the sharp competitive edge of the 1960s.

It was also remarkably convenient in the growing traffic problems. Twenty-seven years after its introduction, it was reprieved again on the basis that it was still selling steadily to customers, two thirds of them women who appreciated its practicality while it had acquired the status of a cult car in so diverse yet stylish countries as France and Japan.

Yet even at its moment of triumph the seeds of disaster were being sown. The sloppiness which had spread through BMC became obvious. The car was launched in the late summer, and it soon became clear that in rain it leaked. Water rose steadily around the passsenger's feet. It was comparatively simple to remedy. But Issigonis' subsequent excuse, that the car had been tried out in dry conditions and that 'when the rain came we discovered that the sealing of the floor imposed too many difficulties under production conditions,'[6] bespoke a carelessness which was to become familiar to too many purchasers of British cars.

But the Mini also showed up a much more fundamental and disastrous flaw in BMC – the same lack of financial control and stringency which had been apparent in Lord's pricing policies to compete with Morris or in the experience of men like Palmer who had worked in the design departments.

Across at Ford, where careful costing disciplines operated, Sir Terence Beckett was the manager of product staff, in charge of all planning for cars. As the Mini captured the public imagination he was pressed by both his dealers in Britain and his bosses in America to produce a competitor. He resisted the pressure with difficulty, arguing instead that Ford should aim at a different target, and that the Mini route was an unprofitable one.

Beckett's view was based on a careful examination of the Mini. His team got hold of one through a BMC dealer a fortnight before it was launched. They stripped it down and costed and weighed every item. The Ford men estimated that they could have taken about £15 off the cost by simplified design, but that even with Ford methods (which were in advance of those at BMC), the car as made could not be turned out at a profit. Beckett commissioned market research which showed that customers would have willingly paid £20 more per car and not a single sale would have been lost. His conclusions were passed on to BMC privately, but rejected.

Looking back now, Beckett blames those attitudes for the subsequent collapse of BMC and British Leyland:

I really do believe that British Leyland's troubles were made in the years 1957 to 1959, with the basic strategy on the Mini. For five years following the introduction of the Mini I correlated their profit and loss account and the increased numbers of

Minis and 1100s they sold knowing their cost disability. As the numbers increased, the correlation was 100 per cent correct. It fatally undermined their profitability. They were locking up something like £170 million worth of assets which was producing them no return.

When you look at their future fortunes and their inability to do this and that in all the generations to come, they had denied themselves that resource and that opportunity. We can talk of all kinds of things they did not do right which caused that decline and demise, but the root of it was in that.

The Sixties
'Time is not on our Side'

The 1960s have been irrevocably tagged as the 'swinging sixties', the years when old inhibitions were swept away and a new British style emerged – a combination of clothing fashions, pop music and artistic style in which the Mini was a potent and recognizable symbol. But in economic and industrial terms, the years of the 1960s turned from dream to bleak awakening. Halfway through the decade the bubble burst, even if it was in a shower of multi-colours. The 'never had it so good' euphoria of Macmillan was replaced by the 'pragmatism' of a Labour Government which came to power warning of 'thirteen wasted years' of industrial decline and a widening gap between what we imported and what we sold abroad. Continuing economic crises and a devaluation of the pound followed.

Behind the swinging facade was a national trauma – a change in the country's view of itself and a national loss of self-confidence which the motor industry typified. In the economic storm, the remaining British-owned motor manufacturers huddled together for survival in one merger after another. By the end of the decade all three of the British-owned Big Five had been taken over by other companies, and the medium sized independents, Rover, Jaguar, Daimler, swept up under their skirts. There were now to be four big companies, three of them American owned. The indigenous industry was controlled by a Lancashire truck and bus maker which had not produced cars for 30 years.

There were cogent reasons for the mergers. They reflected what was happening in other parts of the world. As the market for cars expanded, the stakes grew higher. The launches of new and more sophisticated vehicles became increasingly expensive; the penalties of failure higher. Car makers looked for a more comprehensive spread of vehicles; they came to talk of a 'range' of cars rather than concentrating on particular models. The big companies grew bigger.

When Austin and Morris had merged to form BMC it had been the fourth largest motor company in the world, behind only the American giants. Now, when the enlarged British Motor Holdings was beefed up by the merger with Leyland, which had already taken in Standard-Triumph and Rover, it only took it to fifth place. It was still behind Volkswagen, the fastest rising European company, which had a remarkable re-birth from the ashes of war.

British companies coped with the expansion badly. Between 1960 and 1970, the number of cars in use in Britain doubled to over 11,000,000. Production rose by nearly 50 per cent in the decade. But from 1965 it hardly rose at all. The number of cars made in Britain in 1969 and 1970 were fewer than in 1965. There was to be a small brief spurt in the early 1970s and from then on, decline. British car makers were beginning to lose the battle against foreign competition. Exports reached their ultimate peak in 1969 – 771,634 cars representing about 45 per cent of the year's production.

Imports meanwhile were starting to rise. The high duties, originally imposed by McKenna, had at last to be brought down under pressure of world events. The protective fence which had allowed the British industry to grow was being dismantled plank by plank, and the British manufacturers found it difficult to cope with the cold wind of competition. Between 1962 and 1970 under the impact of growing European free trade and the international Kennedy trade negotiations, the duties on imported cars halved, from 30 to fifteen per cent – making them hugely cheaper. For some smaller countries in the European Free Trade Area, duties were abolished altogether. The result – imports, around seven per cent in 1960 had doubled to fourteen per cent by 1970, and the rise would accelerate.

The industry had erected expensive new plants to make more cars with more modern equipment. The result seemed to be to plunge it into the red. On the shop floor the throwing off of inhibitions which was a hallmark of the 'swinging sixties' seemed to take the form of anarchy, a refusal to listen to union officials as

British forces relied heavily on the American-designed Model T Ford. In the Middle East General Allenby said it was one of the three keys to his victory.

Austin survived in business at first by supplying the Imperial Russian Army for whom it built its first armoured cars.

MGs leaving the Oxford factory for test in 1929 before the factory moved to Abingdon.

In 1930 the sixteen horsepower Austin Burnham was one of Austin's big cars. Note the supervisor with hat, highly polished shoes and top pocket handkerchief; their smartness impressed new recruits.

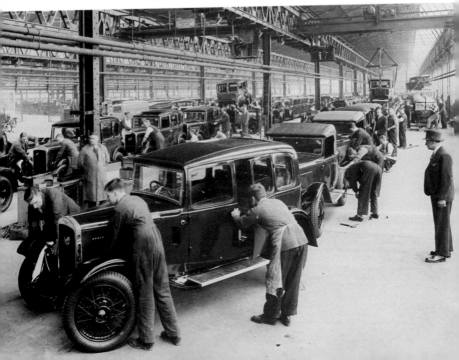

much as to management, which brought a council of war under the chairmanship of the Prime Minister himself.

By the end of the 1960s, the government was no longer limiting itelf to setting the rules for the industry at a distance through taxation policies but interfering directly in day to day operations, intervening in strikes and cajoling and coercing companies into mergers and reorganizations.

In theory the combination of companies was to make them stronger and better able to compete on a world stage increasingly overshadowed by larger and more powerful players. In practice, just as with BMC in 1952, many of the old faults were never addressed and managers found themselves unable to control the sprawling conglomeration of plants and workshops lashed together in a pattern which owed everything to history and nothing to logic. Meanwhile, huge rises in inflation tore apart the self-regulating piecework system on which most of the homegrown British companies had depended for years, bewildering and obsessing workers and managers alike.

It was not a uniquely British malaise, though some of it came to be known as the 'British sickness'. General Motors, the world's biggest motor company, let its British subsidiary, Vauxhall, slip heavily into the red. Another American giant, Chrysler, after sniffing round the industry for years, finally plunged in at exactly the wrong moment, and seemed to lack both the know-how and the will to improve the position of the faltering Rootes Group. Ford showed a growing resilience and consolidated its position. Even so, with a sharp insight into future trends for which British managers give Henry Ford II unstinting credit, its American parent immersed Ford of Britain into the wider pool of a freshly-created Ford of Europe, a merger both strategic and defensive. The result would be to consolidate Ford as the most successful and progressive motor company in Britain, a position which it firmly established in the 1960s, after losing it in the immediate post-First World War years a generation before.

But as the 1960s dawned, greeted with more optimism and newspaper anticipation than almost any decade in the century, it was the British Motor Corporation with its radical front-wheel drive Mini and its forthcoming big sisters, the 1100 and 1300, which held popular attention and a decisive share of the market.

At Ford, Terry Beckett was bombarded with demands from his dealers and from Ford headquarters in Dearborn, Detroit, to do something about it. When the Mini took nineteen per cent of the market in one month of 1961, the pressure was intense. He recalls:

The Americans were constantly telling me, 'Terry, there must be something wrong with the figures. We can do anything these BMC people can do. Why don't you get in; doing nothing is no answer to anything.' I said that my view, based on the very best research of my team, was that if we do, this is going to be an unparalleled disaster for the Ford Motor Company; we'll lose enormous potfuls of money.

What you are faced with in the motor industry is not just the decision of what is going to happen to that particular model; it is denying yourself the opportunity to do anything else for the next five years. You have got to do all the other things. I lost more sleep at that time in my career than I have ever done, before or since.

Beckett stood his ground. Ford's response emerged almost by accident – in the words of one of Ford's senior officers, 'we fell into it' – but when it came, it was the product of meticulous planning and cost control, and it changed the fortunes of British car makers almost for good.

By now the chairman of Ford of Britain was Sir Patrick Hennessy, the tough Irishman who had started on the line at Ford's Cork tractor factory and so thoroughly reorganized Ford's buying policy in the 1930s – 'the biggest dictator I have ever met' according to one of the toughest of Ford executives. Hennessy was unwilling to give second best to anyone, and in the early 1960s he heard that Ford of Germany, whose rivalry with Britain extended to the two companies maintaining separate dealer networks on the Continent, were planning a new medium car, in conjunction with the Americans, to be made and sold both in Germany and the United States.

Hennessy determined that Britain should have a competitor. The German project was codenamed Cardinal; the Dagenham answer was promptly christened Archbishop. Beckett, in charge of the project, says he knew that the Cardinal actually stood for a North American bird, but British executives were ribbed by their American colleagues for years afterwards that they had misunderstood its meaning.

The product planning team puzzled over the size of the car. They decided that there could be a gap in the market in the light medium range somewhere around the very steady but rather stolid performer, the Hillman Minx and the BMC's 1100/1300 range.

A major question was front-wheel drive. The Germans were planning front-wheel drive for the Cardinal. But in Britain a Ford research department in Birmingham had been working on the problem for five years without making a breakthrough. Hennessy and Beckett decided instead for a conventional rear-wheel drive car. When it appeared, it was much less advanced than the BMC range but minutely researched and costed. It benefitted from the successful Kent engine and outstanding gearbox of the Anglia, while Beckett insisted on providing an ample boot (which the BMC range lacked) to please both families and sales reps. He also found that a Ford plant in America had developed a new method of boxed construction for the underbody which reduced weight.

Engineers were given precise cost specifications which they were forbidden to exceed without savings elsewhere. In a last minute decision, a strengthened model designed for the Australian outback was adopted as standard. The car still came in £100,000 under its budget and it was ready 21 months after the first clay model.

The Cortina's first public test came at a test track in Paris, where it was run against its German rival in front of an audience of the company's American management. It was a runaway success. The German cars, after a last minute carburettor adjustment, faltered and dropped out of the race. But the occasion was nearly marred by the enthusiasm of Henry Ford II who, with Hennessy and Beckett in the car, drove a GT Cortina so exuberantly round the track that it almost came off, narrowly missing a tree.

British dealers were at first less enthusiastic. Frankly incredulous that Ford was apparently serving up the same old mixture instead of the advanced engineering which BMC provided, Beckett had to spend over an hour stressing the Mini's inadequacies as well as his own car's virtues – its space, its performance, the clearance on its suspension by contrast to the Mini. The press were less impressed, giving the new car mixed reviews.

But others soon liked what they saw. The car became a bestseller, establishing itself as a favourite among businessmen as well as private customers. Within a few years, government pay restrictions encouraged firms to provide company cars to reward executives and representatives who could not legally be paid more. The new car reaped the benefit selling over a million in five years. Crucially its large size made larger profits. The Cortina was introduced in 1962, and Ford's profits went up sharply in 1963 to over £18 million.

By contrast, the smaller British-owned companies were finding it difficult to make sufficient money to finance their new model plans. Since the war, Standard had relied heavily on boosting its earnings by a contract to make tractors at its Banner Lane plant for Harry Ferguson, the former Argyll apprentice, whose idea for mounting farm implements on the back of tractors had revolutionized tractor design. In the 1950s, tractors produced 60 or 70 per cent of the firm's profits. But in 1953 the Canadian firm of Massey-Harris had merged with Ferguson, and made it clear it was unhappy about manufacture being outside its control. In 1959, it bought out the tractor operation for £12½ million, money which Standard then used to try to boost its car operations. Some went on a new £2½ million car assembly hall but by the time it came into operation in March 1961, its workers were already on short-time, as the company was badly affected by the return of hire purchase restrictions in 1960.

Sir John Black had been forced out of office by his fellow directors in 1954 as he grew increasingly contrary and started to fire long-standing colleagues. His nephew, Alick Dick, took over. Dick was an attractive, hail-fellow-well-met man who called his new car the Herald after his own boat. But even his optimism was now disturbed.

Standard had been the least profitable of the 'Big Five', even with the tractor profits. Its return on capital had slumped and its profits per vehicle were a quarter of those for Ford. Its dodgy finances had been enough to deter Rover from mounting a merger bid in the 1950s to provide extra space for Landrover production. Now its profits were halved, to £2 million in 1959–60, and the credit squeeze made things worse. From being £4 million in the black at one stage in 1960, it slumped to £6 million in the red. In the last four months of the year, the company sold little more than 18,000 cars. Dick, with money pouring out 'like water', pushed up his overdraft limit, cut back on sports car production and desperately tried to negotiate a deal with the smallest of the American companies, American Motors, to use its Rambler body to revamp the Vanguard which he saw as 'dying on its feet'.

It was too late. He was forced instead to open negotiations to sell the company with Sir Henry Spurrier, the chairman of Leyland, the Lancashire manufacturers of commercial vehicles which had been spectacularly successful in post-war export markets and wanted to become an all-round manufacturer.

Leyland was one of the oldest established motor companies, founded in the town of Leyland in the 1890s as the Lancashire Steam Motor Company, and turning to petrol driven vehicles in 1904. Its big production of municipal dustcarts, vans and fire-engines as well as lorries helped it to profits of £100,000 a year on a turnover of half a million pounds by the time the First World War broke out. It had been a carmaker for a short time in the 1920s before difficulties with its commercial vehicle business forced it to pull back. Its products had been at spectacularly opposite poles of the market – a 'straight eight' which had been thought a worthy competitor of the Rolls-Royce, and a utilitarian 'Trojan' range designed for cheapness. Trojans were cars and vans of monumental simplicity and torpor which refused to exceed 35 miles an hour however driven, and were a particular favourite with the clergy. But a solid-tyred version proved to have exactly the same wheel span as the distance allowed between tramlines, and unwary drivers caught their wheels in the lines and found their stately progress directed towards the terminus.

After the Second World War Leyland had mounted a spectacu-larly effective export drive. Its head, the effervescent Donald

Stokes, became a symbol of go-ahead business attack, widely acclaimed by governments as well as newspapers.

The Standard deal nearly failed. Spurrier became increasingly worried about its evidently worsening position, and the deal looked like going cold. Dick solved it in typically car salesman fashion. Challenged in the office of the *Sunday Express* that the deal was foundering and nobody wanted the company, he thought on his feet, and insisted that there was another party interested. It was an act of pure bravado, if not a straightforward lie, but the paper swallowed the bait and putting two and two together to make considerably more than five announced that Chrysler, which was known to have European ambitions, was interested in Standard. Leyland rapidly came back into the deal.

Leyland took over Standard-Triumph International early in 1961. The staff was cut by 800, workers went onto a two and a half day week instead of three days, and the hundreds of company cars issued to staff were sharply reduced. By August, Dick had gone. The company continued to lose money, with a million pounds pouring out in three months. But then the industry was bewildered by yet another twist of the economic regulator as purchase tax was cut back and sales of Standard cars, and the Herald in particular, rose once more.

The new management was welcomed by many at Standard. George Turnbull who became General Manager found Stanley Markland the new managing director 'such a practical Lancastrian, an engineer, with so much common-sense it was not true. He started to put Standard-Triumph back together again from a position where it lost about eight million pounds, which was unbelievable, unheard of, in those days to a small loss the next year, and a small profit the year after.'

For Leyland too, the move seemed a success. Spurrier had made no secret of his ambition to expand Leyland. In articles in the annual *Times Review of Industry* he had expressed his belief that within about fifteen years the European motor industry would be concentrated into a dozen companies – with the clear implication that he intended Leyland to be one of them.

As Standard fell into Leyland's lap, so Rootes was faltering. A combination of ambitious expansion and labour difficulties brought it to the point where it too had to seek outside help in 1964.

Rootes was the first and most obvious victim of the government's refusal to allow motor companies to expand their factories on, or close to, their existing sites and supplies of parts and labour, forcing them instead to site new plants in depressed development areas where they could alleviate the social problems of unemployment. It was another example of how the government saw an apparently strong industry, not as one which needed encouragement but as a milch-cow to sustain national political and social objectives.

The policy was devastatingly successful in the short term. Firms could not build new plants unless they were issued with Industrial Development Certificates. These were simply refused unless the application was for an area where the government wanted new investment. Ford went to Halewood near Liverpool; Standard to Speke, and Vauxhall to Ellesmere Port, just on the other side of the Mersey. Rootes went further still, to Linwood in Scotland where it was close to the new Ravenscraig Steelworks and could take advantage of a new Pressed Steel plant being established there. The new configuration added to supply and transport costs and separated the new plants from the close working relationships with local suppliers which had been a particular feature of the Midlands. In addition the difficulty of training a work force unused to the ways of the motor industry proved much greater than expected, and little or no training was done by the companies.

Many workers saw the new plants as an easy way to big wages and managers provided little or no training in the unfamiliar disciplines of the assembly line. At Ford's Halewood plant the cultural clash between East End supervisors and Merseyside labour was accentuated by the company's decision to pay regional rates of pay which meant that Halewood workers got less than those in Dagenham. In the BMC sprawl it might have been possible; with Ford's centralized union and management operation, it lasted just two years.

The one company which managed to circumvent the restrictions on expansion was Jaguar. Lyons had deliberately moved from the North-West to the Midlands in the 1920s to be closer to suppliers and the kind of workers he wanted. Now he refused to go to a development area.

By the 1960s Jaguar was no longer a tiny company; it was making 20,000 cars and over £1 million a year. The original plant had been expanded tenfold to 600,000 feet by 1950, but Lyons wanted much more. Refused permission to build, he discovered that Daimler were moving out of a shadow factory at Browns Lane and managed with difficulty to rent it on condition he also manufactured a tank engine there. By 1960 Jaguar needed more room still and this time Lyons bought Daimler outright, doubling his factory space. He inherited a badly run-down company which was making cars at far below an economic rate but which also had armoured car and bus production. The Daimler car kept its engine but disappeared into a Jaguar body.

However, the Lyons solution was not available to the larger manufacturers. The Rootes Group, the sweeper-up of traditional small companies before the war, had taken in the bankrupt Singer company in 1955. As he walked nostalgically round the workshops the first Lord Rootes, an apprentice in the company in 1913, was able to point out not just men with whom he had worked but also some of the very equipment which he had used and had survived unchanged.

Now, however, a bigger expansion was afoot. After years of discussion Rootes had decided to go for a small car of advanced engineering design with not only front-wheel drive but a light-weight aluminium engine. It was part of the fashion of extending ranges. Not content with its middle range Hillman Minx and the larger Humbers, the company felt it must supply a full range to its dealers. The Imp was planned to provide the comfort, styling and appearance which the basic Mini lacked.

The plan was to make the new car at a new plant at Coventry or Luton. The Government refused permission. As Geoffrey Rootes (now Lord Rootes) the managing director of manufacture put it:

It was the Government's disastrous attempts to make the industry disperse to the areas of high unemployment. It would have made sense if they had offered major inducements, rather than refusal of ID Cs; we could have made up our own minds.

It entailed moving to Scotland where there was no infrastructure and labour was not particularly suitable. We had inevitable duplication of overheads and practically without exception those factories which they forced the industry to have elsewhere in the country turned out to be failures.

Rootes blames the eventual failure of the Imp on having to build it far away from the expertise of the Midlands. There were also technical troubles, particularly with the advanced high pressure diecasting. But it was serious labour problems which brought the company to the brink of ruin.

Just as the Linwood project was going ahead, there was a major strike at the company's British Light Steel Pressings Plant at Acton in west London. It was an argument over possible redundancy, but the Rootes family saw it as much more: as a stand against the militants, and were encouraged to stay firm by other manufacturers.

The strike arose from fears that the company was going to announce redundancies after the shop stewards combine had noticed apparent stockpiling of components made at Acton. When the company refused to discuss production schedules, a strike was called for 'no redundancy'. In a typically confused motor industry dispute many skilled workers refused to strike but shop stewards rejected an instruction from the national union leaders to return to work. Rootes formally sacked the 1,000 people involved but the strike went on for thirteen weeks before it collapsed after a drift back to work. Few of the shop stewards got their jobs back.

The strike was notable for the strong feelings which it aroused. Geoffrey Rootes, a prominent member of the Engineering Employers Federation, saw it as a test case in managements' increasing worries over unofficial strikes. 'We thought we were fighting a battle against extreme left-wing elements and a battle for the industry as a whole. The background to it was infiltration by left-wing elements.'

It was a costly crusade. The plant made pressings for models throughout the group. The whole company was shut down and lost a third of the year's production – 60,000 vehicles. It was estimated to have cost about £3 million, perhaps half a million of that on paying guaranteed wages to workers laid off elsewhere as a result of the strike.

The Rootes family were already considering how appropriate their family ownership was to the increasingly large scale business of motor manufacture. When the younger members of the family were approached by Chrysler International, they encouraged the chairman, Lord Rootes, and his brother Reggie to consider it seriously.

Chrysler was the one big American manufacturer which did not have large European subsidiaries. With Ford and General Motors both making considerable profits in Europe, it seemed a good idea to invest at that time. It had been sniffing round British companies for some time, discussing a project with Standard to make small cars for Europe in 1956 and even discussing a sizeable holding in Leyland as late as 1962. Now it was to buy into Rootes just when the market started to flatten out.

For the Rootes group, it seemed an attractive deal. Lord Rootes had known the old Chrysler chairman, K.T. Keller, after the war and appreciated his reputation as a great production man. It seemed an ideal opportunity to bring in the manufacturing expertise which it was increasingly clear the company lacked. In 1964 Chrysler bought a majority of Rootes shares – though the Rootes family retained control through the voting shares. A commitment was given to the Conservative Government that Chrysler would not seek to take control against the Government's wishes.

Three years later it was a Labour Minister of Technology, then called Anthony Wedgwood Benn, who was announcing to the House of Commons that Chrysler would now take control. 'The basic fact confronting us was that Rootes was insolvent and that the British employment and expansion plans in that company were threatened. We did not believe that Rootes by itself was a viable organization with or without Government money, owned or not owned by a British company.'

As evidence Benn produced figures to show that over the previous five years Rootes had produced a net return on capital of only 0·3 per cent. It had lost money every year since 1964 – a total of £16·7 million pre-tax. As the Commons Expenditure Committee was to point out, 'The scale of the Rootes operation was too small to enable the company to price competitively in the mass market as well as producing a cash surplus large enough to meet the demands of research and development, new models and expansion. However, Rootes sacrificed its traditional image of quality in an attempt to compete head-on with larger firms in the mass market.'

Gilbert Hunt, who was later to become chairman of Chrysler UK, said: 'When the Rootes company decided to go to Scotland, the act of increasing capacity took it out of its then league . . . if you are going to be in the big league of producers you must make the attempt to reduce your unit costs.'

So it was that the third out of the 'Big Five' companies passed into foreign ownership. It was an unhappy experience. Behind the scenes Benn had tried to get other manufacturers, and Leyland in particular, to take in Rootes but all had refused Chrysler's £27 million asking price. Benn was left to agree a series of conditions which bound the company to maintain its expansion plans and to operate in a British way, retaining a majority of British directors.

Geoffrey Rootes, who had succeeded his father as Lord Rootes, remained as chairman. But the production engineering help which the company had hoped for did not materialize. The only two new models which were introduced – the 1966 Hunter and the 1970 Avenger – were Rootes designs.

Chrysler management was increasingly pre-occupied with its own difficulties in the United States and vacillated about its British subsidiary. Development work was begun on a new large–medium car to replace the Humber range, and then stopped at an advanced stage by the United States management. An indignant Rootes insisted that the American operation bear the cost, as he and others grew increasingly concerned about the daily references to Chrysler for instructions. As one executive put it, 'The company had a very English feeling, and then suddenly there were an awful lot of Americans around. There was a feeling that the Americans would bring a lot of money, though it didn't happen. It rapidly became very Americanized. There was close contact with the States. We would stay night after night up to nine so that we could have an end of the day conference with Detroit.'

The company struggled on, making small pre-tax profits most years and a big loss in 1970, yet managing to produce and sell roughly the same amount of cars as its competitor, Vauxhall.

Indeed, the increasingly public difficulties of Rootes-Chrysler mirrored a serious deterioration in the fortunes of all the car companies in the late 1960s, under the impact of the most severe squeeze the industry had known as hire purchase and credit terms shot up and down like a yo-yo. They changed seven times between June 1965 and November 1967 as the new Labour Government twisted and turned to find a way out of its economic difficulties.

Even Ford's profits plunged; halved to £5·4 million after tax in 1966 and nearly wiped out in 1967, but then recovering to a record £28 million in 1968. Vauxhall made its first loss for years in 1969, embarking on a long-term course which brought only two profitable years between then and 1987; its problems for the time being hidden by the success of its big Bedford truck operation and the long purse of America's most wealthy manufacturer.

Inside the industry people began to feel the ice cracking beneath their feet. The comfortable solidity of the post-war boom was over and it was a time for smaller companies to look for what seemed a safer shore. Even the independent William Lyons, who had a majority holding in his company, judged it was time for alliances and linked up with BMC to form British Motor Holdings in 1966, retaining his position as chief executive of his company: 'In the mid 1960s there was talk about the leading British manufacturers getting together so that as an industry we would be better able to face world competition. I was an enthusiastic protagonist as I believed that this was both necessary and desirable.'

A few months later the last major independent, Rover, merged with Leyland. The Rover company had emerged from its difficulties of the 1930s with a considerable reputation. After pre-war losses had left it short of cash, a designer joining in 1935 described the design office as 'a sort of leaky shed-type building . . . the drawing office staff, which included all engines, body and chassis people, was probably no more than thirteen.'[1] But out of those offices had come a range of stylish middle range cars.

Immediately after the war, the company had made a breakthrough when it invented a successor to the wartime jeep in the Landrover. It was almost accidental – a vehicle developed for use on the Welsh farm of Maurice Wilks who, with his brother,

Spencer, ran the company. A key part of the Landrover's success was that it was built of aluminium and so escaped the difficulties of post-war steel rationing. It was a huge world-wide success.

Rover built a new factory at Solihull which was opened by Sir Stafford Cripps in 1946 and by 1953 its profits of £44 per vehicle were close to Ford margins. But still sore from its pre-war difficulties, it decided against a merger with Standard because it was wary of becoming involved once more with the risks and poor profits of small cars, and because it distrusted the Standard forecasts. Landrover, for which demand far exceeded supply, continued to wait for new facilities.

The same caution obtained in the mid 1960s when a company pamphlet estimated that the cost of development of a new car was about £10 million and went on: 'The Rover company is only capable of developing one basic car at a time . . . a cycle time of approximately five years is required for a car of a new conception.'

In the 1950s and 1960s Rover's design department was particularly fluent, although there was always a question mark about the funds. In 1961 it had produced the Rover 2000. This later used an old Buick engine bought from America and the car created a new kind of market – what came to be called the executive car – an upmarket vehicle with an altogether sharper image and style than the lumbering Humber Super Snipes or Austin Westminsters. It was a niche which was to be hugely exploited, and proved the salvation of a number of makes – including BMW.

In the merger mood of the time, the company agreed to a takeover from Leyland in 1966, anxious to avoid the looming alternative of being swallowed by the bigger BMC, which had just taken Jaguar.

With the wisdom of hindsight Rover was (with Jaguar) one of the two companies most able to have continued on its own. Apart from producing good cars in a market which was expanding and was capable of great development (as BMW was to show), demand for the Landrover always outran supply and it was never built in sufficient quantities. The problem was finance and effective management. In the end, the name nearly perished. In the early 1970s firm plans were laid in British Leyland to eliminate the marque, only prevented by the necessity of spending time on crises elsewhere. It was ironic that in 1986 it became the name for the whole remaining body of British Leyland's erstwhile empire. It was the least tarnished.

But in the 'merger-mania' of the 1960s, it was difficult to see a clear future for a smaller producer, or the deadly perils of over-large units. In addition, the company was bothered, as all the industry's managers were, by increasing labour relations problems. The symptoms of the 'English disease' which came near to wrecking the car industry completely in the 1960s and 1970s and which maimed it for good, are well-known. A huge rash of strikes, large and small, which cost companies sometimes a third of their production, prevented changes in working practices, discouraged new investments, and lost customers for good because of late deliveries and poor quality. The causes are a matter for argument. The easy answer is that the unions were too strong. Paradoxically, a more convincing reason is that unions – along with management – were too weak.

Before the war, the car workers had been largely non-union. disputes were often nothing to do with the unions. Indeed some managements, notably Austin, would call in the union to police the dispute and get men back to work. Post-war, most factories were more or less unionized, although 'Morris Motors', the Cowley assembly plant, did not recognize unions until 1956.

But the impact of unionization was skin-deep. The car workers were loyal to union organization at the gang level; barely responsive to it at plant level, and hardly influenced at all by union organization outside the factory. To full time officials they appeared as freebooters as much as did motor industry managers to the run of their general engineering colleagues.

This was particularly true where piecework operated. Bill Roche was a shop steward in the unionized Cowley body plant, becoming senior steward in 1968, a post he held for sixteen years. He recalls:

Each section and each job was autonomous. It was not unusual for one job to be totally unaware of what was happening beyond them. As a result the people working on the job were the union in effect. They would organize themselves into their own customs and practices within the job and set their own rates. Very rarely would the senior steward be called in.

With piece rates set, earnings could only be improved by increasing production, but when production schedules were reduced, how to preserve earnings?

If you retained the same number of men, then you were earning less money. So it was always for the union as a unit to control labour, and they were pretty vicious, in the sense that it became the norm that each gang looked at its numbers in relation to the amount of money they could earn. They would go to the management and say they wanted one or two less men and those men would leave that gang.

So in the good times, managers could and did leave it to the workers to push production along because it made them more money – but then having largely abandoned control, they became incapable of re-establishing their authority when things went badly.

Piece work rates were fixed at the start of a vehicle's production run and were not altered until the operation changed. So when inflation started to push up workers' outgoings, there were few legitimate ways to increase money – particularly when a sharp rise in the cost of living was usually accompanied by a touch on the Government regulator which meant cutbacks in production, short-time and lay-offs.

It was this kind of situation, encouraged by the easy pay rises since the war as production picked up and managements conceded increases to keep it going, which led to increasing difficulties by the end of the 1950s. Motor manufacturers themselves pressed the engineering employers to do something about unofficial strikes and in 1961, the then Minister of Labour, John Hare, called a conference to discuss the problem, after a big jump in car industry strikes.

It was to be the first of many. The conference called for better training for shop stewards and supervisors, more labour relations personnel and appealed to both sides to stick by agreed procedures. A small Motor Industry Joint Study Group of labour relations managers and union officials started to meet. By 1964 the Ministry of Labour was suggesting, unsuccessfully, the formation of 'flying squads' of conciliators for unofficial disputes.

With the advent of Harold Wilson's interventionist Labour Government, the pace was stepped up. Strikes increased again in 1965. Six million days were lost in the motor industry and the Prime Minister himself summoned car employers and union leaders back from their holidays and grouse moors to tell them to put their house in order, warning of Government action, perhaps compulsory arbitration, if they failed. Out of the meeting came a new Motor Industry Joint Council under Mr Jack Scamp, who became known as the industry's troubleshooter. Its reports revealed a situation of extraordinary anarchy.

At the Rover factory at Solihull there had been 101 unofficial stoppages in a year. The eight manual unions in the plant refused to form a joint committee, and still failed to do so after Scamp recommended that they should. There was high labour turnover – 26 per cent – and an even higher turnover of shop stewards – 131 had been appointed, many 'with little experience of either the industry or of trade union work' – and 80 had ceased to be shop stewards.

Management evidence to the enquiry said that 'the pattern was for men to hold a meeting outside the gates, often at lunchtime, and pass a resolution and then to regard the resolution as overriding any domestic or national agreement. When however, the management drew attention to these agreements and suggested that the matter would be best put in the hands of union officials, they were told "we are the union and the officials are there to do what we want." '

The enquiry found management 'non-plussed by the fact that the new well-equipped P6 line, housed in a brand new factory with good working conditions, has been a comparatively greater source of strife than the older P5 and Landrover lines.'

'The simple truth is,' said the enquiry, 'that neither side has quite measured up to the formidable challenge of the P6 line innovation.'

The Council's descriptions were more powerful than its recommendations. By the end of 1966 it was reporting 600 stoppages in the first half of the year, all but five unofficial. Two-thirds lasted no more than four hours; less than twenty per cent more than a working day. 'One is bound to ask oneself if the problem could not equally well have been resolved without a stoppage of work.' Failure by the industry to enforce agreements could only lead to anarchy, it warned, 'a state which already seems to be not very far away in some establishments.'

'I am very conscious,' Scamp wrote in his concluding paragraph, 'of the present difficulties of the motor industry, which must be having a shattering effect on the morale of both employers and work people. Never has it been more necessary than it is now that the industry should find the means to resolve industrial relations problems while the men continue at their work. Time is not on our side.'

The involvement of the Government, let alone the Prime Minister, at this nitty-gritty level of the industry's affairs was new and unheard of, but it was only the start. The motor industry was the most obvious target of first the Labour Government's abortive proposals for legislation 'In Place of Strife' and its successor, the Conservative 1971 Industrial Relations Act.

And Government involvement was now to go much farther. The temper of the new Government was interventionist and the industry was now clearly identified as a problem for the first time in its life. In 1968, the Government established the Industrial Reorganization Corporation to encourage mergers and rationalization throughout British industry. On its board, amongst others, was Lord Stokes, the highly successful salesman who had taken over as head of Leyland. It was no surprise when one of the IRC's major involvements became the attempt to merge Leyland with Britain's biggest car makers – BMH.

BMC had started the 1960s on the crest of a wave. The success of the Mini had been followed by the 1100/1300 range which adopted the Mini techniques to a larger car, producing an even more popular vehicle which outsold the Cortina almost every year of the 1960s. The Issogonis philosophy ruled. After the 1100, development work went ahead for the Maxi which was effectively a larger brother still with once again, transverse engine, frontwheel drive and maximum internal space. Even the biggest cars – the 1800 range and above – were redesigned so that they had the same look of a small car grown big, with the shortest possible bonnet and boots.

But as the poor sales of the larger cars showed, Issigonis' obsession with the maximum interior space, and designing the car from the inside out, was inadequate on its own. Styling was neglected and market research was non-existent – in sharp contrast to Ford.

British car makers had always been slow to think of customers' needs. Even as late as the 1950s cars like Morris Minors were being sent to Northern Scandinavia without heaters, as they were not fitted as standard items. Issigonis took a particularly puritan approach to accessories. One component supplier, arriving to discuss requirements with him, found him berating BMC's chief engineer for experimenting with car radio fittings. Issigonis' own view was that car radios caused accidents and every kind of driving distraction should be avoided. He even defended the notoriously uncomfortable early Mini seats on the grounds that they helped to keep the driver awake. His contempt for stylists and market research was well-known. He once said, 'Market research is absolute bunk. I design cars without any prompting from my employers to suit what they want from sales. I thought I knew better than market research people, and it showed in the results.' As for styling – 'A stylist is employed to make things obsolescent.'[2]

Issigonis, christened by himself Arragonis, was a dominant and, many colleagues said, domineering figure over the company's design plans, and there was soon no firm hand to control the sprawling empire from above. Lord bowed out of day to day control in the early 1960s, and the company came under the control of George Harriman, a charming and personable manager who had been Lord's number two for years, but who lacked either the vision or decisiveness to get to grips with the company's problems.

The company was run so loosely that Issigonis had refused to let even some of the top BMC men see the complete Mini until it was nearly ready. A Lucas salesman, Charles Davidson, was discussing the tail lights with him when Harriman arrived to see the complete car for the first time. 'He walked round it for a bit and then said: "It's very tiny isn't it, but it's good. When we get the chromium plate on it and get the styling done, it's going to look quite nice." Alec said, "If you do anything to that car I'm leaving. It's finished." It was and it went out like that.'[3]

Under Harriman, the company continued to have a vast range

of unstandardized products – the Mini alone needed 60 different kinds of speedometers for its various versions – and its cars were manufactured in a variety of locations (the Minor was produced in three different places), while dealers continued to compete against each other. The benefits of large scale production of a few models and rationalization continued to be denied.

Sales rose by 39 per cent between 1963 and 1966, profits by 36 per cent. With its big sales, superficially the company seemed in good shape. It had increased production, but it had done so with minimal new investment choosing instead to enlarge the size of its labour force. It was a contrast to other European companies – by the mid 1960s Britain was producing fewer cars per worker than Germany, France or Italy – a change from ten years previously – and the BMC plants were well behind Ford and Vauxhall.

In 1966, the BMH empire expanded still further, buying up its main body supplier, Pressed Steel, and so bringing Joe Edwards back as managing director of BMH. What he found appalled him.

I found that nothing had happened in the twelve years I had been away. The company had unwound. It was the Lord–Harriman regime just staggering from one thing to another.

There was no forward thinking. There was no question of getting hold of new people. They did not believe in training management. The management just was not equipped to run that size of company.

Edwards at last tried to get a grip on the company's purchasing policies, bringing in a new chief buyer from Ford and he began to reconsider the styling. But before he could get into his stride, he found Harriman was involved with the merger talks which were to bring about the Leyland deal.

The problems of the company were now there to be read by those who wished. In 1965 Austin-Morris had held 36 per cent of the market between them – two years later it was little over 29 per cent, only four per cent above Ford's steady performance, with a much smaller workforce.

By now the contrast between the achievement of Ford and

BMH was increasingly obvious. The best tribute to Ford's management expertise was the way its people began to be headhunted for big jobs in other companies. It was no accident that Edwards at BMH and the managers at BLMC after him should turn to Ford for some of their key appointments.

The comparison between the two companies in the 1960s is enlightening. It shows Ford tackling the problems which the sprawling BMC had in even greater measure but did little about – cost control, rationalization, management training, and something largely neglected by the British-owned companies – its network of dealers. Perhaps the most striking thing about Ford was its refusal to venture into the small car market, until it was sure it could make money: a contrast with Rootes as well as BMH. But it was not unalloyed success – Ford too faltered, temporarily in its later Cortina programme after Hennessy's departure, and more lastingly over its labour relations.

The problem about any discussion of Ford's performance and its contribution to the British motor industry is to assess properly the impact of the American connection. Undoubtedly its critics from the left tend to over-emphasize it, while Ford top managers play it down. Many of its policies are thrashed out here without American interference but with the careful preparation and paperwork that is the hallmark of the company. As one of Ford's executives, now with another company, puts it: 'There is a Ford professional culture. If you say you will do something by a particular date, you do it. There is good analysis and factual evidence before any proposal is put forward.'

But throughout the sixties, major investment and product decisions had all to be referred to Ford headquarters at Dearborn where they had to be argued out in minute detail. Ford of Britain also continued to draw on the engineering expertise of the American parent company for the design and production of its new vehicles. So though the British company was only once headed by an American after the war, and saw itself as a distinctively British operation, the reins could be tightened on occasions.

This became even more the case after 1961 when Ford of America bought out the rest of the shareholders in Ford of Britain. With maximum publicity a cheque for £119,595,645.12s was paid into the National Provincial Bank account of the Ford Motor Company Ltd.

Explaining the move, Henry Ford II talked of world competition becoming broader and more intense, a trend likely to be accentuated by the new Common Market and European Free Trade Area. The object was 'greater operational efficiency and marketing effectiveness' in both Britain and the United States. Emphasizing that Ford's stake in the British company would now exceed all Ford's other interests outside the United States put together, he insisted that the British company would continue under Hennessy 'without change in its employment policy or in its development programme.'

Henry Ford's declaration, however, did not prevent the increasingly powerful union activists in the company from blaming the tighter American link for what they saw as a drive to step up line speeds, and firm steps taken against some prominent shop stewards.

The post-war ethos of Dagenham was by now sharply different from the pre-war Manchester days. Ford's traditional leadership in terms and conditions had been diminished by the way the company had had to yield to war-time Government pressure to increase working hours. After the war there was no quick return to 40 hours, and the traditional pay differential which Ford workers had enjoyed over others soon evaporated with the big piecework gains in the Midlands. At the same time, Ford's tough management tradition grew tougher. Outsiders might be amused to find Ford managers aping American styles by wearing trilby hats in the office and speaking with mid-Atlantic accents. But it did not cheer workers who could find themselves being sent outside the factory gate when production was temporarily interrupted, and then facing the sack if they were not still there to be summoned when the line was ready to re-start.

The increasingly bitter tone of Ford's industrial relations had been exacerbated by the take-over of Briggs in 1953. After a war-time court of enquiry, shop stewards – or 'workplace representatives' – had been allowed at Briggs and had achieved the right to hold workshop meetings, something which Ford had never conceded. Shop stewards were involved in bargaining at plant level – unlike Ford's highly centralized system. The Briggs stewards included a strongly disciplined Communist grouping and were well organized. They rented an office over a local shop, paying for a part-time secretary and had their own newspaper – the 'Voice of Briggs Workers' – financed by a raffle and sweep-stakes. In the 1950s they could call on as much as £3,000 a month – while the Austin stewards raised about £150.

Sid Harraway was one of the stewards: he recalls, 'When Ford took over Briggs, we said, "Let's take the best out of both agreements." They said, "Don't be silly, we are taking over."' The result was that the Briggs pay grades were absorbed into the Ford scheme, but as many Briggs workers had been getting more, they were paid merit money which then caused friction within Ford. Local stewards' rights were replaced by the Ford national negotiating machinery which involved national officials and excluded stewards.

As Harraway puts it: 'They were dealing with the trade unions on the basis that the trade union was responsible for the shop stewards and could control them. But at Briggs they had grown up in the situation where workers in a department elected a shop steward and it was irrespective of his union. We looked at the best lad.' So the gulf between union organization and local workers became as critical as in the piecework-dominated Midlands factories.

There was also a growing awareness that Ford workers were falling behind other car workers. As Harraway remembers: 'We felt we weren't getting the return we should have been. It was a peak period for production and wages were being held back. The Midlands lads had broken through – particularly in the toolroom area.'

With Ford's unwillingness to give shop stewards a significant role (it was markedly less than in companies which belonged to the Engineering Employers Federation) a study of the industry's labour relations in the mid 1960s declared that 'large stoppages at the Dagenham plants have been as chronic as those at Austin, but began later and continued into the 1960s', and talked of 'endemic conflict'.

The battles continued into the 1970s in spite of management attempts to discipline and sack leading stewards. The Dagenham body plant, which many of the locals still called 'Briggs's', was a persistent battleground.

In 1957, stewards were disciplined after leaving Dagenham to lobby a meeting of national negotiators. When the news came back, a steward stopped the line by ringing a handbell to call a meeting and was sacked. In the early 1960s another group of stewards were amongst seventeen men finally blacklisted after a strike had led to several hundred at first being given notice of dismissal. Management saw the dispute, over the transfer of men between departments, as a key test of its right to manage.

Official enquiry reports talked of 'a private union within a union enjoying immediate and continuous touch with the men in the shop, answerable to no superiors and in no way officially or constitutionally linked with the union hierarchy', and the company being 'frustrated and put to unreasonable inconvenience by a militant element.' But they also said that although 'Communist influence has made use of the shop stewards' desire to protect their own interests and powers . . . it has not been the prime cause of the trouble.'

Harraway, who had become a Communist in the 1950s after being impressed by their work during one strike, says: 'There was a deliberate campaign to try to offset the democratic system of the shop stewards. Because of the background of Briggs, it was quite powerful.'

Ford's unwillingness to bring stewards into negotiations was only gradually eroded. Eventually convenors were allowed to wait in a nearby pub during national negotiations at Ford's Regent Street offices. Later they were allowed into a waiting room, and finally, in the 1970s, into negotiations themselves.

By then Dagenham militancy had been joined by Halewood militancy, as the new Merseyside plant got off to an unhappy start. It was estimated that many of those who first went for jobs there left after a few months, even though the company had carefully screened them to select solid family men and no-one under the age of twenty. A 1969 strike over company attempts to make lay-off and holiday pay conditional on good behaviour was led by the Halewood men.

Ford's running battles on the labour front contrasted with the effective way it organized its management.

Tec Fawcett was a university student in the 1960s looking for a job with a blue-chip British company. The firms he applied to were the big oil majors, market research companies, but only one motor manufacturer – Ford. He was not aware of any BMC recruiting drive on his campus, and the Vauxhall literature seemed dull:

> Ford by contrast spent a lot of time and effort in trying to attract graduates. It was a lean approach, intellectually equal to the oil companies, and I got a very quick response. You went for interview and ended up at the end of the day with an offer.

Fawcett accepted his offer and joined about 100 graduates on the training scheme moving from department to department. A few years later he was himself running Ford's graduate recruitment, looking for people with commitment, achievement-motivated, with a general awareness of business, and who could present ideas in a clear way.

The company's management training was widely admired. But unions could still point out in the early 1970s that 60 per cent still left within five years. Ford believed , however, that that was still better than most British companies.

The sheer thoroughness of the Ford approach was exemplified in 1963 when it carried out a huge shakeout of its dealers, ensuring those that remained were strong enough to continue to give good service. It was an initiative other manufacturers ignored, only copying it when crisis forced it upon them. Just how necessary it was was shown in 1975 when the Government's think-tank report was sharply critical of the weakness of British dealers – many of whom by that time gratefully snapped up contracts from importers who had not existed in 1963.

In 1975 the 1,258 reorganized Ford dealers sold an average of 245 cars a year. By contrast Austin Morris had twice as many dealers (2,565) – making half as much money – with sales of an average of 135 cars a year. Vauxhall dealers fared worse and other BL dealers, 805 of them, worse still.

Sam Toy was one Ford executive given the job of rationalization. 'I can recall going to one major city and standing on a street corner where I could see two main dealerships and three retail dealerships. I thought, "This is crazy, dealers are cutting their margins to fight their rivals and they are not able to give the customer the service he is entitled to." '

The solution was to cut dealers by a half in five years. Those who remained had to fulfil exacting standards. Ford insisted, and still insists, on inspecting their books and their buildings, working out how much they should sell and earn, and even laying down what sort of bonus arrangements sales people should enjoy – effectively guaranteeing a profitable business.

These efforts culminated in Ford's most crucial move in 1967 when its European manufacturing operations – effectively British and German – were merged into a single company – Ford of Europe. It was a response both to the Common Market and to the growing pressure for the economies of scale that a common range of cars could bring. It was exactly the rationale for the merger of Leyland and BMH – but it was one step ahead – it had the European dimension which the home-grown British industry crucially lacked.

Until 1967, Ford's European operations had been the responsibility of the International Division of the Ford Motor Company in the United States. It had favoured what one executive had christened the 'two fishing line approach' in Europe, with British and German companies competing against each other. Now, on the instigation of Henry Ford II and against the self-preserving wishes of the International Division, it was closed down and a new company, Ford of Europe, created with responsibility for sales, marketing and manufacture of a common line of vehicles. British Ford executives emphasize that it was Henry Ford's brainchild. As one put it, 'He was the one person who was a truly world-wide executive on the US board. The rest looked at us as branches of the US operation. He didn't.'

The result was immediate. European managers were told to come back with plans for an integrated operation, in some cases overnight. Ford of Europe's headquarters was established at Warley in Essex, and the German factories, which were short of saleable products switched to production of British successes – the Capri and the Escort.

For British plants, it was a double-edged sword. Integrating all manufacturing on a European basis and leaving national companies effectively to run the sales operation had two effects. It meant that British factories were competing with German and Belgian plants to produce cars, and as Britain became increasingly less efficient, British sales increasingly came from cars brought in from abroad, while the profits made on those imports helped to keep the British company solvent. Without the link, Ford in Britain might have gone the way of the British-owned companies.

Bill Hayden was the first Briton to become a corporate officer of the American parent company. As Vice-President in charge of all European manufacturing, he has no doubts about the effect of the deal on British and German operations. 'It saved both of us.'

Sir Terence Beckett says, 'There is no doubt that it put us in an entirely different league than if we had attempted to remain little Englanders. Of all the postwar developments, it was strategically the most important. As the sixties went on we had begun to see an enormous increase in the development costs of a new car-line. The vital thing was that it gave us enormous economies of scale.'

An indication of the growing costs was that Ford's Anglia had involved about £10 million worth of expenditure in 1959 while its 1968 Escort was reckoned to have cost the British company $39 million.

If BMC, with its inadequate control and monitoring of costs was slower to see the writing on the wall, its underlying difficulties did not escape the eye of the new Labour Government. It was increasingly worried by what it saw as the shortcomings of British industry which were most clearly evidenced in the embarrassing monthly gap in the balance of payments and reflected in the devaluation of the pound in 1967. Stokes' export success for Leyland made him appear a potential saviour to a Government obsessed with the trade balance. Amongst those who had been given the task of surveying the motor industry was Michael Shanks, author of a best-selling critique of British industry, *The Stagnant Society*, who was working as a temporary civil servant in the new Department of Economic Affairs, which drew up the National Plan:

We were looking at the structure of British industry, particularly the problem areas. And the biggest crisis area was the British motor industry and particularly BMH. It was the flagship of the British motor industry, enormously important and it was going bankrupt. It was going bankrupt because it had run out of models. It had very few new models in the pipeline. The models that it had were old, and not very effective, with the exception of the Mini – and it had an enormous dealer structure with far too many dealers trying to sell too few products.

You could see this huge company headed for the scrapheap – what did you do about it? You could either let it go or you could find somebody to take it over, and really the only candidate was Leyland, which was a much smaller company.[4]

With the aid of its new Industrial Reorganization Corporation, the Government set about the merger, but met with resistance from BMH which took a less pessimistic view of its future and saw Leyland as a small upstart which knew little about cars. There was reluctance from Stokes who had now taken over as Executive Chairman of Leyland and had cold feet about the enormous task. To push things along, the Prime Minister, Harold Wilson, invited Stokes and the now ailing Harriman to Chequers for dinner. Afterwards Harriman was heard to say, 'When the Prime Minister asks, it is not a good thing to say no.'

Both sides bandied conflicting profit forecasts, with Leyland increasingly concerned about what they saw as the over-optimism of BMH's figures. As the devaluation crisis of 1967 intervened, BMH shares slipped and Leyland's rose.

The deal was finally struck early in 1968. Not all were happy: BMH's financial prospects worsened between the agreement in principle and the acceptance of the deal by Leyland shareholders; Joe Edwards refused to serve under Stokes and left the company for good.

As the Government welcomed the rationalization of the industry under what they saw as successful management, it agreed that the IRC should provide a loan of £100 million. It was the first direct Government financial support for the industry, the beginning of a long and bitter road. Up to now the Government had been content to milk the industry, to influence its decisions by restrictions and prohibitions, but now it was having to put money out to achieve the results it wanted; some in the industry said to undo the harm it had done. But as the BMH leviathan drifted towards the rocks, it needed more than money for the small Leyland boarding party to wrest it onto a new course and inspire its quarrelling crew.

As Leyland looked at its prize, it was apparent that time was not on its side; things were worse than it had thought. Shanks was by now working as an assistant to Stokes and he wrote an analysis: 'The dangers facing the motor industry are so serious that they will demand radical changes in method or organization to exploit the opportunities created by the merger. These will in any case take time, but we may not have all that time available.'[5]

And so it was that 95 per cent of the remaining British-owned motor car industry came under the umbrella of a single company. The merger captured the British headlines. The fact that the same year the production of the Japanese motor car industry surpassed both Britain and France for the first time, leaping from 1·37 million to over two million cars in a year, hardly rated a footnote. Little over 2,000 of them came to Britain.

12

The Seventies (1)
'This Wonderful Merger'

The establishment of the British Leyland Motor Corporation in the early days of 1968 seemed to many the fulfilment of a dream. Here at last, it appeared, was all the British-owned motor industry that mattered under one roof, with an effective management and proven success in the export markets of the world. It was an opportunity for a British firm to take the world stage and even to dominate it. It was a chance to end the process where, in the words of a later chairman of Jaguar, Sir John Egan, all too often 'the standard performance for a British car company even by then was to do badly and go out of business.'

George Turnbull moved from Standard Triumph to manage the mass production car business of the new corporation:

> 'We started off this wonderful merger with all these wonderful ideas about being the greatest organization for the production and sales of motor-cars in the whole world.' At the shareholders' meetings in February and March Stokes found himself showered with congratulations, but vainly tried to inject some caution with a warning that 'you cannot take two large complex companies and put them together and reap the benefit. There is much planning, much rationalization to do before the extra profits come in.'

What the shareholders would have been stunned to learn was that in the event they would have been better off selling their shares. The company's future profits, even in its best years, were never to exceed the combined profits of its constituent parts before the merger. Within six years, it would be effectively taken over by the Government and before ten years were out there would be real doubt whether any mass production motor cars would be turned out in Britain at all – with not just British Leyland, but Chrysler, Vauxhall and even Ford teetering on the brink. Chrysler shareholders were only saved from the fate of BLMC shareholders by the persistence of the Rootes family which ensured that Chrysler bought out their shares in 1973 only three years before the Americans were to offer the company to the Government for nothing.

The most astonishing and alarming thing about the decline was that, although it was precipitated by the collapse in world-wide car sales after the Middle East crisis which trebled the price of oil in 1973 and changed the face of world trade for ever, it had begun while companies enjoyed the best years for sales the motor industry had ever seen.

The reasons were many and various. The British amateurism and sloppiness about planning and researching new models finally found them out. The lack of investment as British companies put less and less money into their firms than their continental competitors and relied instead on taking on more people to boost production, began to take its toll. The dismantling of tariff walls against imports allowed British customers to appreciate the style and performance of cars designed on the Continent and in Japan at a competitive price, and which were available without long delays in delivery.

Anarchic industrial relations became even more out of control as inflation and successive Government pay policies turned the industry into a more obvious political battering ram for the left, and in two consecutive years, 1973 and 1974, nearly a quarter of the industry's production was lost from strikes.

In short, the decline was a result of the refusal to manage the industry over the previous post-war years; the chickens came home to roost. But once again the extent of the decay was concealed. Its dimensions were only guessed at until the avalanche of reports which started to tumble from the Government presses in the mid 1970s; from the House of Commons Finance Committee, from the Trade and Industry Committees, from specially appointed enquiries, from the Cabinet's own think-tank. Thousands of words of explanation and excuse were poured out by queues of manufacturers, suppliers, trades union-

ists and outside experts who traipsed through the nineteenth
century corridors of the Palace of Westminster to give their
analysis of the causes of twentieth century industrial decline. By
then it was far too late. While the glum statistics could tell the tale
of past troubles and tussles, the conflicts remained unresolved
and still prevented a lasting solution.

Even from the inside, the sheer extent of the problem was not
always apparent. So sharp-eyed an observer as Sir John Egan,
who was recruited to look after pricing at BLMC in 1971, for all
his trenchant views about past failures, could still believe at the
time that 'British Leyland was grappling with its many problems
and one had the feeling that they could win. They had a remarkably good range of cars; they really should have been world-
beaters. If they had made them well, they probably had the best
range of cars in the world.'

Pat Lowry was the head of industrial relations at the Engineering Employers Federation, recruited by Stokes in 1970 to tackle
the new corporation's multitudinous labour problems. He had
already had an inside track at some of the bitterest conflicts in the
industry and could still believe that the new Corporation was
'solid, substantial, here to stay. I had no reason to think my future
should be in any doubt at all. But I very quickly began to realize
that it wasn't so.'

For Leyland's negotiating team the doubts had begun as they
cross-questioned BMC's profit forecasts more and more in the
last stages of their merger talks. The troubles of the Austin-
Morris group, which dominated both the old and the new
company, were stark.

Lord Stokes says:

> We found that Austin-Morris was more of a problem than we
> had ever dreamed of; there was a complete lack of new models.
> It should have been marvellous actually. I still think it could
> have been. Apart from our inexperience in managing such a
> huge organization – we had about 200,000 people – I don't
> think that was the problem. We managed to get that more or
> less sorted out. But at that stage the unions were all-powerful
> and whenever we tried to institute any reform, we came up
> against insuperable union barriers.

I think there were three obstacles. One was getting a management team which had enough experience to run a 200,000 strong company. I think the plans and policies were right. Our thinking was quite logical. The tremendous problem was translating that down the line to middle management where you had these 50 or 60 different companies all trying to retain their independence even though they had been taken over. Then down below that you had a very strong, very powerful trade union movement. They could call out people at the drop of a hat; they didn't have ballots or anything and even if we were right we couldn't resist a long strike because we didn't have financial backing. The other thing was that although the Government of the day said it wanted a viable, strong motor industry, it did nothing to assist it by, for example, its public purchasing policies.

Stokes tried to solve his problems with a mixture of new ideas and new management. Pulling together the best he could find from the Midlands and Northern managers of his own smaller company, he tried to marry it with the best of the Ford experience, recruiting considerably from Ford, and putting in some of the systems which Ford employed to run its company on a centralized basis. The tension between the two schools of thought was not always creative and became an easy stereotype of the continuing argument about what sort of company BLMC should be – centralized or devolved.

Michael Shanks was fascinated by the contrast between the two styles, of the Leyland and BMH approach and what he saw as Ford's American way:

You issue memoranda, everything is put down in writing, and if it isn't put down in writing you don't need to bother about it. But it means that when instructions are issued people read them and carry them out. Now the culture in BMH and Leyland was quite different; it was that you never had any time to read anything, and if you were sitting at your desk reading a paper, you were obviously not doing your job properly. So the only way that people in Leyland and BMH would respond was if somebody picked up the telephone and told them.

The Morris Eight was the best-selling small car pre-war. Here Lord Nuffield (centre) hands over the 100,000th in 1936. Leonard Lord, who designed it, stands, glum as ever, on the left.

Ford's first small car, the Model Y was designed in six months and launched in 1932. In 1935 it boosted its flagging sales by a big advertising campaign and by cutting its price to become the first £100 fully-equipped car.

It can be yours –

THE £100 FORD SALOON

The 1922 Austin Seven. This is the Chummy version; the ladies are
Herbert Austin's daughters Rena and Zena.

The Ford family celebrates the driving of the first pile for its new
Dagenham works. Edsel Ford, son of Henry Ford waves his gloves; the
boy is his son Henry Ford II while Lord Perry looks on.

It was all verbal culture. Anything that was written down in memoranda just went straight into the filing system without anybody acting on it.

That difference in culture really pervaded the whole atmosphere. That meant that many of the Ford people who were extremely good at their kind of organization just foundered in British Leyland because they couldn't come to terms with a totally different way of communicating.[1]

The contrast between the two styles was highlighted by the rivalry for the succession to Stokes between the two most powerful men in the group – John Barber, the former Finance Director of Ford who was doing a similar job for BLMC, and George Turnbull. They seemed almost the living embodiment of the best of the cerebral and practical approaches.

Barber, the only man to have been on the boards of both the two major car companies, had been brought in by Stokes from AEI where he had fought a determined but unsuccessful campaign to resist take-over by GEC. Regarded by his contemporaries as something of a cold fish, his cool exterior hid a passionate fascination with motor cars.

George Turnbull, whose father had been the world-wide service manager at Standard, was born and bred in the Midlands and the trench warfare of the shop-floor. A former Coventry rugby front-row forward and captain of Warwickshire. He relished the cut and thrust of hands-on management, always ready to discuss past battles and his fight against Sir John Black's 'Yellow Peril', the yellow-covered set of agreements with the unions at Standard which in Turnbull's view told supervisors to appease the stewards to avoid strikes. Standard-Triumph's £15 million profits, achieved while Turnbull was general manager, was one of the reasons why Leyland was able to launch its bid for the much bigger BMC.

Both men entered the merger with high hopes. Both were appalled by what they found. As Turnbull put it:

It was the hardest five years of my life. It took me a year to understand the people in the organization, and what strings to pull to try to bring it together. There were so many different models being made in so many different places. It was like topsy; it had grown and there was a huge rationalization job to be done.

We had started off this merger with all these wonderful ideas about being the greatest organization for the production and sales of motor cars in the whole world, and here we were, in trouble with the trades unions with strikes in the factories. Frankly we had a strike a day in the factories – and those were only the ones I heard about.

From his more detached perspective away from the hurly-burly of the shop floor Barber had some more fundamental criticisms. They did not endear him to his colleagues but went to the heart of some of the failings of the home-grown British motor industry – its inability to move on from workshop production to the essential international business perspectives. He recalls:

It was unbelievable. BMC was a national institution and the names of Austin and Morris one had grown up with. Although seeing it from the outside in Ford we could see the mistakes they were making, it wasn't possible to realize just how bad they were.

It was an incredibly shattering experience. If you are looking at fundamentals, I think my worst shock was the quality of Midlands management. The management had been so bad since 1946 that labour had got out of control; the unions had taken control and the thing was getting chaotic.

The other thing that I noticed immediately was the lack of interest – and that is not too strong an expression – in motor cars. Everyone in Ford lived cars; they couldn't help it. You were always watching what the customer wanted and looking forward to market requirements, whereas in BMC they didn't seem particularly interested in cars. They weren't interested in competitors. I remember asking a BMC director who had a problem on something, 'What do they do at Volkswagen at Wolfsburg?' He said, 'I don't know; this is what we do at Longbridge.'

Whereas in Ford you would be looking at the competition

all the time to find a better way of doing things, the in-bred Austin-Morris people weren't interested. They weren't interested in competitors' cars, whereas in Ford you were constantly driving other makes of cars. I remember when the Austin people were developing the Allegro, we were talking about its handling and roadholding. In those days the small car with the best roadholding, I thought, was the Alfasud. I kept nattering on about it and said, 'Why don't you get one?' Eventually they did and they said 'We see what you mean; we have something to beat.'

It was a mass of unrationalized production plants, and unrationalized products – umpteen engines, umpteen gearboxes, umpteen axles. The thing wasn't rationalized at all; they weren't ready to compete in the world league although British Leyland was still number ten in terms of units produced in the world.

Whatever their differences, both schools of thought, the cerebral and the pragmatic, could unite in the early days on the need to bring about rationalization and above all to bring on new models. It was urgent; the Mini, though still selling well, was beginning to decline, the 1100–1300 range was showing its age, while the new middle car, the Maxi, had had a disastrous launch. Stokes particularly disliked it: 'It was ghastly. The concept was quite good because Alec Issigonis was good at concepts. But as for a marketing machine it was absolutely impossible. It looked wrong; you couldn't change gear on it; it just wasn't developed.' The Maxi, which had many of the features to be found in medium cars in the 1980s, was improved but never sold well. Issigonis was sidelined to do concept research, shifted out of his design and production function. Stokes' view was that 'he was a charming man; you couldn't help liking him. But he was an autocratic individual in the sense that only Alec Issigonis knew what the public wanted – whether they wanted it or not. Nice as he was, you can't run a big motor factory designing cars on the back of dirty envelopes.'

Out with Issigonis went his project for a new small hatch-back car to replace the Mini. Called the 9X, it was a favourite of the design team which produced it. Stokes says he never saw it:

'There were all sorts of odd cars, none near the production stage.' Barber remembers that it was smaller than the existing Mini. But with the market for small cars fading in the days before the sudden rise in oil prices put a premium on economy, the company thought it prudent to concentrate its limited resources on a new medium car which would take on the Cortina. They were looking back to the car which obsessed them, rather than forward to the new markets of the 'super-Mini' which the continentals would meet.

However, once again old problems, like the failure to sort out the dealer network, came home to roost. To keep both Austin and Morris outlets happy, two cars were projected: an Austin which would continue the front-wheel drive innovations and a Morris which would be more traditional – like the Cortina. The result was the Austin Allegro, based on the engineering of the 1100–1300 but with less room when first developed; and the Morris Marina, designed to use components from the Morris Minor first put into production over twenty years before. Neither car was to sell as many as the models they replaced; the Allegro in particular never reached the annual sales figure for the 1100–1300 range. The two cars also competed against one another; if Ford of Europe had abandoned the two fishing-line approach, it was alive and well in the smaller British market.

The Marina was hurried through using some parts, though fewer than at first intended, from the Minor. The company needed a new car quickly and it was relatively short of funds, but Barber insists that there would have been sufficient for a totally new car; what got in the way was the management philosophy BLMC had inherited.

Sir John Egan, coming into the company from General Motors, is blunt about it:

They were setting out to design cars with resources that were usually a third or a half of what their European competitors were putting into designing and developing cars. I know it was very difficult to make the money available, but I don't think they aspired to do it. You were always trying to do as much as you could with as little as possible. In reality a car is such a complicated thing that you have actually got to put the re-source up front or you are not going to get very much out of it.

On the shop-floor at the Cowley body plant, Bill Roche had a dramatic demonstration of how far his company's investment had fallen behind. As a member of the Transport and General Workers' Union National Executive Committee, he had the opportunity of looking at Continental car plants as part of union delegations. He found them scrapping the very equipment which BLMC was installing as a modern improvement to build the Marina bodies. He says:

Up to the Marina we were building cars at Pressed Steel effectively by hand, almost everything had to be worked and re-worked. It was the old way of building a motor car. You built it from the rear end, then the front end, and a middle post, and a floor and a roof from different components all made separately in different sections and then brought together and assembled. You can imagine that if they didn't fit, which they never did, everything had to be changed – resoldered and rewelded – that sort of thing.

But with the Marina they installed the gate line which meant that the two sides were each built in a jig and then the two were put together. But when I had the opportunity to go to Renault and Fiat in the early seventies, I found that our competitors were disposing of the gate line as obsolete. So we were ten years behind them – and that's forgetting the Japanese.

Lord Stokes says:

Before the Marina went into production I was assured that it was going to be quite reasonably costed because we were going to be able to use a lot of the facilities available from the Morris Minor. Later on, I found that a lot of the machine tools they said they were going to use were so obsolete that we had to get new ones and we would have been better in retrospect to have designed a brand new car altogether. But we were in such a hurry; we had to get something. We had nothing to sell. It was marvellous getting that Marina out on time. Although it didn't really hit the markets, it did quite well.

But 'quite well' was not sufficient for a company which was striving to push up its profits in the face of the increasing difficulties caused by industrial disruption. George Turnbull had been brought in to run Austin-Morris, and the Marina and Allegro were his projects, but before they could come into production, he found his industrial relations falling to pieces.

The main problem was that the piecework system on which the Midlands motor industry had run was collapsing. It could not cope with the constant changes that adapting the model range required, and it was also becoming a casualty of inflation. In 1967 inflation had been two and a half per cent; in 1968 it nearly doubled to 4·7 per cent, rising to 5·4 per cent in 1969 and 6·4 per cent in 1970. In 1971 it jumped to 9·4 per cent.

Bill Roche felt the effect on the shop floor. 'Piecework could not have continued. It thrived when inflation was fairly static. Rates were steady and you only had to earn another two or three per cent by stepping up the rate a bit. When it went up to ten per cent or so, more piecework didn't have a meaning in terms of money.'

From the management side, Stokes remembers:

You couldn't change any design without renegotiating the rate. I remember when people complained about the position of the instruments in one car; that you couldn't reach them without having an elastic arm, we couldn't move them without retiming the piece rate arrangements for the whole car, because years before someone had negotiated an agreement that if you altered anything the whole car had to be re-timed. It was impossible to carry on making motor cars in the old way doing piecework.

Piecework in the Midlands is marvellous for little backyard workshops and it worked very well over past generations. It does not work in a modern car factory. I don't know one that operates a piecework system.

Just how confused the situation had become is illustrated by Geoffrey Whalen who was brought into the assembly plant at

Cowley by Turnbull to try to sort out the problems. Whalen, now the British Chief Executive of Peugeot-Talbot which builds cars in the former Rootes plant at Ryton, had entered the motor industry with General Motors after being a Coal Board industrial relations negotiator in the traditionally militant Scottish coalfield.

His first shock came when he contrasted the well-drilled professionalism of the mineworkers' negotiators, pillars of the community within their pit villages, with what he found in the motor industry. He recalls: 'I was surprised at the relatively poor standard of union officials; they were neither so dedicated nor so professional. On the whole they were of poor quality though there were obvious exceptions.'

His second shock came when he arrived at the Cowley assembly plant, the old Morris Motors, in 1970:

The piecework system there was completely irrational and discredited. There were for example 80 different rates of pay for inspectors. It had all been based on giving extra bits of money for different responsibility. It started in the days when management had complete control, and that, I suspect, included blue-eyed boys. The mixture of paternalism and autocracy had continued after the war and they carried on managing ineffectively and inadequately. Then the unions became stronger and in the 1960s the plant at Cowley had become a hotbed of dissension. It was as if the management had restrained the unions completely and then once the floodgates were open and the militants in the union were strong, the result was dissension and difficulty and strikes. When I went there, that year on average there were two and a half strikes a day – over 600 stoppages in the year.

To try to tackle the mushrooming labour relations difficulties which were blocking the reorganization of the company, Stokes brought in Pat Lowry from the EEF. Lowry spent six months analysing the problems and then produced the company's first industrial relations strategy in October 1970. Warning that they 'must not expect too much of union officialdom' and that problems must be tackled on the shopfloor, it talked of a decline of union authority at the centre and an increase in the authority of shop stewards. The Corporation, it said, 'should seek to discontinue present piecework systems.' While Lowry conceded that its replacement, 'measured daywork', which set targets for people to achieve, would take years to prepare for, 'the situation is too serious to allow of a perfect solution.' Thus began the drive to change working practices, but it was to take a generation for the company to fight its way out of its industrial relations jungle, with compromises and setbacks all along the way.

Not everybody was immediately convinced of the need for such a major change. George Turnbull, just anxious to get as many cars produced as possible as the customer demand for his cars picked up, had been sceptical at first. But once he was convinced, he made it clear that the Marina would not be built unless the unions at Cowley agreed to measured daywork. The first deal was concluded in the Cowley Body plant, a unit with a reputation for comparatively few disputes but markedly high earnings – some managers said because too much had been conceded for fear of stopping the line. The deal, signed on a Saturday afternoon, was seen from the trade union side, led by David Buckle, as the best they had ever made. Among the small print, the management had conceded what became a union rallying-call – the concept of 'mutuality', which meant that manning levels and line speeds had to be agreed with the unions. It bothered senior industrial relations specialists in the company, but they saw it as a necessary price for the negotiation of a breakthrough, but something which might have to be clawed back in the future.

After the breakthrough at Cowley, the new payments system was extended to other plants. At the increasingly militant Cowley assembly plant just across the road, where the company was putting in a £50 million investment, the deal was accepted by a mass meeting even though stewards in charge tried to claim it had been defeated. Whalen watched from his office. 'The shop stewards came to tell me the vote had been against. I said, "Well in that case why are they all coming back to work?" '

The introduction of the new systems was no immediate panacea. While piecework gangs had tended to regulate themselves, anxious not to have too many men in a group to share the earnings, with daywork the argument about numbers worked the other way. At Cowley the almost immediate result of measured daywork was to increase the numbers on the Rover body line by a third. It all helped to produce the overmanning underlined by the Central Policy Review Staff. Its report to the Cabinet in 1975 said that many of the plants where daywork had been introduced were 'substantially overmanned and the grounds for dispute have switched from piecework rates to manning levels.'

At the same time men like Lowry and Whalen began to try to change the atmosphere in the company by a programme to improve carworkers' conditions. They had both been struck when they first arrived at the way the casual nature of the industry had persisted in its arrangements for sick-pay, pensions and lay-off. Lowry found that there was no real sick-pay or lay-off schemes and that pensions were based on a scale which provided a measly £12.50 per year of service. Workers, uncertain about how long they would remain employed, had opted to maximize earnings. He argued that if the upward drift in earnings could be checked, some money that might have gone on earnings could be used instead for lasting benefits.

As Whalen puts it: 'We had to persuade the men that benefits of stability and continuity and some moves towards better fringe benefits and lay-off pay provisions were better than the existing piecework system.' It was a logical aim; a philosophy which Whalen was to extend further when in charge at Peugeot-Talbot. But in BLMC at the time, Lowry says ruefully, 'sadly they were not the motivators I had hoped they would be.'

The initiatives and the changeover to daywork did little immediately to reduce the Corporation's strike-proneness. Lord Stokes says: 'The strikes and the money we spent changing over was just absolutely out of this world. It crippled the company in the end.' Lowry found himself explaining to colleagues that although strikes might not be fewer, they were 'better quality' strikes, often now about management reasserting its forgotten authority.

For managers in the plants, this was long overdue. Lowry's temperate prose in his strategy document that 'in the present environment the improvement of our industrial relations must essentially be tackled on the shop floor' covered a situation where shop stewards were so much in control in some plants that union officials, to whom they were technically responsible, were told to keep away by often highly politicized shop stewards. This was particularly true at the Cowley assembly plant, where union recognition had only come in 1956.

Whalen describes the scene:

> Piecework was an engine not just for wage increases but for shop stewards' control. And some were not just interested in Cowley and its work problems but wider political things. Trotskyists had a disproportionate influence particularly in the Transport and General Workers' Union, and they were skilful adversaries.

David Buckle was the TGWU's Oxford District Secretary, a former Cowley body plant worker who on occasions had worked in the assembly plant and tried to recruit there before the union was recognized. He now found himself being warned off by a senior shop steward when he attempted to visit the factory, where the politics which were never far from the big car plants had reached extremes.

Buckle's own explanation is that when management conceded union recognition in 1956 they still insisted in keeping local union officials out, preferring instead to deal with shop stewards who were almost hand-picked. But when they gave few concessions, the stewards lost credibility and the way was open for more radical representatives to take over, and force concessions by industrial action. Buckle recounts:

> The shop stewards had this taste of power over the management without any outside interference by the trade union movement and the extreme-left shop stewards were using the name of the TGWU and the AUEW but were not prepared to have the organization outside the plant in any way affecting them or influencing them inside.

Inside the plant the militant leadership had consolidated its grip. The senior shop steward was elected by the other stewards, and they in turn were effectively selected by him; it was a self-perpetuating system. It was not until the end of the 1970s that Buckle reorganized the branch, splitting it and arranging election by secret ballot.

Outside the gates the Cowley plant became the meeting place for all kinds of political grouping and workers were showered with propaganda leaflets from every sort of political party from the far left Marxists to the National Front. Inside it, workers were encouraged to make huge demands. Buckle remembers: 'I was told by one left-winger that the trouble with the Transport and General Workers' Union and the Labour Party was that they were obstacles in the way of the real revolution which has got to come in this country. I asked, "Does it make sense to put in for massive increases in wages which we know we can't win?" Then I was told, "We encourage workers to put in claims for substantial pay rises because we know they will be defeated. The working classes have got to go down to one defeat after another until they learn the only way to change is by revolution."'

But even leaving behind these farther shores of ideology for more mainstream politics, industrial relations in the plants were further complicated by changes inside the trade union movement nationally.

The whole shift to what was variously called 'shop-floor' or 'shop steward power' was given official sanction by the two very different men who, in the late 1960s, had been elected to the leadership of the two biggest unions. Jack Jones of the TGWU, and Hugh Scanlon of the Amalgamated Union of Engineering Workers, who were once known as 'the terrible twins' by their political opponents, both insisted that more attention should be paid to shop stewards. It was a mixture of philosophy and a realistic assessment of what was happening.

Hugh Scanlon, now Lord Scanlon, explains his view:

Before I became President, the whole of our energies had been concentrated on trying to get increases in the national pay rate for engineering. But the amounts that we got were those which the smallest and least efficient companies could afford, and so meaningless did these national increases become that the better paid – particularly in the motor industry – knew that

they could get more in half an hour's downer – as they called a
strike – than we could negotiate in two or three years. So we
were more than anxious to say, 'Don't give so much emphasis
to national negotiations – give more to company
negotiations.'

Scanlon blames the unwieldy procedures for dealing with
disputes in the industry for the prevalence of wild cat strikes.

The negotiating procedure as it then was almost invited direct
action because of the long time it took to exhaust the procedure, at the end of which there was inevitably a failure to
agree. Workers quickly found they got a solution quicker by
direct action than by negotiation.

This union resistance to change did not just affect the day to
day management of the factories, but also BLMC's ideas about
reshaping the whole enterprise. Leyland's advance planning had
been rather perfunctory. Stokes, at one morning meeting with
Harold Wilson at Downing Street, had referred generally to its
strategy and had been asked to produce Leyland's plan that
afternoon. Returning hurriedly to his office, he had asked his
central staff under Barber to draw up a plan for dealing with
BMC by four o'clock that day. But when the merger took place,
a series of about 50 working groups were established to draw up
action plans over a wide range of subjects.

One of the key questions was how much to rationalize the
sprawling factories of the group, and its 200,000 work force. For
this there was both a precedent and a caution. A few months
earlier, Arnold Weinstock of GEC, like Stokes an exemplar of
the effective businessman and much favoured by the Labour
Government, had taken over the heavy electrical firm of AEI,
merging it with his own GEC group. Weinstock, who ironically
employed Jack Scamp whose experience was drawn from his
numerous motor industry enquiries, embarked upon a programme of wholesale redundancies and cutbacks at AEI, closing
its south London factories.

In spite of furious union reaction, Weinstock succeeded and
then instituted an effective devolved management style for his

enlarged empire with individual companies having general autonomy, but the centre retaining financial and policy control. It was
the sort of pattern which many think would have been appropriate for BLMC, but ironically the success of Weinstock's efforts
seemed to close off the option for Stokes. The company had
identified a possible cut in the work force of 30,000 but never
even tried to implement it. Stokes says, 'We realized as soon as
we took over that we needed a cutback of about 30,000, but it
proved impossible. Just before we took over, GEC had taken
over AEI and had a huge redundancy programme, and when we
tried a similar programme there was a tremendous resistance
from the unions.'

John Barber says:

> Looking back, Donald Stokes was in many ways too kind a
> man to have taken over BMH. What it needed was a really
> ruthless rationalization – models, people, the lot. He tackled it
> the kind way, setting up working parties covering every aspect
> of the company. He tried to do it in a consensus way and if you
> start off that way, you don't get things achieved as rapidly as
> they are needed.

George Turnbull, however, was not keen to make cuts at
Austin-Morris. While he wanted rationalization – cutting the
number of paint colours available in some plants from a hundred
to a dozen; trying to get more common components – he also
wanted production. He resisted cutting numbers. He recalls:
'There was no point in firing everyone in a plant when all of a
sudden you have deprived yourself of 250 vans or whatever it was
that you were selling. My problem with Donald was to convince
him that we couldn't reduce the numbers until the new product
was in. All we could do was trim down, keep the labour
working, try and get some discipline, try and improve
communications.'

Turnbull was fighting both to get his new models ready and to
get his old models out – a problem made more difficult by strikes
in most of his major component suppliers – Pilkington, Lucas,
GKN – with an impact on Austin-Morris he describes as horrific. In 1969–70, BLMC lost five million man days – and its
suppliers as many. Turnbull says:

It was quite obvious that the only way we could put some rationale and some productivity and efficiency into the overall company was to bring in some new models, source them in a much more effective and efficient way so that we had all the body being made in one place and the painting and assembly done adjacent to it, without this transportation of sheet metal in the form of bodies and fresh air. At the time, the Minor, for example, was being made and put together in all sorts of places – in Coventry and Birmingham as well as Cowley. We replaced it with the Marina at Cowley – that was the major strategic plan.

In 1969–70, Austin-Morris lost £16 million – a huge sum, though the combined company struggled to profits of £4 million before tax. The Marina was launched at the Motor Show in the autumn of 1970. Its original development cost was to be £10·2 million. The car aimed to get away from the 'ultra-compactness' which had been the Austin-Morris trademark, and was to be 'a lot of car for your money' with a big boot and a style that one brief described as 'exotic and tending towards the wild but tempered with a high degree of good taste'. The costs rose as a larger engine was put in after market research, and a Triumph gearbox and rear axle were pressed into service. The cost went to £16·7 million and then to £21 million with hoped for production of 300,000 a year and a target of between nine to eleven per cent of the market.

In the event, in its best year in 1973 it sold 115,041 in Britain and took less than seven per cent of the market. It found itself up against not just the Cortina but also a new model from the recently taken over Rootes Group, the Chrysler Avenger. Chrysler's last stand helped to blunt BL's recovery.

The Avenger came out just before the Marina and superficially had many similarities. Although it never did as well (in 1972 and 1973 for example, it sold over 78,000 compared with 104,000 and 115,000 for the Marina and 187,000 and 181,000 for the Cortina), it was competing for much the same market – the increasing proportion of cars bought by companies for fleet operation or to reward executives whose pay was restricted by the Government anti-inflation pay policies which were a feature of all governments in the late 1960s and '70s. By 1975 a third of all car sales were in company names – 550,000.

The success of the Avenger (which had been designed before Chrysler took over Rootes) helped the company to maintain its respectable market share, and to compensate for the failure of the Imp. Intended to provide the style and comfort which the basic Mini lacked, its sales did well if they reached a third of the Mini's. In 1965 when the Mini had sold over 104,000, the Imp sold just under 30,000, and by 1973 when the Mini could still notch up 96,000 sales in a year, the Imp was down to little more than 15,000.

Helped by the Avenger, Chrysler's market share, which had slid to just over ten per cent rose to 12·4 per cent in 1971 before coasting down on another slow decline. But it was simply living on borrowed time – the clock set in motion by Rootes, and given a brief wind by the Chrysler funds, was running down. The American company put in no new investment and no new models. The simple answer was that the company was making no money. After losing £10·8 million pre-tax in 1967, it made £3·7 million in 1968 and a mere £700,000 in 1969. By 1970 it was losing again – £10·7 million in the year and the combined profits of the big sales years of 1971 to 1973 failed to reach £6 million.

But the decline was more cynical than that. American companies, above all, are aware that without new products motor companies have one foot in the grave, and Chrysler's treatment of its British subsidiary contrasted with that of its other European possessions, as well as with the Ford approach to integrating European operations. While some integration did take place in research and managerial and financial planning, and British engineers at Whitley near Coventry were responsible for the design of Chrysler's new Alpine which was only made in France, technical and production integration was found by the House of Commons Expenditure Committee in 1976 to have been 'almost non-existent'. Mr Marc Honore, Chrysler's director for Product Planning (Europe), told the committee that the company in Britain simply had not had the necessary resources for any significant alteration to their car range in the 1970s.

The American company also showed itself unable to handle the difficult labour relations of the British industry. British manufacturers were doing, it seemed, equally badly but those involved in the hugely publicized Chrysler strikes in the early 1970s (the 'shoddy work' dispute at Ryton and the long electricians' strike) saw them as stemming from the interference of American management. The Americans passed the worst possible messages to the strikers – first standing resolutely firm, and then capitulating stunningly. When, years later, Turnbull took over the plants under the banner of Peugeot-Talbot, he saw his first essential job was to re-establish managerial credibility. As one of the English executives closely in touch with the day to day running of the big Chrysler dispute put it: 'They were erratic. They would take a very hard line, and then quite suddenly in the last few days they would cave in.'

The strikes were clearly an element in discouraging both investment and integration with Europe. They cost Chrysler UK nearly fourteen per cent of its possible production in 1972, over 22 per cent in 1973 and seventeen per cent in 1974.

Vauxhall's performance was, if anything, more puzzling. Roughly the same size as Rootes-Chrysler, with a similar large American parent but much better established, its financial performance was similar and sometimes worse. It lost almost as much as Chrysler in 1970 and in 1972 and 1973, when Chrysler made (a little) money, it lost over £7 million. To date, it has only made a profit in one year since – in 1978. The company's production had come to depend on the success of a single model, its Viva, a small medium-sized car which was an immediate success when first introduced in 1963, selling a quarter of a million in two years. It was regularly updated and remodelled and by 1971 it was outselling the company's unsuccessful bigger car, the Victor, by three to one with regular sales of nearly 200,000 a year and even giving Ford's successful Escort (which usually, but not always, passed the 100,000 mark) a close race.

General Motors' willingness to allow Vauxhall to perform so poorly remains mysterious. In part the company's attitude was clearly affected by the success of the Bedford truck and van business which was located cheek by jowl with the car plant in Bedfordshire, and the losses were minuscule compared with the big profits General Motors made globally. GM management were much more interested in their Opel subsidiary in West

Germany. The consequences however of the fool's paradise in which Vauxhall continued to exist were to be severe. It fostered complacency once again, and ensured that when hard decisions about global sourcing for General Motors' new car range were made, that British plants, even those established recently like Ellesmere Port, came out almost empty-handed.

By contrast to its American-owned competitors, Ford pressed ahead with both integration of its European operations and a new model programme. In 1968 it replaced its Anglia with the Escort which it also made in Germany, the forerunner of a car to be as successful as the Cortina. Once again, the new vehicle showed a clever marketing shift. The Cortina over its career had moved up slightly, from the small to medium bracket to medium and now the Escort nudged up slightly from the Anglia, leaving a larger gap available for the B car, the small vehicle which Ford were increasingly being pressed by its US parent to build in Europe, but for which it could still no more get the sums right than Beckett had been able to when the Mini first appeared in the late 1950s.

Building the same cars in Europe as in Britain was to have another growing consequence – depending on cost and availability of plant Ford's market could now be supplied from Cologne and Saarlouis if Dagenham and Halewood did not perform. And increasingly in the 1970s the British plants did not perform – as Ford's industrial relations were as combative as any in the motor industry. Tellingly, the performance of its plants, making like with like, could be compared directly. In the period 1970 to 1974 Dagenham produced fifteen vehicles per employee and Halewood nineteen – a British average of seventeen. In comparable European plants, at Genk in Belgium production was 27 per employee and at Saarlouis in Germany it was 23 – a continental average of 25.

The difference was not quite so stark when costs were worked out because European wage levels were higher, and British plants got less investment because labour was cheaper. In evidence before the Commons Trade and Industry Committee in 1974, the Ford of Britain Chairman, Terry Beckett, was asked whether Ford's British operations would continue to be more labour intensive. His reply was 'probably to the extent that our wages are lower than German wages, from an economic view it probably is likely to continue. To answer you candidly, yes.'

According to SMMT figures, Ford still had the largest fixed assets per worker. As a measure of investment, it came top in Britain with £2,657 per man. But it was still well below its German plants which had assets of £3,608 per man; that was streets ahead of its British rivals – Chrysler with £1,456, Vauxhall with £1,356 and BLMC trailing with £920.

The company's willingness to invest in new products was pointed up by the $39 million it put into its Escort in Britain for its launch in 1968. Another $11 million was spent in Europe. Then $56 million was spent for the 1971 Cortina three years later, and $58 million in Europe.

The money was invested in spite of increasingly difficult labour relations. The introduction of the Mark II Cortina in 1971 had been accompanied by a long strike. Ford's share of the market which had climbed to something like 25 per cent in the mid 1960s to over 27 per cent by the end of the 1960s fell back to 18·8 per cent and did not return to its peak levels until the end of the 1970s. As one Government pay policy and contract after another came into operation so the Ford workers were seen as the standard bearers for workers in the private sector intent on busting the norms and limits in the same way that on the same date the National Union of Mineworkers with its national strikes of 1972 and 1974 was seen as the Praetorian Guard of the public sector workers.

It was an uncomfortable spotlight for management and also for many workers. Outside the gates of Dagenham, an extraordinary section of far left groupings handed out leaflets and sold their newspapers from Trotskyist splinter groups with names like Big Flame or Socialist Worker, from orthodox Morning Star Communists as well as the Communist Party of Great Britain (Marxist–Leninist), a sect which professed allegiance to Chairman Mao Tse Tung of China and included among their handful of adherents the Engineering Union's national executive member responsible for negotiations with the company, Reg Birch. Personally charming but highly irresponsible in industrial terms, Birch could enliven a long sullen negotiating committee with a sudden spiritualist knocking from under the table and a quavering voice would demand to know if improved death benefits were retrospective. But he scandalized the Commons Committee enquiring into the industry by refusing to take them seriously.

With its European structure, Ford had an answer as the anarchy outside its gates was increasingly being reflected inside its plants. By the end of the 1970s it was bringing in almost half the cars it sold in Britain from abroad.

Ford's European moves were encouraged by one of the largest changes which was to shake the insular British industry. This was the big fall in import duties which reversed the decades of protectionism under which the industry had grown up since the First World War. At the beginning of 1968 duties for cars coming into Britain (with the exception of tiny Commonwealth imports and those from the European Free Trade Area which included only Sweden among significant car making countries) were at almost original McKenna levels – 25·2 per cent for petrol engined cars. Imports in 1967 into Britain were 92,737.

But later that year under the impact of the Kennedy round of trade negotiations intended to encourage more world trade, the duties were cut and by 1972 they had been more than halved to eleven per cent. Over the same period, imports of cars grew more than four times to reach a figure of 450,314 in 1972. They were led by Volkswagen which notched up British sales of over 66,000 (half as many as Vauxhall), closely followed by Renault with over 60,000, while there was a huge jump in cars from Japan. With only about 9,000 imports in 1971, they rose to over 36,000 in 1972, doubling again to almost 74,000 in 1973, a position from which they were hardly ever to decline. Even Chrysler's European plants joined in the attack on the British market, with nearly 33,000 vehicles sold in Britain.

By contrast British exporters seemed to gain little from any freeing-up of world trade. British exports of cars peaked in 1971, at 721,094. It was equivalent to over 40 per cent of production, three times the imports coming in, a major achievement. But other countries were now doing much better. Western European manufacturers exported roughly half their production. By 1976 the number of cars imported into Britain exceeded our exports for the first time for half a century.

Again there was a combination of reasons. But with Britain

sending a much higher proportion of exports than her European competitors to places other than the United States and Europe British trade was particularly vulnerable to the big expansion of Japanese exports. They rose from 400,000 cars a year in 1968 to 1·7 million in 1974, directed not just to Europe but to many of the old Commonwealth markets in which Britain had enjoyed a favoured position.

Britain had benefitted from one striking export success. In November 1964 the overseas projects manager of Rootes, Ted Justice, received a telegram from his agent in Iran. It told him that a certain Ahmed Khayami would be at the Hilton Hotel in London the following Sunday and wished to talk to manufacturers about establishing an assembly plant in Teheran. Justice, who had already arranged assembly of Rootes products in countries which included Venezuela and Turkey and had made an abortive visit to Teheran three years before, decided to go along. He recalls: 'What we didn't know at the time was that the same cable had been sent to all the British manufacturers. But nobody turned up other than the Rootes group.

'We met a chap we had never seen in our lives before who had hardly any English but who said that what they wanted to do was to set up an assembly plant.' To this day Justice is surprised by the speed with which events moved. Rootes took the Iranians to see its own plant and within four months a deal was signed to build an assembly plant for 7,000 cars a year to be constructed from kits supplied from Coventry. 'Basically I think the reason was that they found someone they could talk to and trust. There weren't big teams in the Rootes group; it was just me and about four others.'

However small the start, the contract was by any standards huge, worth something like £150 million a year to the company at its height and taking something like 60 per cent of production from the firm's engine and powertrain plant at Stoke near Coventry in the good years – providing over 2,000 jobs. It lasted for over twenty years from February 1967 when the first car – a version of the Hillman Hunter called the 'Paykan', meaning 'arrow', was produced until it petered out amid currency difficulties after the Iranian revolution in the 1980s. It was the industry's biggest-ever contract. The car became a national institution in Iran – a vehicle which the middle classes could afford, if only they could get on the list. Arranging to get a Paykan became almost a way of life for some, notwithstanding that the car was the butt of regular television jokes, the car, it was once said, 'that could have an accident on its own' – a reference, it was fondly thought, to Iranian driving.

The car's Iranian sales turned what was a very modest competitor on the British scene into one of the biggest selling British cars of all time. Even in 1987, over twenty years after it was first made, there were still Iranians prepared to pay £35,000 for one, simply in order to get their hands on a car.

Rightly or wrongly Justice remained convinced that the contract was one big reason why Chrysler was interested in Rootes. 'They were after our overseas network,' he claimed.

Through the 1970s, the kits poured out to Iran even after the movement to encourage world trade, which the cuts in import duties reflected, had reached its apogee in 1973. In Britain, it was signalled by the 'dash for growth' of the Chancellor, Anthony Barber, and the tides of economic encouragement took the British motor industry to its highwater mark in 1972.

In 1972, production of new cars in Britain reached its record level – just short of two million cars – 1,921,311. Of these cars, 627,479 went for export while the record figure of 450,314 imported cars boosted overall sales of new cars in Britain to 1,702,211, a record which stood for seven years. The 'Barber boom' was blamed for sucking in imports but British manufacturers counted their profits too. In 1972 British Leyland took over 33 per cent of the market with sales of 542,440 cars spread over eighteen different models; Ford with only five models took just over 24 per cent (401,994) while Chrysler and Vauxhall level-pegged with between nine and ten per cent. On the crest of the boom, B L M C made one of its best profits – £21 million after tax, while Ford made £28 million. Chrysler made £1·6 million, but Vauxhall lost £4·1 million after tax.

As for the international perspective – in 1973 Britain joined the Common Market. As it did so, B L M C had slipped to become only the seventh largest producer in Europe with 8·6 per cent of the market. Fiat led with eighteen per cent followed by Ford of

Europe with twelve per cent. Citroen and Peugeot, whose recent merger paralleled Leyland's, had 11·6 per cent between them, Renault eleven per cent and VW and General Motors 10·4 per cent each.

It was not a propitious moment. BLMC did not have its own sales organization on the Continent and two thirds of sales were down to the Mini; Vauxhall's exports (rarely directed to Europe) had sharply fallen away, and Chrysler did not regard its British-made cars as even suitable for the European market. And as British regulations were redrawn to harmonize with European practice, there was a last twist of the old taxation screw which for so long had used the industry as a regulator and an easy source of revenue. Purchase tax, which stood at 25 per cent, was abolished, and in its place came Value Added Tax at a standard rate of ten per cent. But to compensate the Exchequer for the money which would have been lost by the reduced tax on cars, a new tax was created – the ten per cent car tax – which brought the level of taxation almost back to where it had been. Once more car manufacturers were being singled out for special treatment; when VAT rates moved sharply upwards a few years later the car tax remained the same.

Therefore, under the best conditions the industry might have hoped for, its performance had been indifferent. Its foundations were now too fragile to sustain the shock when the sands of time ran out, shifted by the earthquake which up-ended the world trading system when the OPEC oil producing countries suddenly managed to unite and force up the price of oil threefold in 1973 after the Arab–Israeli war. As the price rose, so the sales of cars tumbled, carrying with them most of the hopes and expectations on which the car companies had rested their plans. In Britain the industry's problems were exacerbated by the collapse of the Conservative Government's anti-inflation strategy in a three-day week, power cuts, and victory for miners in their pay strike.

From the high sales figure of 1·68 million in 1973, the number of cars sold in Britain in 1974 was only 1·27 million, a drop of almost a quarter; production dropped from 1·7 million in 1973 to 1·26 million in 1975.

They were the kind of figures and change no manufacturer

could sustain without severe difficulties. Now they were compounded by the huge increase in inflation as a result of the rocketing oil price – already over nine per cent a year in 1973, it rose to 16·1 per cent in 1974 and on to 24·2 per cent in 1975. The collapse of motor manufacturing companies could be only months away.

By July 1974 Lord Stokes of British Leyland was forced to negotiate with the big banks for money to keep his capital spending going. As the group headed for a £23·9 million loss, the banks argued and negotiated without agreement. By November they were refusing to allow the company to extend its overdraft, and Lord Stokes turned to the Department of Industry under the then Anthony Wedgwood Benn for help. Without 'money from somewhere' the company would have to contract in a major way.

Six months after Leyland's crisis had been dealt with by a huge commitment of £1,400 million of Government money, and effective nationalization with the Government taking a huge controlling shareholding in return for its investment, it was Chrysler's turn. Its American masters, their American company heading for the rocks even more rapidly than BLMC, delivered the British Government an ultimatum – take it over too, or we close it down.

Both crises were predictable, given the inherent weaknesses of the industry: the inability to make big enough profits to put in the new investment and to finance the new models on which companies depended.

In Leyland's case, the group had struggled bravely but increasingly ineffectively once the opportunity to make major changes at the start had been passed up. Its mass car division, which took so much of the resources which Leyland or Landrover or the specialist cars might have made effective use of, never achieved its breakthrough. Following the Marina's holding operation, the company launched the Allegro in 1973 to succeed the 1100/1300 range. Its unexciting lines and modest performance were disastrous. While the old range had sold over 100,000 cars in its last full year of production, Allegro sales never got much beyond 60,000. The company's market share plummeted from 41 per cent in 1971 to 32 per cent by 1974 and was to go on its way to as little as 23 per cent by the end of the 1970s. Its failure to take a bigger share of the company fleet market left it vulnerable to the growing attractions of imported cars which proved particularly alluring to customers who had to buy their own cars – the traditional patrons of the Austin-Morris dealers who were concentrated in smaller outlets, often in country areas in contrast to the larger and more urban Ford dealers.

George Turnbull believes that given the huge demand BLMC could still have done much better had it been able to build more cars in the face of its countless labour disputes, not always of its own making. At one point in 1972–3, he estimated he had made £15 million in three months but saw it all wiped out by a three week long strike by delivery drivers in an outside company which prevented any cars being moved and so stopped production. 'It was heartbreaking,' he recalls, 'I had £15 million profit in Austin-Morris after three months. But after the fourth month and the strike it was all gone.'

John Barber says:

> The oil crisis had an enormous effect on the market. It caused an awful lot of pessimism in British Leyland. We hadn't been doing all that well; we weren't making enough profit and while five years earlier we could have raised cash and it would not have cost so much, by 1973 it was becoming a problem. In the 1970s I think we failed to devote enough attention to product. I remember sitting in a meeting with Stokes and all the top management and we were talking about the model programme. Stokes turned to me with his usual grin and said to me, 'The trouble with you, John, is that you are a car nut.' I thought that was indicative of the problems of the group – instead of ten car nuts sitting round, there was only one.

The unresolved conflicts in the company's organization also took their toll with a line-up of powerful barons, Turnbull, Barber, Lyons and Sir George Farmer of Rover, fighting in their corner. One of the most successful efforts of the talented Rover design team was a mid-engined sports car, highly regarded by engineers who studied it and enthusiasts who drove it. But the project was killed by the opposition of Sir William Lyons of Jaguar, jealous of Jaguar's position as the specialist luxury sports car maker in the group. Another Rover project, the SDI, for an executive saloon, took a lot of management time and would eventually win a European Car of the Year award and become the standard car for executives of British companies, but it was not to start production until 1976, and in the meantime the £100 million its new factory was costing was a drain on the company's resources.

The undecided clash between centralization and autonomy of individual units came to a head in 1973. Turnbull left on what he saw as a principle, resisting moves which would have given the car division less autonomy under a new corporation-wide financial set-up. Turnbull went on to a successful career overseas, establishing the South Korean motor industry with Hyundai and later running the Iranian Paykan assembly plant before returning to Britain to look after the Peugeot-Talbot take-over of the British Chrysler empire.

But Stokes and Barber soon found themselves under an uncomfortable microscope, after Stokes' approach to the newly elected Labour Government which was attempting to run the country on the basis of a social compact with the trade unions, many of whom had been passing resolutions at their conferences for years calling for the nationalization of the British motor industry.

Stokes now sounds wistful about his overture to the Government. 'We ran out of money. We were building a new factory for Rover which was over £100 million and we had a cash flow crisis. All our overseas markets suddenly dried up. But I think the Government, and Benn in particular, was determined to get British Leyland nationalized. The only way they would give us any extra facilities was by taking the company over. All we wanted – though we probably would have needed more than that – was £200 million. If they had left it to private enterprise, desperation would have driven us into effective economies. But they just poured money in.'

In December 1974 Mr Benn announced in Parliament that he was seeking authority for a £50 million guarantee to British Leyland while a team under the head of the proposed new National Enterprise Board, Sir Don Ryder, would advise on Leyland's situation. Its remit was 'to conduct in consultation – I stress that – with the Corporation and the trades unions, an overall assessment of BLMC's present situation and future prospects.'[2]

It was a small committee – just five people – headed by Ryder, who had been boss of the Reed International Paper company and including an accountant and a senior trade unionist, Harry Urwin, the deputy general secretary of the Transport and General Workers' Union.

Stokes and Barber were sidelined. Barber remembers:

What they did was to ask some of our management and particularly our finance director, Alex Park, to prepare a plan on completely ideal assumptions – what would you do if you had all the money you wanted. Then they immediately grabbed it and didn't discuss it with me or Stokes or anyone.

Ryder had a session with Stokes and me initially, which was very perfunctory and then disregarded the Board completely and talked to people down the line. At one point Stokes said, 'I am the chairman of the company and we do have some directors.' Ryder replied, 'All right, let's have a meeting.' He produced his team and we produced ours and he asked what we wanted to talk about. We said, 'Tell us what you are doing.' He said, 'We are doing fine thanks . . . any other questions?' He was almost insolent to Stokes.

Stokes, who was chairman of what was then still the twelfth largest company in Britain, found even his good humour taxed by the enquiry behaviour. He says:

It was quite obvious they were not going to discuss anything. We were never asked any reasons why anything had been done or what the long term thinking behind it was. If you go round any company and you ask people to tell you what's wrong, you will get a whole host of stories. I think it was quite reprehensible the way they went snooping round asking people for comments and doing it without anyone being there who would have told them the answers they were getting were absolute rubbish.

I thought they were an incompetent lot. They published a

report which was bland and innocuous itself and then
mysteriously added that there were certain pages which were
not for publication – and they were equally bland and
innocuous.

The report was highly critical of the company's performance.
It emphasized the truism that profits had been inadequate, and
was sharply critical of the fact that the company had looked after
its shareholders instead of investing. All but £4 million of the £74
million it had made in six years had been paid out to shareholders
as dividends. The reports stated: 'In our view this policy was
clearly wrong.'

But even if all the profits had been ploughed back into the
company, they would still have been inadequate to remedy a
situation where investment had been so neglected that more than
half the machines and equipment were over fifteen years old. In
most motor companies, equipment was replaced after eight to
twelve years.

The report concluded that there was an overwhelmingly
strong case for the Government to provide the huge sum of
£1,400 million over eight years 'because of BL's importance to
the national economy' and its inability to generate sufficient
funds itself. It recommended a new organization based on four
separate businesses – Cars, Trucks and Buses, Special Products
and International. As for the work force, it hedged. It announced
that it did 'not subscribe to the view that all the ills of BL can be
laid at the door of a strike-prone and work-shy labour force.
Nevertheless it is clear that if BL is to compete effectively there
must be a reduction in man-hours lost through industrial disputes.' A separate table showed man-hours lost through
industrial disputes rising from five million in 1969–70 to eight
million in 1970–1, ten million in 1971–2 and falling back to 7·4
million in 1972–3. Disputes had delayed one new model, lost a
South Korean contract and cost fifteen per cent of production, yet
days lost per worker were still astonishingly lower than at Ford
or Chrysler. In the first nine months of 1974 all three companies
had lost the equivalent of more than a week's production for
every single worker.

Yet against Lowry's strong advice the report laid no requirements on the labour force. (It set out an elaborate system of councils and committees to try to bring workers and managers together in the planning of the company). It was left vague whether the proposals would result in any cutbacks. The only sanction it suggested was that the investment programme should be staged and that payment of each stage would depend on 'evidence that some tangible contribution is being made both by BL's work force and its management to the reduction of industrial disputes and the improvement of productivity.' Here was a recipe for Government interference and confusion with a vengeance – a no-win situation for any Minister at the Department of Industry who had to decide whether he could really pull the plug on the company if it remained at any time afflicted by industrial disputes.

The biggest weakness in the report was its extraordinarily optimistic view of the possibilities for a company whose share of the market was palpably slipping, even as the review team sat. It expected a minimum 33 per cent share of the British market, and talked of pushing up its market share in Western Europe from three per cent to nearly four – an increase in sales as the Commons Expenditure Committee soon pointed out of nearly 200,000 cars given the expected growth in the market.

Few reports have received a more rapid refutation. In August 1975 after extensive examination of witnesses, the Expenditure Committee published its own report. 'In our opinion,' it intoned, 'resources on a huge scale have been committed without sufficient examination of the aims, mechanics and desirability of such a step.' It went on: 'an apparent eagerness to adopt highly convenient assumptions has robbed the report of a degree of objectivity,' and it suggested that the team had relied too heavily on the BLMC concept study which had assumed 'a fairly free availability of cash'.

The report brought the unions into the centre of the company's planning process. It set out an elaborate system of councils and committees to try to bring workers and managers together in the discussions about overall company policy, with a cars council at the apex of the structure. Union officials, including Bill Roche, and the Longbridge convenor, Derek Robinson, sat in on some discussions between the company and the National Enterprise

Board. It was the biggest advance in participation the unions had ever made in the industry, and like the wartime arrangements which had only come after Government encouragement and regulation, it had once more depended on the action of a sympathetic Government. At the centre of the Labour Government's thinking was the belief that for British industry to perform properly, the energies and enthusiasm of the work force must be released and harnessed, and that would only come about through the trade unions.

The Expenditure Committee report queried Ryder's market forecasts. It suggested that the committee had simply produced the answer it had been expected to provide, noting that the Department of Industry was already staffing up before the Report in anticipation of its findings. It believed, it said, that 'the Government's initial Ministerial stance conditioned the findings . . . Dissent from the original view became steadily more difficult, and, in the end, impossible.' Its conclusion that 'we do not wish to see the only way of correcting a fundamental mistake in the Ryder report turning out to be payment from public funds' was horribly prophetic.

The Ryder report was extraordinarily optimistic. It simply avoided hard decisions about whether it was possible to continue making mass-produced cars at sufficient profit or any profit at all, and it dodged the horrific problems of manning levels. Its assumptions on market share suggested BL could sell about 1·1 million cars in 1985; in fact in 1985 the BL companies made less than 490,000, still trying to make both specialist and mass-production cars.

But the Government accepted it and the proposals for worker participation were set in train. Stokes was given an honorary role; Barber, told by Ryder there was no place for him, left. The new managing director was Alec Park with a part-time chairman but Ryder, as chairman of the NEB which had to approve each slice of the new funds, maintained an obsessionally close watch on what was happening.

But no one had watched more carefully the British Government's willingness to shell out money to keep its motor industry afloat than the American bosses of Chrysler. Now it was their turn to arrive on the doorstep of the Department of Industry – but theirs was a very different approach, one which the Prime Minister, Harold Wilson, himself described as a 'pistol to the head'.

On 29th October, 1975 the Chairman of Chrysler, Mr John Riccardo and his second-in-command, the President Eugene Cafiero, held a press conference in Detroit to discuss a loss of $231 million in nine months. The company had warned of 'extraordinary action' over operations where there was a probability of continuing losses and Mr Riccardo announced that Britain was the biggest single problem and that 'anything was possible'. 'The United Kingdom situation,' he said, 'is a very grave one. The economic situation is not so good and unfortunately it seems to be getting worse rather than better.'

Through the autumn the company had been discussing the possibility of a £35 million assistance from the Department of Industry to launch a new model at last. But now the prospect of complete closure took the Government by surprise and by November 3rd Mr Riccardo and his team were in London meeting the Prime Minister and the new Industry Secretary, Eric Varley, who had taken over from Tony Benn.

The company's proposals were blunt – either the Government could take over Chrysler for nothing or they could have an eighty per cent stake with the American company retaining twenty per cent. Otherwise it closed.

For the Government the implications of closure had been set out in black and white in the think-tank report in the autumn. It had estimated that unemployment in the Glasgow area would grow by fifteen per cent, and in Coventry by 42 per cent but about 60 per cent of Chrysler's sales would be picked up by other British based manufacturers, so mitigating the effect overall. It soon became clear that no other manufacturer was interested in taking over the Chrysler plants, and Varley fought vigorously against the suggestion backed by his predecessor, Benn, that the company might be nationalized or merged with BLMC. His view, strongly endorsed within BLMC, was that it would prejudice their chances of survival.

An extraordinary six weeks of negotiations came close to bringing down the Government. Varley himself remained in favour of closure, hoping some parts might be sold and believing that Volvo might be interested in buying Linwood. But Harold Wilson took a different view. Without Varley's knowledge, another Cabinet Minister, Harold Lever, was encouraged to start secret talks with Chrysler to see whether some plants could be retained under Chrysler control – if the Government would put in money. As the bargaining mounted to over a hundred million pounds, it became clear that Chrysler could be interested. A series of options involving the closure of different plants was discussed until eventually Chrysler offered to build the 1975 Car of the Year, the new Alpine, at its Ryton factory from parts made in France. The price was a Government commitment of £162·5 million over three years; the Alpine came into Ryton; the Avenger went to Linwood, and just over 8,000 of the company's 25,000 workforce were made redundant. It was a huge price to pay to keep on employment – a clear signal, it seemed to many that the Government would tolerate any behaviour from the car industry and still preserve it.

Varley, his stand against a deal backed by other Cabinet Ministers like Shirley Williams, Roy Jenkins, and the Treasury Minister Edmund Dell, resisted and pondered resignation. The Cabinet Secretary warned him that the Government could fall if he resigned. The motor industry was at the very centre of the political stage. In the event Varley decided to stay even if he lost, though he kept the decision to himself. As he waited to go into the Cabinet Room for the crucial meeting, Wilson warned him of the loneliness and lack of prospects out of office. Varley lost but stayed and for the second time in six months the Government was paying huge sums of money on questionable advice to keep the British motor industry going into a yet more uncertain future.

So the direction of the British motor industry which some in Government had wanted to exercise from the 1940s was now in its hands. But the industry it had grasped hold of was now at once so shrunken and yet still so unwieldy that it was left not with the direction of success but the management of decline.

The combination of poor management, bad planning, labour indiscipline and, not least, Government interference had turned the once golden goose into a lame duck. In some ways, it was an ideal test for the new National Enterprise Board set up by the

Government to show how a partnership between Government and industry could help revive Britain's industrial base in a thoroughly modern manner. But in other ways, it was the last refugee the Government wanted. The NEB, it had declared, would not be the hospital for lame ducks but a hatchery for new industries which had taken over the plumage of modernity once worn so proudly by the car industry.

13

The Seventies (II)
'The More that can be Saved . . .'

The new start at British Leyland could scarcely have begun under more difficult circumstances. In 1975 inflation had climbed to over 24 per cent and was not to dip below fifteen per cent until 1978. It put all the fine plans into doubt and created enormous pressures on the company's labour relations which were already a battleground for national political arguments over wage restraint.

The situation was made worse by the fierce competition. In 1973, British small cars had tended to have a price advantage of about twenty per cent over imports, but a year later this was largely gone. Between 1973 and the beginning of 1977 the last duties on imported European cars were abolished, falling from 8.8 per cent to nil as Britain's entry into the Common Market took full effect.

Although the British companies started to compete with each other in price again in a way they had hardly done since the war, with both Ford and Vauxhall introducing special economy versions of their popular Escort and Viva models, prices of British cars still regularly went up by more than even the high inflation rate. Imported cars looked a better and better buy for the harassed customer.

By the middle of 1977, for the first time since the earliest days of the motor industry, imports accounted for more than half the sales of new cars in Britain. Over the year, the total was 45.4 per cent, with over ten per cent alone Japanese in spite of eleven per cent tariffs.

By the end of the year British manufacturers were forced into a panic mission to Tokyo to try to agree with the Japanese industry a voluntary control of imports to Britain, while there was talk, less than convincing, of more import controls if they did not agree. The deal was done; the Japanese agreed to what was called 'prudent marketing' which was interpreted as between ten and eleven per cent of the British market, but usually came out nearer eleven per cent.

It was another extraordinary and humiliating turn-round. Twenty years before the Japanese motor industry had come to Britain for the plans to build its post-war models; now it had developed them to such an extent that British manufacturers had to go on bended knee to ask them to restrain imports of their successors which tariff barriers could no longer keep out.

The Japanese honoured the agreement for a decade; imprecise it might appear to be, but the Japanese motor manufacturers' association precisely allocated the share between its member companies.

They were difficult years for any manufacturer, let alone one like British Leyland engaged on major reconstruction. In addition, the problems of wage restraint under a social contract agreed between Government and unions and the strong left-wing push to challenge it found a ready cockpit in the industry. In February 1977, the convenor of the Longbridge plant, Derek Robinson, told a Communist organized meeting in London: 'I'm quite prepared to lead a mighty orchestration of workers so that we can move towards smashing the social contract.' Robinson was a man who management had found not unhelpful but he was the latest in a line of Communist party leadership in the plant. His predecessor, Dick Etheridge, had once told a manager that the reason for his politics was his revulsion for the dinner jacketed customers who would visit his father's coffee stall in the middle of Birmingham in the early hours of the morning.

So the new team at British Leyland set about their task of establishing new forms of organization and consultation – designed to break down some of those old divisions. Names like Austin and Morris and Rover vanished like Russian Politburo members after a purge. The new name for the Jaguar assembly plant became the Brown's Lane Plant: Large/Specialist Vehicle Operations. At the same time, the committees for participation were established. But even the efforts to involve the unions brought setbacks. The old Triumph plant at Canley in Coventry refused to allow its powerful union convenor to sit on the council; withdrawal from participation became a sanction with which unions could threaten the new management. Roche, chosen as secretary of the Cars Council, says, 'I welcomed the Ryder report. One felt here was an opportunity but it all went disastrously wrong. We failed initially because we didn't start with the membership. If we had had time and it had been practicable we could have had shop floor elections for people to go forward. Then not only would we have had different people but they would have had a stake in it. At the end of the day the committee was trade unionists looking after their own – and their own trade unions.'

While many in BL were manfully trying to make the new structures work, and the industrial relations team worked towards getting company-wide bargaining for the car plants, the company's lifeblood, its market share, continued to slip away. From 30 per cent in 1975, it was down to 25 per cent by 1977, well below Ryder's projected 33 per cent.

The new Rover executive car came out in 1976, but labour disputes and production problems with its new metallic paint and poor quality prevented it ever being made or sold in the numbers hoped for. It rusted, its boot leaked and it broke down. And even after modifications its electrics proved unreliable for years. BL's purpose-built new factory turned into a white elephant, with only two of its three production lines being utilized. Plans for a smaller two litre Rover which might have provided an upmarket alternative to the Marina (there were plans for a more utility version to be made by Austin-Morris) were dropped. In the aftermath of the oil crisis, which revived the attraction of economical small cars, a Mini replacement was worked on.

But once again it was all well behind the game. The think-tank report in 1975 had illustrated how the British manufacturers, with their obsession with the success of the Cortina, had ignored what came to be called the 'super-mini' market – the improved small car represented by the Fiat 127 or the Renault 5. In the small car market the twelve-year-old Mini and Imp were competing against thirteen foreign models, some only a few years old, where the import attack was concentrated. The British cars, it noted, often came off badly in terms of performance and extras offered.

After a good start to 1976, BL lost production equivalent to 200,000 cars. By mid February 1977, 20,000 workers had been laid off in three separate disputes, the most serious of them an indefinite strike by skilled toolmakers who wanted separate bargaining arrangements to enable them to correct a complaint as old as the industry itself, that they believed they were being paid badly in comparison with production line workers. By mid March the numbers laid off had grown to 40,000 and the Industry Minister, Mr Varley, had issued an ultimatum that unless there was a return to work the company's future investment programme would be cut back. An instruction to return to work from the Confederation that brought together all engineering unions fell on deaf ears. Engineering Union President Hugh Scanlon warned that unless they went back to work there will be no British Leyland with which to discuss the problems. 'It really is,' he said, 'the question of the employment or not of thousands of our members.'

Still the toolmakers refused to budge, as the union's executive member responsible for Leyland, Terry Duffy, declared, 'We are on top of the precipice going over.' Finally the management decided to issue an ultimatum to the toolmakers – 'Come back to work or be sacked.' In the event, it proved a well-timed final straw and the men went back. But not before it had demonstrated the extraordinary bureaucratic Government grip in which British Leyland was now enmeshed.

The decision to issue dismissal notices was made by the industrial relations team under Pat (now Sir Patrick) Lowry after discussions with union leaders. He informed the managing director of the cars division, Derek Whittaker. Whittaker then referred it to the Managing Director, Alex Park. Park agreed but felt he should telephone Ryder at the National Enterprise Board, who had considerable day to day involvement. Ryder refused to approve it without consulting Varley. Varley in turn asked the Leyland team to go to the House of Commons at ten that evening to brief him so that it could be discussed the following morning at the Cabinet. Lowry, to his acute embarrassment, had to adjourn his meeting with the increasingly suspicious union leaders until the following day, when permission was granted.

Lowry says, 'I can always remember Scanlon and Moss Evans

coming up to me afterwards and saying, "Don't ever do that again; it destroys our credibility and your credibility".'

Scanlon says, 'There were constant political interruptions in the role of management. Before they could really answer yes or no in national negotiations, they had to see father. I hope that doesn't imply that I am against Government overseeing any nationalized industry, but the day to day running of the company must remain in the hands of the managers. There were a number of good trade unionists on the NEB who would bend over backwards to do anything to assist the establishment of a publicly-owned British motor industry, yet we collectively reached the stage where the NEB could not keep offering money because it was only going to finance strikes rather than get involved in production.'

So the great Ryder experiment was dead in the water; for all the soft words about workers' responsibilities and the attempt to involve unions in elaborate constitutional frameworks, the company was being destroyed by industrial relations difficulties. A new approach and new leadership had to be tried.

From the Department of Industry, Varley watched with increasing concern. He recalls: 'It had started with a market share of 33 per cent and it was shrinking all the time. By any standards it was awful; in terms of productivity; in terms of model range. There was only one thing you could do which was to get the best possible management available and back it to the hilt. The problem was – they weren't exactly tumbling over themselves to take the job. No prominent well-known British industrialist or businessman wanted the job.'

Varley watched while Leslie Murphy who had taken over at the NEB from Ryder canvassed a range of people. One name mentioned was David Plastow, who had been running Rolls-Royce Motors. An approach was made to bring back George Turnbull who was finishing his contract in Korea. But Turnbull was anxious to spend another year out of England for the purposes of overseas investment. He was not prepared to live in Britain for another twelve months – an impossible position for a chairman. He offered instead to become a director and take over in a year's time. Finally an approach was made to Michael Edwardes, the South African born businessman who was chief executive of the Chloride Group.

Edwardes was a diminutive but forceful figure. Trade union negotiators, forced to give him best, were reduced to calling him Mr 'Head and Shoulders' because of the way he appeared to them over the negotiating table. Admirers gave him the flattering nickname of the 'Mighty Mini', reflecting the impatient urge to succeed which, like many other small men, marked him out. Opponents in BL were to call him 'poison dwarf'. Love him or hate him he was always an abrasive and challenging presence, whether with managers or suppliers, ministers or the press – and like a number of other prominent businessmen he took with him his own personal public relations adviser, John Mackay, who was one of his first appointments to British Leyland. Mackay guarded Edwardes' image as carefully as that of the company.

Edwardes' background was the outdoor world of South Africa. He had deftly reorganized Chloride's interests in the old Central African Federation in a touchy political climate as Northern Rhodesia became Zambia, and Nyasaland, Malawi. The company brought him to Britain at the point where Southern Rhodesia declared UDI in 1965. Later the Government was to delay his appointment to the NEB while his links with the rebel regime were investigated.

At the NEB he had a ringside view of Leyland's problems, and was appalled at Ryder's performance and his attempts to try to exercise day to day management control in the business. He saw it as interference which undermined management. He was alarmed to find his own suggestions and those of the rest of the NEB Board cursorily dismissed on the grounds that it was not their business. Ryder viewed it only as his own as the Government's industrial advisor. The illusion that the Ryder report was still valid was described by Edwardes as a 'charade'. He was being asked to sort out the consequences of its failure.

Edwardes had already impressed the Government as an effective modern industrialist. Chloride's profits had risen from five million pounds in 1972 to £26 million in 1977. The first offer was that he should be BL managing director while the part-time chairmanship was held by Ian Macgregor, the Scottish American businessman on whom Murphy had relied considerably for advice in his role as a non-executive director of Leyland. Edwardes insisted on being an executive chairman. He told

Murphy by telephone from Washington, 'I couldn't accept less than the combined role of Chairman and Chief Executive. I want a free hand including the right to change the Board on "day one".'

His salary of £80,000 was well above the rate for chairmen of nationalized industries. But it was rapidly approved by the Prime Minister, James Callaghan himself, and in October 1977 Michael Edwardes took over the company for a five year stint which was to reshape not just Leyland but also the climate of industrial management in the country.

Michael (now Sir Michael) Edwardes arouses strong emotions, a man to whom it is not possible to be indifferent. To many he is a business hero, the man who did for British industry what British managers should have done long before – stood up to the unions, closed plants and gave his managers back the pride and commitment they were in danger of losing, inspiring their counterparts in companies all over the country. To them his qualities are those of a dedicated man who did not flinch, as did so many before him, from confrontation, who was prepared to go to the brink and beyond and who singlehandedly changed the climate of British industry by the way he sacked workers and cut back the sprawling corporation to a size where it might just become viable.

To others, typified by David Buckle, he was simply 'a tyrant; an industrial dictator'; the person who abolished any chance of a cooperative approach to BL's problems, instituted an authoritarian management which made managers as hagridden as the workers whose schedules they increased, and produced a combative and difficult relationship not just with the unions, but also with suppliers and anyone with whom the company did business. To them Edwardes was the man who did the will of monetarist Government masters and did not mind what he closed or whom he sacked. 'Ruthless and cynical' was the description given to him by Derek Robinson, the Longbridge convenor controversially dismissed by him.

To others still, including the very Prime Minister, Margaret Thatcher, to whom Edwardes' philosophy most approximated, he was a man of great achievement but nonetheless one who had extracted a billion pounds from the Government coffers on the basis of an eventual break-even which perpetually receded.

What no one doubted was his intense commitment, thoroughness and personal bravery. He became a symbol of a re-born management which was not only aggressive but realistic and competent. Allied to Edwardes' strengths, such as his analysis and vision, his aggressiveness could be a benefit – the problems came when some of those he promoted, less able, turned the tough style into an ultimately self-defeating policy of macho management for its own sake.

While the unions might try to diminish Edwardes, there was also a healthy respect for his achievement in salvaging what was by any standards an appalling mess. Harry Urwin, who sat on the NEB with Edwardes, and opposed his first plant closure at Speke on Merseyside, said: 'the man did make a contribution. He had no friends at all when he went in, but when he was working with the NEB and accepting our monitoring I thought he was doing a first class job. It was when Sir Keith Joseph made him directly responsible to him that unnecessary harshness was introduced, and I disagreed with the things he was doing. When he left he wrote to me and said that he knew that I had disagreed with him but that he had been determined to preserve a British motor industry and had done so.'

Edwardes' own aims and his public image were furthered by a shrewd manipulation of public relations in conjunction with Mackay. He limited his exposure to the media except when he wanted to say something particular, often confining it to selected journalists. At key moments, carefully pre-arranged chance appearances in his car on the ramp of his office car-park enabled him to make comments which might influence union mass meetings. His autobiography, *Back from the Brink*, setting out in great detail his own account of his years with BL, was published the year after he had left, deliberately enshrining his version of events, which he says proudly, have not been contradicted. It was a new departure for a motor magnate, but once again the trends he set were soon being copied by others in wider industry.

In terms of cars, he will be remembered as the man who launched the Metro – the first wholly successful mass production new car launched by the group for twenty years, and who started the rescue of Jaguar from the slough of unreliability and poor quality which threatened to choke the life out of it. He set BL on the road to cooperation with the Japanese with a deal to collaborate with Honda that saw Cowley building a Japanese car, the Acclaim, under licence. But he was also the man who ended an era in sports cars, closing the MG factory and, soon after, discontinuing Triumph sports car production.

Edwardes took over a company which still employed 195,000 people, almost the same figure as when the great merger had taken place eight years earlier. In the first eight months of 1969 the company had sold 241,000 cars and taken 25 per cent of the market. When he left five years later there were little more than half the number of people – 108,000 and they were selling twenty per cent fewer cars – 204,873 in the first eight months – eighteen per cent of the market. In financial terms, the company had made a bottom line loss of £51·9 million in 1977. With high investment and redundancy costs, the losses over the five Edwardes years came to £1,489 million.

Edwardes now says, perhaps surprisingly:

> When I went in there no-one thought we could keep the whole thing together in the form it was. There was never any question in my mind that you could cure the thing as whole and have it as an on-going long term proposition. The debate that went on, the argument with the Government in 1979, 1980 and 1981, was that whereas we could save chunks of the business the bulk of the money I needed was actually for retrenchment, cutting back people, therefore even if the business subsequently failed, I argued, or bits of it failed, the money was not wasted. It would have to be spent to close down anyway.
>
> If you analyse the chunks of what I took on in 1977 the bulk of it will be saved; a lot of it is profitable and a lot not linked with BL in people's minds today. I never had a thing about British Leyland per se. I saw this as 40 different businesses, and the more that could be saved the better.

It is fair to say that the outside world did not always see it like that as they watched the company go to the brink time after time with warnings from Edwardes that he would close it down if he did not get agreement on a series of industrial relations ultimatums.

His own view of BL when he took over was that:

It was an industry that was torn apart by industrial relations disputes. Companies like Jaguar and Landrover were being emasculated by the Leyland Syndrome where the management was trying to impose the Leyland umbrella on individual marques. Productivity was low; quality and reliability even on Jaguar was low and market share was declining at an alarming rate. The company had virtually no overseas car outlets. The average person was crying out for leadership, but the vocal militants were being led by the nose by ideological extremists.

Amongst his first actions was to override internal advice and to re-establish the individual identities of the companies that made up BL, reversing the obsolete Ryder recommendations. He instituted an urgent overhaul of accounting procedures to try to establish the profit and loss on individual cars – information which astonishingly was unavailable. He says: 'The previous Board knew the total costs and the total sales, and they knew what the loss was, they did not know the detailed costing of individual cars. It took me six months to find out that MG was losing £26 millions a year.'

Meanwhile the new Board reviewed the model programme. The Mini replacement had reached the stage of road tests, but Edwardes' doubts about its viability were confirmed by European consumer tests of the new car which showed little enthusiasm for it. The company decided to alter the project, redeveloping the car into what it nicknamed a Mighty Mini in the class which the Europeans came to call the Super Mini. Production of the car was put off from 1979 to 1980 but in the meantime £275 million was invested in the new West works at Longbridge to establish the most modern car production plant in Britain equipped with industrial robots and sophisticated computer controls. For a while it was the case that the majority of robots in British industry were in that one plant.

Edwardes' approach to labour relations was even more radical. A huge programme of interview and psychological testing was instituted for the 300 top managers; many left. Sixty came in from outside. The NEB were told that there would have to be redundancies of 15,000 in cars and about 2,000 in trucks.

Edwardes characteristically took the fight to the unions, arranging to address a meeting of 720 shop stewards and union representatives at Kenilworth on February 1st, 1978, at which he set out his recovery plan, and then to the union's astonishment forced a vote. Only five voted against even though Edwardes had warned of contraction of at least 12,500 car jobs.

This was rapidly followed by the announcement of the first closure of a plant – the Triumph factory at Speke in Liverpool which built sports cars. Production was to be transferred to Coventry. The decision was a watershed. Edwardes' claim that no-one had closed a major factory in Britain for ten years was effectively true. The received wisdom in many quarters was that in union-led Britain it would be near impossible to carry through. In the event the Speke workers, exhausted by an earlier strike, accepted it. It was an astonishing change of attitude; management was back in the driving seat.

In the event nineteen out of the 55 factories were to close under Edwardes, including, unbelievably, the brand new Rover plant built only a few years before. The impact of Speke was reinforced with a training programme to advise management. He wrote: 'Act firmly, put some backbone into it and you will be backed. Repercussions? Yes. Of course there will be, but I give you my word you will not be let down. The old ways are out – your job is to manage your part of the business.'

Industrial disputes still dragged on. A toolmakers' strike at the SU carburettor plant in the summer of 1978 threatened to stop production, but women at the factory, encouraged by a personal visit from Edwardes, kept working and the company faced down the strike. In early 1979 car production at Longbridge was hit after pay parity payments bringing plants towards the same level of pay were stopped because productivity levels had not been reached. But in April an attempted repeat of the big toolmakers' strike fizzled out without a car being lost.

Edwardes' own explanation for the change was that this time a hundred senior managers had spent hours on the shopfloor walking round and explaining why the demands could not be met. The decision had been taken not to rely on the unions to communicate management offers to the work force but to speak directly to them and use leaflets and letters sent directly to workers at their homes.

By the middle of 1979 lost production was 110,000 cars for the year, less than half what it had been the previous year. Days lost from industrial action had reduced. It was a time of what Edwardes called later 'the illusion of progress'.

At the same time a huge rise in the value of the pound after the Conservative election victory was threatening to wipe out the company completely. As successive Confederation of British Industry annual conferences argued the pros and cons of an appreciating currency without firm conclusion, about a third of British manufacturing industry disappeared, including famous sections of BL.

The most celebrated closure was that of the Abingdon plant of MG. For the board the financial reasons seemed overpowering – each car built there was losing something like £1,000 in its principal market, the United States. It was a direct result of the huge appreciation of sterling. It was the decision car enthusiasts most remember Edwardes for – why not, they say, have held on until the exchange rate improved as it eventually would? The closure was announced shortly after the company had celebrated its 50th anniversary with a pageant of old vehicles through the streets of Abingdon from where the company drew most of its 4,000 workers; many of them keeping employment within the family.

There was talk of consortia taking over the plant, and union leaders claimed that American dealers said the price could have been greatly increased, but nothing was agreed. Edwardes says, 'At the beginning one wouldn't have foreseen Abingdon going. Sports cars depend on the production of volume parts which are then woven into a sports car design. But over the years it had become more and more unique, as they failed to adapt the sports car to what was happening on the volume car side. You ended up with a product that was totally incompatible. All a change in the exchange rate would have done would have cut the loss down to break even. You need to make at least £1,000 gross profit on a vehicle like that.'

The exchange rate had now become a bigger threat to the company than labour relations or the policies of the incoming Conservative Government.

The new Secretary of State for Industry, Sir Keith Joseph, a fervent opponent of state aid and nationalization, was greeted

with a warning that unless the company got £500 million more
from the Government it would effectively go to the wall, with
horrific redundancy costs. Instead the board prepared a Recovery
Plan involving 25,000 redundancies and the closure or cutback of
thirteen factories.

The unions demurred and suggested double the money from
the Government; Edwardes decided on another bold initiative –
he went out to a ballot of the workforce warning that anything
less than a 70 per cent 'yes' vote would mean the dismantling of
the company. It was a typical Edwardes brinkmanship and he got
an 87 per cent 'yes' from those voting.

The characteristics of the Edwardes' style were by now
established – give managers and supervisors back the responsibilities and the backing they had lacked for years; argue your
case with the workforce without relying on the unions; argue it
out with the unions but if they don't agree, go over their heads for
a workforce ballot – and when that doesn't work (as at least two
ballots did not) argue some more, and ultimately threaten to close
the place down.

The strategy worked through a series of knife-edge situations –
none more dicey than the decision to sack the long serving
Longbridge convenor, Derek Robinson, over his endorsement of
a pamphlet urging resistance to the closure under the Recovery
Plan. It had followed a warning given earlier but industrial
relations professionals in the company were never sure it would
have stood up at an industrial tribunal. Like Speke, getting rid of
so prominent a figure was breaking recent new ground.
Marathon talks with Robinson's union, the AUEW, bought
time by instituting a union review; by the time a mass meeting
voted on a strike tempers had cooled and the vote was lost, again
in the face of warnings that a strike could spell the end of the
company.

It was coolly calculated. Edwardes, agreeing it was risky, says,
'We did it exactly a year before the Metro was launched because
the car's management told me that they could not meet the
productivity requirements that would get Metro down to budget
costs unless they could manage Longbridge, and they could not
do that with Robinson running his own private disruption.'

The 'Red Robbo' affair was followed by the imposition of new working practices which swept away the mutuality agreements, and confrontations over pay in both 1980 and 1981. In the meantime the pay structure was reformed – to give skilled men better differentials and reintroduce a bonus system based on the number of cars produced.

Behind the scenes battles with the Government sometimes seemed even more perilous than those with the unions. The Conservative victory of 1979 had replaced a Labour Minister, Varley, who had adopted a largely hands off approach, with a Government ideologically suspicious of paying large sums out to lame duck industries and a Prime Minister accustomed to asking, 'Michael, what are you doing about your militants?' By the mid 1980s both civil servants and Sir Michael Edwardes were made sharply aware of consuming Prime Ministerial interest in even the smallest questions relating to BL.

The early 1980s were a disastrous time for car companies the world over, following the further increase in the price of oil and the beginning of the world recession. Both Ford and General Motors in the United States joined the near-bankrupt Chrysler in the red by 1980. In Britain, even Rolls-Royce was in trouble from falling demand as well as declining quality. In 1982 it cut back production and made about 2,000 people redundant.

But the huge subventions required by BL were still political poison for a Government paying out vast sums to other failing nationalized industries like steel and desperately opposed to the successive attempts of its predecessors to get a direct handle on the motor industry. It was the greatest irony that the largest sums of money for the state-owned motor industry should have come from a Government more opposed to public spending than any in the industry's history.

In 1980 BL had received £450 million from the Government, but by the end of the year Edwardes was on his way to Downing Street to argue that even more money would be needed – an eventual £990 million over two years – not far short of the £1·4 billion which was estimated as the cost of closing the company. Argument dragged on for months and was only finally resolved in an extraordinary Cabinet debate, even though the industry secretary, Sir Keith Joseph, whose own department had backed the deal, spoke out against it.

A few days later Mrs Thatcher gave her view in a television interview: 'It was a difficult decision, I don't conceal that . . . I never want to take on another British Leyland. We shouldn't be in it at all, but now we are in it, we have to choose the time and back Michael Edwardes' judgement. He is the manager. I'm not the manager.'

Edwardes was pressed to put privatization – a new political catchphrase – ahead of a return to viability, but he told the Commons Select Committee on industry in 1981: 'It is a pie in the sky to believe that any major unprofitable part of BL is ready yet to return to the private sector on its own. As to the profitable parts we need the active parts of the business to attract the strategic collaboration we are actively seeking . . . and to fund our cash flow.'

The new determination for Government to get something back for its money was eventually seen in the privatization of Jaguar in 1984. But its recovery was a close run thing. Even the Ford motor company had decided against buying it because it believed that it had become a liability – that its quality and its long queue of pending warranty claims were something to beware of.

Edwardes had started the rescue by turning the old companies back into separate businesses. But Jaguar was still part of JRT – Jaguar, Rover, Triumph – when he approached John Egan to return to run it. Egan declined. He recalls, 'I was wary how much could be done. I thought he was still too optimistic about what could be saved. But when a couple of years later he asked me to come and run Jaguar, I thought it stood a chance.'

Egan arrived to find the factory on strike over new working practices. After three days he got them back to work. 'The workers were saying, "You have done everything else to us; you might as well close us down." I was the only new ingredient.

'It was a complete shambles, there were a load of quality problems, very low productivity and it was losing money at an alarming rate. We homed in on improving quality and getting the workforce to understand that quality was the number one objective. We had technical problems with the bodies from the Castle Bromwich plant – we had to repaint them here, and they could only supply three colours – red, yellow and white. But I viewed the car as eminently saleable if only we could make it work.'

Egan was appalled by the components supplied to him. 'There were tyres that weren't round; radio aerials which wouldn't go up and down; switches that failed; leaks.' Jaguar started a 'black museum' of failed parts to show to directors from the supplying companies and agreeing action programmes for improvements which were then monitored.

Meanwhile productivity was improved. A third of the work-force went between the end of 1980 and the middle of 1981, and the same number of cars were still produced.

Customers were wooed. A programme of telephone inter-views of 300 customers a month to ask about their satisfaction with both cars and dealers was begun in four countries. In 1980 only ten per cent was prepared to say they would buy another Jaguar; by 1986, 80 per cent would. Edwardes argued for new investment; £100 million of the 1980 money went to Jaguar.

The climax came in 1984 when Jaguar was sold to the public – the shares flotation raised £297 million although the Government held a 'golden share' to prevent the company being swallowed by an unwelcome buyer at least until 1991. A key part of the deal was the gift of £450 worth of shares to workers in the company; four years later, 90 per cent still held them. One of the characteristic sights at the Jaguar factory, startling, given the industry's history, is the moment on a Monday afternoon when the supervisor comes round a shop and announces the share price plus any other factory notices – such as a works Guy Fawkes bonfire, or car production figures.

The company's progress had been rapid, helped involuntarily by improvements in the disastrous exchange rate which had slashed American sales. It had been close to disaster in 1980 when it made fewer than 14,000 cars and lost £52·2 million after tax; by 1982 with the workforce cut back from 9,700 to 7,500, it was back in the black and making over 22,000 cars and by 1983 was building up the numbers employed once more to meet demand. In 1986 Jaguar produced a record number of cars – 41,437 with 11,300 people. In 1987 the number of cars produced per employee, a crude productivity measure, was 3·8, nearly three times what it had been in 1980. In 1986 the company made a profit of £83·4 million and exported about 80 per cent of its production, and launched its new XJ40 saloon which received rave reviews and, more important, proved a sell-out at home and abroad. Not dissimilar to its predecessor, still showing the distinctive Lyons styling, the company claimed that the only part that remained the same was the badge on the steering wheel.

Egan's view of the benefits of independence are unequivocal, rejecting the arguments which took Jaguar into a wider grouping in the 1960s. He says:

> People have overestimated the advantages of economies of scale and underestimated what good people can do if they all pull in the right direction. I don't think that in any case it costs us more to do things for ourselves than BL charged. Their economies of scale did not give us value for money. We buy in about half the car and make about half – which is what almost all car companies do – we make our own body, engine, trim, axles and so on. But of course with our cars people are willing to pay for individuality and excellence.

His target in 1987 was 'to make better and better cars more and more cost effectively.' He says: 'Unless you are keen to be the best in the world on something complicated like a car, you simply are not going to exist at all. These days there aren't any bad cars.'

Egan prides himself in the investment that is going into engineering development. In 1986, £90 million was spent; in 1987 – £140 million. Jaguar is developing the old Whitley research centre that once belonged to Rootes and Chrysler into an ultra-modern development centre, spending £50 million in a wave of investment, although some of its motor industry neighbours wonder if this can be sustained. It is part of a very conscious policy of learning from the mistakes of the past, and Egan's criticism is that the old British Leyland 'never really put anything like competitive amounts of money into new investment', and that the benefits of state ownership did not greatly show either.

'I think we will have invested more since privatization than in the entire existence of Jaguar before. The stewardship which the Government gave to Jaguar was very poor. When we took over, all the roofs leaked; we have had to repair all the floors, and the tracks were secondhand in the 1960s. No money was spent here at all.' The £100 million for the new car and engine was paid back to BL, and Egan took some delight when showing the Prime Minister round Whitley in 1987 in pointing out it was one of the few car engineering establishments in Western Europe built without any Government money.

Another innovation at Jaguar's Browns Lane assembly plant has been the provision of a two-storey prefabricated canteen block alongside the plant; something which provides facilities which amazingly were not available before. But then even in 1912, *Automobile Engineer*'s correspondent in America was contrasting the lack of canteens and other facilities in the British industry with what he found in the United States.

Some things remain the same. Egan, a particular critic of trades union practice, complains that only very few unions understand the pace of technological change and the training and investment needed. Union leaders tend to come for social meetings, but not when the company is making presentations of its plans. Some still block the formal establishment of 'quality circles' which discuss how production could be improved. He says, 'It is still a difficult environment for all but the most determined managers. If we ever caved in to the wages demands we would be bankrupt. Even today we are getting things like a 30 or 40 per cent demand from people who are already the best paid in the industry.'

Jaguar has been the most spectacular rescue job from British Leyland. But even so its production is only a tenth of what is still produced by the Austin Rover division of its old parent – or four per cent of total British car production.

Edwardes' work on the volume car side had much more mixed results. He too was deeply concerned by the lack of good engineering facilities and good engineers within the company. In 1977 new cars still had to be tested on the public roads because the company had no test track of its own and millions of pounds were put into new engineering facilities and a test track at Gaydon. At the same time the company estimated it was short of 1,500 trained engineers, a persistent problem in Britain where even Ford claim that identical production facilities on the Continent have a much higher number of engineering staff attached to them – with hugely beneficial results for productivity.

The launch of the Metro enabled the company to invest in high-quality up-to-the-minute engineering and computers and push through flexible manning arrangements it had long wanted. The launch of the car in October 1980 was a major success. The company was at last learning the lessons of the past; a year before its advent the car was tested carefully against British and continental competitors, and the lessons learned were incorporated into the new model. Production at Longbridge, supervised by Harold Musgrove, a former Austin apprentice brought back from Leyland vehicles, was rigorously controlled and cars carefully checked and stockpiled ready for the launch, getting away from the embarrassment of only a small number of poor-quality vehicles being available for a well publicized new range.

But, as contemporary reports pointed out, one small car alone was not enough to turn the company around. Edwardes was well aware of the huge gap in the middle range of cars, which could not be bridged simply by the £2 million facelift of the ageing Marina, re-styling it as the 'Ital'. The new medium cars which BL were to launch, the hatchback Maestro and the larger Montego, both came after Edwardes left the company, in 1983 and 1984. While reasonably received at first, neither made anything like the waves of the Metro, and the Montego earned a reputation for embarrassingly poor quality which began to evoke memories of the early Marinas. By the middle of 1986, BL's market share was down to below seventeen per cent and the company was once more retreating from any possibility of break-even. As a new executive chairman, the Canadian, Graham Day, was brought in, replacing both Edwardes' lieutenants Musgrove and Ray Horrocks who had run the business with a part-time chairman; the company's brightest stars remained the Metro and cars designed in a collaborative deal with the Japanese company Honda, which was one of Edwardes' most important legacies.

By 1977 British Leyland had already realized that it would have to consider some form of international collaboration in an increasingly internationalist scene. It held extended talks with Renault, but the difficulties of dealing with a very much larger company, Government involvement and strong nationalisms on both sides, prevented rapid progress. The gaping hole in the middle of the car range where traditionally the biggest profits are made could not wait. Edwardes arranged for a colleague, the former Ambassador to Japan, Sir Fred Warner, who was on his board at Chloride, to sound out the president of Honda about a collaborative deal as early as September 1978. Honda was much smaller than the big Japanese producers but had a reputation for excellent engineering, and, like BL, was a leader in front-wheel drive. Under the deal signed in December 1979, BL bought a Honda car which it assembled in Cowley as the Triumph Acclaim but, more significantly, began a programme of collaboration which resulted in February 1981 in agreement to join forces to design and build a new executive car to replace the Rover. Known with suitable mystery as the XX, it was launched as the Rover 800 series and the Honda Legend in the summer of 1986.

The Acclaim appeared in 1981 and proved a popular and trouble-free addition to the BL range, bobbing in and out of the list of the best selling top ten cars in Britain. It was also a further education in production techniques. At Cowley where it was made, it seemed to the workers to be the first car they had built on what felt like a modern system with equipment and robots imported from Japan, similar to those in use in the Honda's home plants. The car's successor, the Rover 200 series, was based again on a Japanese design but considerably modified by British engineers with many parts made in Britain, which included the engine for the successful 1·6 version. In the mid 1980s it had established a growing reputation and was selling over 45,000 a year.

The Honda deal was not the only international link. BL's deficiencies were such that it decided to buy a Volkswagen gearbox for middle range versions of the Maestro and Montego, while another German company, ZF, supplied automatic gearboxes.

However, the most far-reaching plan – codenamed Gemini – was to merge BL with the American-owned Vauxhall. The idea was hatched by Bob Price, the American chairman of Vauxhall in 1978, a man who had so impressed Edwardes that he had already unsuccessfully tried to persuade him to join BL. Now Price had a suggestion to make.

General Motors' ten year review of its European operation had concluded that it needed more factory space – an expensive investment. Why not, Price suggested, build GM cars in BL's underused factories, let GM provide the engineering which BL lacked and form a joint sales company which could market a complementary range of trucks and cars while developing Land Rover and Jaguar. Tellingly he said, 'We think that your Austin Morris problem is bigger than you think it is, for we believe that you need not one, but two new models in the mid-car sector. But you don't have the people resource or the cash resource to do it. And time is against you . . . We could build on our mutual strengths – we think that the Mini can be developed, and your new LC8 (Metro) would give us a ready made car in that sector. We can solve our mid-car problem quicker than you can.'[1]

It was a sharp and momentous analysis. To this day, Edwardes regrets that it did not find favour in Detroit. A slimmer version of it – with GM merging its truck operations with BL and Land Rover – was the subject of long negotiations in 1986 before being torpedoed by the British Government with maximum political embarrassment. Gemini would probably have suffered the same fate – but it indicates how far the British industry would have to travel away from its insular attitudes to face up to a world where international collaboration was becoming not merely common-place but standard practice.

14

The Eighties
'We Couldn't go it Alone . . .'

The effective collapse of British Leyland in the 1970s ended its last chance to make a major breakthrough in what was becoming an increasingly international world of car making. As Edwardes had quickly analysed, if it was to be any sort of international force, if indeed it was to survive, it had to draw on international expertise, for joint designs and components.

The established American companies in Britain, Ford or Vauxhall, were even better placed to draw the same conclusions and act on them. The story of the British motor industry in the 1980s is not so much about the continuing difficulties and disappointments of what was first called BL and then the Rover Group, but of a major switch of car and component making and design out of Britain into other parts of the world. Throughout the British industry's history the consequences of bad habits and poor performance, unnoticed at first, has often had a devastating impact a few years later. So the traumas of the 1970s taught lessons to multinational companies planning deployments for the 1980s, from which British plants were now often excluded.

A graphic sign of the new order of things came in 1978 as the new regime at BL struggled to impose its mark. As it did so, so the other Government rescue of 1975 unravelled. At the Chrysler offices at Ryton in Coventry, a sealed letter from Chrysler Europe arrived at 9 a.m. on the morning of August 10th for the managing director, George Lacey, with instructions that it should not be opened till 10 a.m. It was placed on the board-room table and executives sat looking nervously at it as if it was an unexploded bomb, waiting for the hands of the clock to reach ten o'clock. Its message was straightforward: the Corporation had sold out all its Europe interests to the French company Peugeot-

Citroen. It was now up to the French to dispose of the plants which the British Government had paid over £160 million to save with guarantees from the American company.

If that was one indication of the seachange in the British industry's place in the world, the escalating scale of things was demonstrated by the cost of the introduction at the end of 1976 of the small car which Ford had been considering for years.

The oil crisis of 1973 had hit all the big American motor companies. In the United States, Ford had lost $3·8 billion between 1980 and 1982 and had been significantly helped by hundreds of millions sent over by its European companies. In 1983 Ford of Britain was making almost as much profit from the money it was sending to its American parent (about $645 million) as it was from sales. In Britain Ford had seen its profits plunge to £3 million in 1974, even though it held on to its market share. Throughout it all, however, the company had clung jealously to what it called its 'crown jewels' – its model plans.

Ford's corporate identity and culture is a powerful one. Talk to Ford men and they tend to come up with many of the same adages and assertions. They like to talk of 'product', by which they mean the cars, and one of their deepest held and most repeated beliefs is that 'you don't cut back on product': you make sure you have a competitive range of cars even if that means changing successes like the Cortina while their sales are still high.

Sam Toy, former chairman of Ford of Britain, credits the American Chairman of Ford of Europe, Bill Burke, with sticking to the line in the early 1970s. He says,

> We got to the stage where because of short-term financial problems, a lot of pruning took place, but Bill said, 'Hold it, without product you don't survive.' It's the last occasion I guess when it was debated within Ford what you do about the future when you have short-term financial problems. The last thing you do is to take money out of your product programme. Everyone else has learnt the hard way, and some people still haven't learnt. Within Ford you stay with that product programme and bite the bullet on something else. But you don't denude it because in four, five or ten years' time you will be benefitting from it.

The cost of the 'product' which Ford introduced at the end of 1976 was a billion dollars. Called the Fiesta, it was the small B car which Detroit had wanted to build for years. It had set up a task force as early as 1969 with a hundred thousand dollars budget but it was not until December 1973, with the oil crisis giving an extra boost to smaller cars, that the decision to go ahead was taken.

The green light was only given after a new factor had come in to change Ford's calculations. The company was increasingly interested in the growing Spanish market from which its cars were effectively barred by high import tariffs. The answer would be to build a factory in Spain; the problem that it would have to supply other markets as well. But by combining two investments – the Spanish factory and the costs for the new B car – the sums for both made sense, particularly as there seemed to be a big market for the B car in France and Italy, both close to Spain.

As Toy puts it:

> The Spanish business was wholly incremental and there were two huge B sector markets on Spain's doorstep. So from a geographical view it was the obvious choice. One hears an awful lot of nonsense talked about cheap labour and non-unionized labour. It was absolutely nothing to do with that; without the sales we were going to make in Spain, we were not certain we would get even that miniscule return on investment.

Original plans were for the car – the Bobcat project which was renamed the Fiesta when launched – to be made in Spain and at Saarlouis only. But when Ford decided it needed more capacity, Dagenham was added to the production centres. Toy says, 'We estimated that we would get the Fiesta share in Britain up to four per cent of the market, so it made good sense to put it into Dagenham.'

The Fiesta, launched in 1976, proved much more successful than Ford had hoped, notching up a seven per cent share in Britain alone. But the way the whole project was argued through and directed from Detroit, with US executives falling over themselves to claim the credit, and with production ending up almost as an afterthought in Britain, showed how much more international the focus of what had started effectively as a merger of British and German Ford companies had become.

Another effect of the merger was that once common model production was established, Ford of Britain could do what other British manufacturers could not – measure themselves against European competition. As Paul Roots, later the head of its Industrial Relations, put it, 'Ford was in a unique position; we were able to make proper comparisons between what we were doing and our continental plants who were making the same models to the same standards, often engineered by the same people. We really were comparing apples with apples.'

What they found did not make happy reading. In the period 1975–79 productivity in Ford's main British body and assembly plants at Dagenham and Halewood dropped – from an average of seventeen vehicles per employee to only thirteen. At the same time, German productivity, already ahead, improved still more, from 25 to 31 cars per employee – nearly three times the British performance.

Indeed at times Ford's industrial relations performance seemed no better than British Leyland's even without the handicap of a maze of different companies and plants. It showed the characteristic British patterns. 'Our problems were fundamentally the same; the big problem was to get continuity; we were unable to get continuous production because of stoppages. The typical strike in the British motor industry involved few men and lasted less than a shift; they were sorted out quickly but they stopped the line. The big staged strikes – which they had on the Continent – were not so much of a problem,' says Roots.

As always it was the body and assembly plants, employing the largest number of men on the most repetitive work which bore the brunt. Other plants, like engine or transmission factories, were much less affected and productivity was better. At Dagenham, although the old Briggs body plant had the largest history of industrial disruption, by the mid 1970s the resentments caused by the continual stopping and starting because of the irregular supplies from the body plant was causing strife in the assembly plant too.

In 1976 Ford had managed to launch two new models in a year, for the first time in memory, the Mark IV Cortina and the Fiesta, but congratulations did not last long as its problems worsened and management found themselves spending almost their whole time dealing with disputes. There were many similarities with what was happening in BL – strife between the skilled and semi-skilled (that old perennial problem), taking the form in this case of arguments about how many shop stewards each was allowed; difficulties of encouraging both the confidence and consistency of its supervisors eventually dealt with by months of weekend training sessions; the vast proportion of management time spent on disputes rather than planning and production.

With its high profile, Ford suffered too from the politics of the social contract. Just how fragile matters were in the plants was brought home to me in September 1977 when I wrote a lead story in the *Sunday Telegraph* saying that, 'Ford will offer below the Government's ten per cent pay limit when it starts pay talks with the union this week.' The article caused a walk-out in one shop in Halewood on the Monday because they claimed the company had been leaking to the press. (It is perhaps the only tangible effect that I can measure in sixteen years of industrial reporting.)

A few weeks later Ford was caught between union militancy and Government pressure in the same negotiation when it secured peace for twelve per cent – markedly above the Government's ten per cent guideline. As a result the Government imposed sanctions on the company cancelling the Ministry of Defence contract for Cortinas. A furious Terry Beckett lambasted the Government, and the sanctions were dropped, but few episodes demonstrated more clearly the difficulty of running a car factory in Great Britain at the end of the 1970s.

Nor were workers in the plants greatly impressed with the situation. Their turnover at Dagenham reached 25 per cent a year in the mid 1970s as workers looked elsewhere for easier conditions and comparable or better money with local councils and public corporations like British Telecom.

The problems of the shopfloor then knocked on to other areas. Anyone who visited the German plants, as supervisors and workers were increasingly encouraged to do, found a much greater proportion of trained engineers on the shopfloor, which greatly helped the efficient running of German plants and their better productivity.

By contrast in 1973, Ford of Britain was reduced to commissioning a Gallup survey to try to improve its faltering recruitment of graduates. Tec Fawcett says, 'We found that industry was bottom of the league, the car industry was bottom of that and Ford was the bottom of that; I think because people found its work ethic too demanding and thought of it as a materialist ratrace.' With typical thoroughness, Ford later set up a scheme whereby senior managers each 'adopted' a particular university and tried to encourage links with the company to bring in more graduates of a better quality. Bill Hayden, Ford of Europe's vice-president in charge of all the manufacturing plants, says:

> Our plants in Germany are not only more efficient because of the unions but because we can actually get a better calibre of individual on the shop floor. In Britain our people tend to want to take commercial degress and until three or four years ago we could not entice qualified people on to the shop floor.
>
> The Germans look on manufacturing as a career in itself. In Britain we were always able to get all the finance people and all the marketing people, all the product engineers we wanted, but the actual people we could entice into plant management were very few.

Hayden, a tough expansive East-Ender brought up in West Ham is something of a legend in his own lifetime amongst British Ford people. Starting as an accounts clerk in Briggs, after a brief spell as a Stock Exchange clerk he became the first Briton to be a corporate officer of the Ford Motor Company of the United States.

'I had an interest in cars; and it was an expanding industry. The car industry attracted me – also Ford was part of my background. You can't live in this area and not know someone working for Ford.' So at the age of 21 Hayden joined Briggs, thinking he might get farther with a smaller company. He was scandalized to find that when in February 1952, King George VI died, the company observed a two-minute silence, but when W. O. Briggs died soon after, the plant was stopped for a full three minutes.

When Briggs was taken over, Hayden found himself part of

Ford and for more than fourteen years it has been on his desk every morning that production details of all Ford of Europe's plants arrive. He was responsible for bringing plants in Spain and France as well as Bridgend in south Wales into operation. It is to him rather than to the chairmen of what are effectively Ford's sales organizations in different countries to whom the car makers look.

When he warned in the 1970s that Ford might have one too many European plants because of over-capacity, people sat up and speculated about the future of Halewood, then the least productive plant. 'What I was trying to point out,' he says, 'was that there was no automatic salvation. You only survive if you make profits. There was a stage in the middle of the depression when the whole industry thought someone would have to shut a plant.'

The message from Ford in the 1970s was confused, however, by the fact that far from closing down in Britain, it decided to put £180 million into a new plant to build engines for its European cars at Bridgend. There were strong reasons – a huge package of Government aid and the fact that Henry Ford was personally courted by the Labour Prime Minister, Jim Callaghan.

But the siting of the new plant also reflected the fact that Ford needed to stay in Britain – its best European market and the only major market where it ran ahead of General Motors – and that whatever might be said about its assembly plants, Ford found British workers particularly effective in engine manufacture. As Sam Toy puts it, 'The British are good at chassis parts like engines and gearboxes – the Germans are better at bodywork – and it shows.'

In the event the Bridgend plant went ahead after assurances from Callaghan about the good behaviour, not so much of the car workers but the construction unions, and he was called on to use his influence to ensure it was completed in time.

While the Bridgend message appeared to be that Ford was committed to Britain, the company's sales figures told a rather different story – fewer and fewer of the cars sold here were made in Britain.

In 1978 when Ford had 25 per cent of the market, nearly two thirds of the cars (64·7 per cent) had been made in Britain. By

1982 when it had over thirty per cent, little more than half were made in Britain (51·49 per cent). While Ford's share of cars sold was going up, the actual numbers made in Britain were going down. In 1979 the number had been just over 400,000; by 1984 it was below 300,000 for the first time since the 1950s. Ford's exports from Britain, once a matter of intense pride, had almost disappeared. In 1975 Ford exported 103,671 cars; in 1984 it was down to 19,583.

The result of these changes was that for the first time since the First World War Britain started to run a balance of payments deficit on motor manufactures. After a brief revival, it was back in the red in 1981 and grew rapidly to a deficit of £3,887 million in 1986. Of that Ford on its own was accounting for £854 million and Vauxhall for £650 million, importing more than some foreign manufacturers.

The multinationals were shifting out of Britain – none more so than General Motors, the owners of Vauxhall. Whereas Ford's centre of operations in Europe had traditionally been in Britain, GM had always regarded Adam Opel in Germany as the jewel in its crown. By the early 1980s the British Vauxhall plants were becoming virtual assembly stations for parts designed and made in Germany and in other GM factories round the globe.

It had not always been so. Pre-war, German influence had shown on only occasional models. But the first Viva, the HA, had an engine based on a German design; because of problems a few parts were actually made in Germany and calibrated metrically.

General Motors' commitment to Britain had been reinforced by the construction of its Ellesmere Port plant on Merseyside in the 1960s, where the Viva was largely built. But by the time its successor, the hatchback Chevette, arrived in 1975, the car was a straightforward copy of the German Opel Kadett – a result of what Eric Fountain, a long serving Vauxhall director who was formerly the Ellesmere Port manager, says was, 'a clear realization within Vauxhall that we couldn't go it alone any longer with a totally separate model range. We had too little capacity and the cost of designing and producing new models was just too much.'

Therefore, the German and British operations were brought closely together with the British end inevitably being overshadowed by the more powerful Opel. Instead of effectively two models, Vauxhall was to offer a whole range – but they would not all be made in Britain. The pattern was a repeat of what the company was doing on a worldwide basis – the Chevette, made in Australia, Japan and the United States as well, was GM's first attempt at what was to be known as the world car.

There are two different definitions of the world car – one is the car that can be sold in markets all round the world – the other, perhaps more apposite, is the car assembled in different parts of the world from parts which come from all over the world. This development came on apace just at the moment when Britain's performance was at its worst; the result was therefore inevitable – the work went elsewhere.

The key decision came in the mid 1970s when General Motors was deciding where to make its power train – its engine and transmission system – which is the most skilled and most expensive part of the engineering of a vehicle, and one for which Ford, as we have seen, thought British workers had particular aptitude.

Now different national companies belonging to GM including those in Japan, Australia, Germany and Britain competed for the business; in the event engine production for various models was split between Germany, Australia and Brazil while transmission was allocated to the Japanese company of Isuzu which is 40 per cent owned by General Motors. Fountain says, 'We lost out at the end of the road because of the strike situation that existed at the time. We would have had to make about 300,000 engines and about half would have gone for export – and that's the reason we lost; it would have been too much of a risk.'

So when the Astra replaced the Chevette at Ellesmere Port, the huge engineering workshops which had turned out engines and transmissions and other highly skilled products fell silent, their workers made redundant or drip-fed into jobs in the assembly plants where the Astra was largely built from parts, including metal body pressings, not only designed but made abroad.

The highly popular Cavalier introduced in 1978 came at first from the company's Antwerp plant in Belgium, merely being fitted to a slightly different specification and given a distinctive radiator grille. Later it was assembled at Luton from mainly

imported materials. When in the early 1980s the British Steel
Chairman, Ian Macgregor, managed to persuade General Motors
that they should take British Steel once it had improved both
quality and price, there was no market for it in Britain – it had to
be shipped to Europe where the principal pressing work was
done.

Therefore, in 1984, when the Mark II Cavalier was being
assembled in Luton, one could watch parts coming together on
the assembly line delivered from almost every country but
Britain – the basic engine was made in Australia; if the gearbox
was automatic it was American; if it was manual it was Japanese.
The distributor and much of the pressings came from Germany;
the carburettor by courtesy of the French, while the oil filter,
some glass and the wheels, but little more, was British. The
British content of the car only reached 60 per cent with the help of
a calculation which counted half that as being the labour costs.

The arrival of a new multinational in the shape of the French
firm of Peugeot-Talbot did not at first have the effect which many
had predicted. The French company signed a declaration to take
on all the obligations of Chrysler and to view its British operations 'in the same manner and in all respects on a par' with other
companies in its group. It pledged to give the 'fullest opportunity' to the models it inherited like the ageing Avenger, its
derivative, the hatchback Sunbeam, and the Alpine and to continue to use cars from Britain to meet the valuable Iranian
contract. It resurrected a new name for its Chrysler products,
calling them Talbot after the Earl of Shrewsbury who had
imported cars in the early years of the century. It brought back a
stalwart of the Midlands motor industry, the ever-green George
Turnbull, from running the Iranian end of the contract to become
chief executive. When he stood firm in a pay strike that lasted
twelve weeks, the French company did not second guess him or
order a climb down, in sharp contrast to the company's experience under Chrysler.

Linwood continued for a while, but with no new investment it
withered away. The company's share of the market declined and
it became increasingly clear that in future Talbot would give way
to Peugeot. More than 2,000 workers went from Linwood in
1979 and the remaining 5,000 were made redundant in 1981.

Meanwhile the Iranian deal was thrown into chaos by the Ayatollah's revolution. As payment trickled through only occasionally, hundreds of workers at the Stoke plant which serviced the contract were put on a one day week, with Government support.

In the first half of 1982, the company, its Iran sales almost at a standstill, lost £40·6 million. Yet after cutbacks, a sudden return of Iranian sales and a better share of the British market, the company actually made a small £1·5 million profit in the first half of 1983.

At the same time Turnbull launched a major programme of communication with the work force introducing a series of what are called 'team briefings' where information about the company's performance and plans are passed on in a series of set meetings from management to supervisors to the work force. It was highly praised by the Industrial Society although it seemed to have little direct impact on the company's difficult labour relations.

A further blow to the industry came when the French company decided to move its design facilities out of Britain, accomplished it almost overnight and presented it to the British Government as a *fait accompli* in 1983.

The big question —, whether, unlike Chrysler, Peugeot-Talbot would invest in Britain —, was answered in 1985 when £30 million was spent on re-equipping Ryton for production of the Peugeot 309. The first cars were produced in 1986 and the plant reached the highest production levels it had seen for ten years. There was even talk of putting on a night shift in 1987.

Meanwhile the slow improvement of industrial relations under Geoffrey Whalen, who had been brought in by Turnbull as personnel director and had succeeded him as Managing Director, was showing results. Workers from the firm were enthusiastic about the new cars; eager to go to dealerships and presentations in the centre of Coventry to show off their new product. Whalen himself was attempting to alter established traditions in the industry by proposing a more trusting system: not docking pay for late arrival and moving towards harmonizing the conditions of staff and manual workers. It was a bid to try to end what he saw as the old adversarial relations in the industry – an attempt in

Austin's new post-war small car, the A35, at Longbridge.

The Vauxhall Victor, introduced in February 1957, showed clearly the American influence and ownership of the company. It became Britain's No. 1 export car for a while – many going to North America.

The small car dream of the forties and fifties – Issigonis' Morris Minor.

The most profitable British car ever was the Cortina. Terry, later Sir Terence, Beckett led the team that produced it.

This is how the first Minis were advertised when they appeared in 1959.

By 1965 they were celebrating the first million. Designer Sir Alec Issigonis is immediately to the left of the car in a tweed suit.

The face of a modern body line. Robot welding on the Ford Sierra production line at Dagenham.

The Jaguar line. One of the first Austin Swallows, a rebodied Austin Seven, made by Sir William Lyons, and the latest post-Lyons Jaguar XJ6 still showing his distinctive styling.

In the fifties British patriotism celebrated the performance of Jaguars at Le Mans.

some ways similar to what the incoming Nissan motor company would do to try to break the mould. It was part of the changing face of the multi-nationals; another side of what for British managers and workers were often harsh consequences of facing up to international realities.

The British Government could chart the multinational shift away from the United Kingdom production but had little power to alter it. It could only ensure that incentives for companies to invest in Britain, such as Ford in its Bridgend engine plant, were as attractive as possible. But for regions desperate for employment, such as Wales or Northern Ireland, the new mobility seemed to offer a tantalizing opportunity if only it could be grasped.

Tragically, but typically, the project the Government appeared to succeed with most brought with it the most spectacular and embarrassing disaster. The British Government's attempts to intervene in the motor industry have throughout its history been mainly ill-judged and ill-timed and usually calamitous. Its support of John Zachary DeLorean, the flamboyant former executive of the American General Motors corporation, was no exception.

DeLorean's dream of his very own sports car manufacturing plant was hawked around the world in an unashamed Dutch auction until the promise of loans and grants which added up to £54 million secured it for Northern Ireland in 1978 against the competing claims, and promises, of the Irish Republic and Puerto Rico. Briefly it would provide jobs for 2,000 people. The car, a stainless steel sports coupé, whose opened doors rose like gull-wings from its body, was developed with the help of the Lotus car company, the prestigious British sports car which had grown from the manufacture of kit-cars in north London by its founder Colin Chapman after the war. But although Lotus' owners benefitted from the millions poured into the project, and the cars became collectors' items, the DeLorean company was never viable and turned repeatedly to the British Government for an endless drip-feed of extra assistance to stave off closure.

When it eventually closed its doors in October 1982 after its founder had been arrested in the United States on drug-running charges, of which he was later acquitted, it had cost the British taxpayer £85 million and crushed the hopes it had so cruelly raised of worthwhile employment amongst the hundreds it had taken on in an unemployment black-spot.

Throughout the history of the British Motor Industry, hope and enthusiasm have tended to overrule commercial common sense. The DeLorean episode was perhaps its clearest example in Government.

The decision of the multinationals to make more and more elsewhere had a savage knock-on effect on the British component industry, once regarded as one of the strongest and most successful in Europe and accustomed to point proudly to the high proportion of cars like the Swedish Volvo which came from its factories. It had long been seen as a mainstay of the industry with a considerable balance of payments surplus.

Now it was struggling in two ways – the drop in the number of British cars made slashed its market, denying it economies of scale and cutting its chances of profit, in turn affecting the prices it could offer manufacturers at home or abroad. And the shift of design out of Britain had another telling effect. As Fountain bluntly puts it: 'With manufacturing, where design goes so does most of your component production.' At the same time, as manufacturers like Edwardes and Egan tirelessly pointed out, the component makers were suffering from the same sins as the assemblers – erratic delivery because of industrial troubles and embarrassingly poor quality.

Since the war the tendency for component makers to solidify into a smaller number of larger groupings had continued. The biggest growth came from the steel products group GKN, which had used some of the funds from the compensation for the nationalization of its steel-making plants to finance a vigorous buying-up of motor component manufacturers which seemed to offer good prospects of profits.

GKN's most significant purchase was in 1966 when it took over the Birfield group of companies. This provided it with two key elements of its future success – the Hardy Spicer transmissions and constant velocity joint expertise, and a Continental outlet in Uni-cardan of West Germany. By astute development and engineering, GKN has preserved and increased its lead in constant velocity joints of all sorts, with both licence agreements and a share of manufacturing plants in most major car-making countries – it supplies most continental manufacturers from its plants in France and Germany. When US attempts to make CV joints faltered and American companies turned to Europe for help, GKN established a factory dedicated to supplying Ford, and later a second plant in North Carolina. It still supplies a large amount of Ford's needs and is the sole supplier to Chrysler, with manufacturing also in places like Brazil, Mexico, Korea and Taiwan as well as Japan. Of the billion pounds its motor business earns a year, over three quarters comes from outside Britain. It is also closely involved abroad with the latest developments in four-wheel drive and transmission and suspension systems. Its international success is demonstrated by the way that parts from its German factories are made into units which are shipped from Germany to Luton to be built into British Vauxhall cars. But it has still cut back enormously, reducing its British work force from 84,000 to 27,000 in ten years.

By the middle of the 1980s one famous name after another was hoisting distress signals. Lucas also expanded into Europe, successfully with its Girling brakes, less so with its electrics. In the 1970s, the French Government thwarted an attempt to take outright control of Ducellier, its French equivalent, and Ducellier's fortunes later declined. Meanwhile, faced with the challenge of electronics, Lucas's reply in the motor sector was inadequate.

Another major name, S. Smith, re-named Smith's Industries, had decided to get out of the motor business altogether by 1983, selling its heater business which once had employed 5,000 people in Oxfordshire and merging its remaining electrical and instrument business into a new Lucas company, Lucas Electrical systems, with Government assistance.

John Thompson, Smith's deputy managing director, says, 'All the instruments in vehicles used to be electro-mechanical. The design hadn't changed for years. Then they all went electronic. If we were going to compete realistically with Japan and the USA, we needed a wider package. If you wanted to be a mainstream player, there was no second division; you had to get into the bigger league.'

But the new company was not a success and Lucas' problems

continued to mount. Its automotive section had been overtaken by its aerospace interests and in the summer of 1987, while a House of Commons committee was actually examining the future of the components industry, it announced the sale of its motor lighting business, the foundation of its original motor interests in the days of Joseph Lucas, to a foreign company which was a subsidiary of Fiat. Other parts of its motor business were for sale.

The biggest crash of all was that of Dunlop. It had linked in 1971 with the Italian Pirelli company, a costly and unsuccessful merger. Dunlop had lost millions helping out Pirelli, but when the two companies split it proved unable to manage its own affairs. By 1985 it was being described in the newspapers as 'the biggest industrial casualty in Britain's private sector', was burdened with over £400 million of debts and was sold to the take-over specialists BTR, once the junior neighbour of the great Dunlop empire as the Birmingham Tyre and Rubber Company, for £33 million.

By that time the company had stopped making motor tyres – the once mighty Fort Dunlop and the company's few remaining car tyre factories, including its German operations, were sold to a Japanese company, Sumitomo Tyres, which had been set up as a Dunlop subsidiary 70 years before, and was by then making more tyres under the Dunlop name than Dunlop itself. The company had plunged from one of the most prominently quoted blue chip stock market firms to losses in 1982 which amounted to a fifth of its capital and reserves. The BTR move followed a drastic pruning by a rescue team led by none other than Sir Michael Edwardes. By the time Sumitomo took over, renaming the Dunlop production in Britain S.P. Tyres, the number of Dunlop workers making tyres had fallen from 11,500 in 1978 to about 3,000.

How had it all gone so wrong? There were external reasons shared by other manufacturers who had also sharply cut back, and run into trouble. Michelin's losses, which reached over four hundred million pounds in a year, dwarfed Dunlop's and were due to two common problems – the huge rise in the price of oil, and the way tyre manufacturers became just too good at their job – tyres lasted longer and they sold fewer.

Dunlop had been overtaken by Michelin in the 1960s. Its problems were compounded by poor management which decided to expand on forecasts of a growing market at just the wrong moment; it was slow both to respond to changes in tyre design and to improve its productivity. In a fearfully familiar British motor industry fashion it had failed to shake off the complacency of the days when Britain could sell all the tyres it could make. Dunlop representatives in Europe in the 1960s preferred to get their tyres from their European factories because they could get them weeks quicker and better made than from a Fort Dunlop which took three weeks to send out a tyre from stock. In the 1960s the tyres the company had provided for Jaguar had not been tested at all on hot continental autobahns, only on the M 1. By the 1980s Jaguar could still complain that some of the tyres supplied were not even round.

Therefore, when in the summer of 1987 the Commons Committee came to report on the British component industry, its conclusions were almost as gloomy as its predecessors' verdicts on the motor assemblers twenty years before, reports which had then gone out of their way to stress the health of the component sector.

So in the event it was no surprise that when the domination of Ford in the big selling medium car market was challenged after twenty years of the Cortina, it was not homegrown BL which did it, in spite of all the money poured in, but another multinational – General Motors with its world-produced J car – the Mark II Cavalier. With its front wheel drive, sportier feel and plenty of the extras which British sales reps and motorists liked more than their continental counterparts, it even overtook Cortina sales in some months in 1981 and 1982 as Ford waited for its new design.

Ford's new car, the Sierra, was launched in September 1982, proving that even multinational backing and the best market research does not always get it right first time. The new car was the particular brain-child of Bob Lutz, the American chairman of Ford of Europe. It had many of the Ford virtues – simple, effective engineering and a basic design which inherited the simplicity of the Cortina. The company had spent quite a lot of money on it – $813 million of which almost half was in Britain.

But that was a lot less than the $1,076 million, three quarters of it in Britain, which had been spent two years before on a brand new front wheel drive Escort. Ford had decided that in spite of the remarkable success of the Escort, front wheel drive, which was, anyway, less of a bonus on the bigger car, was just too expensive to put into its new model.

In many ways the car was a Cortina twenty years on, but there was one major change of approach. While the old car had been conservatively styled, the Sierra appeared with an aerodynamic body which soon was disparagingly christened the 'soap dish' by the largely conservative salesmen to whom their companies allocated it. It was not helped by an extremely plastic interior which contrasted with the by now established Cavalier, and there was no version with a boot – what by now was being called in the motor trade jargon, a 'notch-back'.

The merits or otherwise of the Sierra were of more than motor enthusiast interest. The intense competition it sparked off coincided with, if it did not actually cause, a huge price war between the manufacturers which ended up beggaring them all, and which Ford, with the longest purse, was most able to stand. The least robust inevitably was BL, waiting for a new model and as always, short of money, yet deciding to discount as fiercely as the others.

By the middle of 1983, as the Sierra struggled to outsell the Cavalier, a huge spiral of price cutting had begun – something relatively new for recently introduced models. Some motorists found they could get reductions of as much as £800 – well over ten per cent off the price, while dealers could earn £350 extra for every car they sold over two thirds of their allocation.

BL's attempts to use price cutting to stay in the market showed in its figures. It lost nearly £300 million in 1982, £151 million in 1983, and only went into the black in 1984 because of the sale of Jaguar.

By the mid 1980s as Government investment continued to pour in – £260 million in 1982, £200 million in 1983 – and its middle range cars, the Maestro and the Montego, began to appear, it became evident that there was to be no easy salvation for the company. The new cars were competently engineered, reasonably well-received by the press but failed to set the market alight. The Montego in particular began to exhibit the same sort of niggling quality problems and unreliability which had been a trademark of the early Marina. The Metro continued to be the star, fighting a fierce sales battle against the Fiesta, and there was still demand for the Mini. But things were just not going well enough, particularly when the truck operation was making big losses because of a world-wide collapse of the market.

The company looked to its new executive car project with Honda – the excitingly titled XX. The chief executive of the cars division, Ray Horrocks, travelled backwards and forwards to Tokyo. He was filmed making a presentation Japanese style, with much bowing, at one moment and then at another was seen brandishing an imported hammer from the rostrum at the old imperial seaside resort of Eastbourne, complaining about the flood of imports into Britain.

BL arranged to adapt another medium car from Honda (what was to become the Rover 200), as the prestige name of Rover was allocated to cars made with Honda. It was remarkably successful, before long outselling the company's homebuilt Maestro.

The old abrasive image which was a hallmark of the Edwardes era still persisted. There were more ultimatums to the work force; a fiercely fought and ultimately successful drive to get bell to bell working at the company's plants, cutting out the practice of finishing early to get cleaned up. Relations with big customers and suppliers of components alike were spikey; some customers complained of the take it or leave it attitude of 'these cars are good, why don't you buy them?' A supplier, like the successful GKN (which found itself still supplying far more varieties of its CV joints to medium sized BL than to its bigger customers on the Continent) found that it was easier to get inside Japanese plants than into BL's nearby factories.

For the Government the company still remained a hostage to fortune; an uncashed open cheque of potentially huge proportions. So when the multinationals, which even with their vast resources were finding the going increasingly expensive, came knocking at its door in 1985 with schemes to collaborate with and even take over parts of the company, it was worth taking further.

The sharp-eyed Edwardes had seen the possibilities of a link with GM; now the project was partly revived. The world collapse of truck sales had affected all the European commercial vehicle manufacturers, and GM's Bedford subsidiary was worse hit than Leyland. With huge over-capacity, putting the two together made big commercial sense. Involving the fourwheel drive Landrover and Range Rover which had never had sufficient investment or been properly marketed in the United States, made sense too. What neither Government nor GM bargained for was an explosive outburst of patriotism which saw the success of the Landrover as almost as much a national symbol as the union jack.

On the cars side, an even more radical approach had come from Ford. The company was increasingly aware of the spiralling cost of new investments and by 1984 with three new engines planned it was looking for collaboration with other companies – it had talks with Mazda in Japan and wide-ranging discussions with Fiat. But by 1985 it was clear that the talks were failing. Then it occurred to Ford that Austin-Rover, jointly arranging a small engine development with Honda, might be a possible partner.

Sam Toy, then chairman of Ford of Britain, was the British motor chief most worried about the Japanese threat. 'Just as we were looking at the huge sums of money involved in the engines we started to ask, "What's a British company doing going to Japan to buy engines when we are investing this huge sum? Is there some way we can cooperate and avoid Austin-Rover becoming more Japanese?" '

Ford's approach was received coolly by the Austin-Rover management, though some talks did take place. But it swiftly set Ford thinking about the advantages of an even bigger link-up.

Ford of Europe has what it calls a European Advisory Council which consists of its senior executives plus important industrialists from different countries. It meets in different European centres and the normal practice is to invite top politicians to come and address its dinners. In 1985 it met in London and its guest was the Cabinet Minister, Norman Tebbit. Originally invited when he was Secretary of State for Trade and Industry, by the time the dinner was held, he had become Chairman of the Conservative Party, but was still a Cabinet Minister.

The Ford executives suggested to Tebbit that some sort of link with Austin-Rover was worth talking about. Tebbit, anxious to privatize BL, agreed to talk to his successor at the Trade and Industry Department, Leon Brittan, and to report back.

Toy says, 'One of our reasons was that we were seeking some form of arrangement between Ford and BL which would provide a great big substantial British manufacturing bloc to fight the importers more effectively.'

A series of meetings followed with ministers meeting Ford and then a small team of four from Ford and five from Austin-Rover being brought together for talks. They were strictly exploratory, starting with no precise proposals, but whereas in Whitehall there was considerable excitement about the prospects of the deal, there was resentment at Austin-Rover. Harold Musgrove complained bitterly to David Buckle in Oxford that on Government instructions they were being asked to show Ford confidential market projections. From the Ford side, there began to be a feeling that the talks were treading water; there were unexplained blockages.

The whole enterprise exploded in the early part of 1986. The Government was in political trouble after the Westland affair – a row over whether European or American companies should take a big share in an ailing helicopter company, controversially resolved in favour of the American Sikorski company. Somehow it had split the Cabinet so badly that two ministers, including Brittan, had resigned. In the wake of it, all talks about American deals were in jeopardy and disclosure of the GM talks about Landrover caused a huge political storm about selling British industry to the Americans. The Government withdrew Landrover from the deal, causing GM to pull out.

As he went to the House of Commons to explain, the new Minister, Paul Channon, was quickly briefed to answer questions about the secret Ford talks, if necessary. But none came. However a few days later, the story of the Ford–BL talks was leaked to Labour Party spokesmen who demanded a Government explanation. A rapid pull-out followed. On the morning of the Cabinet's weekly meeting Ford telephoned the Trade and Industry Department to be told that the talks were still on; by the time the Cabinet finished, it had decided that they must end, to the intense disappointment of both the civil servants and the

Ministers at the Trade and Industry Department who were aware of yet another deterioration in BL's finances.

It was time for more traditional solutions. Once again there was a change of management. The idea of a part-time chairman was scrapped, and a new hands-on chairman and chief executive on the Edwardes pattern was appointed – a tough Canadian, Graham Day, who had been running the heavily loss-making British Shipbuilders for the past two and a half years.

Day, hard-working and disciplined, came with a strongly transatlantic flavour. Trained as a lawyer, he had worked his way through college selling shoes and moonlighting as a broadcasting producer where he claimed to have helped discover a famous Canadian singer called Anne Murray. He took the common North American view that every success in business must first have learnt to be a salesman and liked transatlantic aphorisms like 'when push comes to shove' or more disconcertingly, 'my name's tucker not sucker'.

He was a resourceful man as was shown in an account of a successful mission for Canadian Pacific to sell coal in Japan. Day, in some trouble making the sale, had noted the Japanese big business practice whereby firms employ hostesses in formal geisha houses to research the business interests of their business clients and competitors. Day asked one to work for him to discover who the key decision-maker was in the company to whom he wished to sell, and what his tastes were in food and music. In due course he entertained him suitably and clinched his deal.

It was a colourful indication of his savvy and thoroughness although his experience of British industry was rather more mundane. Impressing as the executive overseeing merchant ships being built in a British yard for his company, Day had been brought in to sort out the shipbuilding interests of the private Laird group, and later, after nationalization, the problems of state-owned British shipbuilders. Here he had impressed Mrs Thatcher with his straight-talking approach, promising only to 'save the saveable', but cutting back manpower and yards without major trouble while fighting hard for orders for the most productive. Describing himself as a professional manager, he had obeyed Government instructions to privatize yards and seemed an obvious man to deal with the continuing problems of BL.

Day did not endear himself to the industry by remarking that he knew nothing about motor cars, but that selling cars was much the same as selling shoes, but his new approach soon showed. Declaring that 'the most important thing is "if you love your customer to death, you can't go far wrong"' he set about establishing the marketing department which BL amazingly lacked, and announced his intention of backing out of the price war. Faced with a sliding market share before his arrival, he made clear that he was not prepared simply to buy a bigger share but would concentrate in making the company profitable.

Internally he was amazed to find the huge amount of paperwork that passed between executives – a contrast to the old Midlands manufacturing days – and cut down his own daily briefing to a few key figures. At the same time he clashed with what he styled a pseudo-macho culture in the upper reaches of the company which he felt inhibited discussions on what the company should do. His own view was that Edwardes had dealt with manufacturing but the key effort was now needed on marketing – which suited his temperament.

One of his first decisions was to reprieve the Mini, which Harold Musgrove had marked down to finish in 1988. Day's research discovered that it had not been advertised for years and that many people thought it had gone out of production. In fact several hundred a week were still being produced and its sales in Japan and in France, where it was still a cult car, were increasing. He instituted a modest advertising campaign for it and production of what he called a 'nice little earner' increased. As for those who had tried to kill it, Day remarked curtly, 'They are no longer with us.'

Helped by good relations with the Government (he addresses Mrs Thatcher as ma'am) Day got approval for a new corporate plan and arranged for the sell-off of the troubled commercial vehicles section to a joint company with Daf of Holland and a cancellation of the enormous debts it had incurred. He stopped the slide in sales, instituted a quality drive, and sent a senior executive round component firms to try to establish less abrasive relations, announcing that he wanted a smaller number of favoured suppliers.

It was an energetic and encouraging start helped by an American export drive for the new Rover 800, which had been introduced just before his arrival. But the question remained whether, without the startling success in the market which still eluded it, the company, now renamed the Rover Group, could survive in the new international world without a merger, politically difficult as it might be.

As Day took over, the first trial cars were being assembled by the newest British mass manufacturer – the Nissan company of Japan, at a purpose-built factory on the old airport at Washington in the north east of England. It was being variously regarded as a Trojan horse whose proposed 100,000 cars a year would take sales away from British cars in general and Rover Group in particular or as an object lesson in manufacturing which would demand good quality from British component manufacturers; a company which would in any case go elsewhere in Europe if it did not manufacture in Britain.

The Nissan company had come to Britain for its first post-war models, arranging to build the Austin A40 Somerset in Japan in the early 1950s. Joe Edwards remembers, 'They wanted a car and were prepared to pay for a licence for it. They went to Rootes and they came to us. Len Lord and I took them to lunch at Droitwich – and don't forget it was the fifties and there was a lot of anti-Japanese feeling. I asked for the head waiter but they said he would not come as he had been a Japanese prisoner of war. We ended up signing a deal whereby they paid us, I think, about two million a year and we gave them all the drawings and so on.'

Now 30 years on there was a big debate within Nissan whether to manufacture in Britain at all where they were the most successful Japanese importer. It had announced plans in 1981 but then postponed them in 1982 after boardroom disagreements. But on February 1st 1984, an agreement was signed in London between the Government and Nissan for a plant which would produce 24,000 cars a year from imported parts. Production would start in 1986 with an option to move to a second phase by 1990 involving full manufacture of 100,000 cars a year in Britain, with eventually 80 per cent local content – a markedly higher proportion than the British Government had managed to squeeze out of Vauxhall. In late 1987 it set a new target: 200,000 cars.

The Government view, expressed by Mr Tebbit, was that, 'it will introduce a major, efficient new domestic customer for the UK components sector, and it represents a constructive step forward in the dialogue between Europe and Japan on trade and investment.' From the Japanese point of view it provided a base within the tariff barriers of the Common Market from which to expand.

By the summer of 1986 the first Bluebird cars were coming off the production lines on schedule, and by December full production was reached. By March the company was announcing the go ahead for its phase two and by May a stepping up of car production which would bring another 300 jobs a year ahead of schedule. It announced that it was buying parts from 37 British suppliers – traditional British names like Lucas, for some batteries and electrics, and Pilkington for glass, but also some with Japanese connections like S.P. Tyres and Ikeda-Hoover. The company's production controller, Ian Gibson, announced, 'Japan is a long distance away as a component supply base. The easy parts have been done now. We are now working through the component make-up of the car in terms of difficulty.'

Gibson was one of a team of British managers recruited to run the plant under a Japanese chief executive. As the senior British manager, he, like another key appointment, Peter Wickens, the personnel director, had had long experience with Ford, being one of a team of managers sent to try to sort out Halewood's problems in the 1970s and becoming the acting manager of the assembly plant there in 1979. He had also worked in Germany.

The British managers were soon able to announce that using the same rigorous quality testing methods employed by all Nissan factories that the cars turned out in Washington by the 500 workers were better than those being made in Japan.

The plant itself, though modern, had few revolutionary features except, in British terms, its organization. It was built on Japanese lines but presented an instantly familiar appearance to anyone accustomed to British factories. It had fewer robots than some British plants, as a result of a sharp appreciation of the poor economics of expensive robots for some relatively low volume jobs. Its biggest revolution was in its handling of the work force – recruited from an area far removed from traditional car production but still known as conservative and dominated by heavy industries like shipbuilding and generating-plant construction. Under the guidance of Wickens, who had already set up a new factory in Wales for an American company, Continental Can, a single union agreement – a Japanese condition for the go-ahead – was made with the Amalgamated Engineering Union, though by summer 1987 only 25 per cent of workers had joined the union.

Although the single union agreement was envied by other car makers, the company's most significant change was in the way it treated its work force. Everybody was put on a salary and started work at the same time – a sharp break with the traditions in most motor plants where office workers are on salary and start later, and the production workers are often defined as 'the hourly-paid'. At Nissan pay was not docked if workers were late or sick.

At the same time all employees were expected to attend section meetings for five minutes at the start of every day in special rooms by the production shops which served as meeting place, supervisor's office and recreation area. At the meetings, workers were encouraged to discuss ways of improving their operations and much of the equipment lay-out was rearranged to meet their suggestions.

On the assembly line, vehicles were tilted in order that workers did not have to stoop or bend unnecessarily, and the company broke with the system of 'tag relief' common in most British plants where workers take tea-breaks individually while the line continues to work. Instead everyone takes a break at the same time with production stopped.

The Nissan system puts much of the responsibility on the supervisor. With an average of twenty people under his control he is involved in recruiting. It is he and not the personnel department who rings up applicants and asks them to join his team. He is also given the difficult duty of line balancing – arranging the workload so that different operations dovetail together – a far cry from the days of Midlands piecework.

'In most other companies,' says Wickens, 'the role of the front line supervisor has been reduced to almost zero responsibility and authority. The result is that good calibre people do not want to go onto that particular job; that's true of British industry in general.

What we have tried to do is to break the mould by having high calibre with high responsibility.'

Gibson's view is that:

Essentially we treat our people as responsible adults who are as much in control at work as you or I am – that has not been the approach of mass production industries in the UK. They have tended to want to withdraw that individuality from the job in order to feel in control. You feel in control by telling the guy, 'If you don't turn up, we won't pay you. Don't argue about what you do; do what you're told. If you need something doing, yell for the fellow up the street because you aren't capable.'

Our approach is very much the other way round, saying, 'You are a responsible member of the team; you raise it with the supervisor if you think the job is wrong, and we will listen.'

It is early days still for Nissan, and whether its tough and idealistic start can be maintained as numbers build up and different shifts are employed remains to be seen. But its new management approach may be almost as significant as the novel manufacturing methods introduced by Henry Ford into Britain 70 years before in the last major arrival of a foreign manufacturer starting from scratch.

It poses a major international challenge. What the effect of a successful Nissan, even exporting a large part of its production, will be on the old-established British companies in a limited market is a key question as the British industry approaches its centenary in the 1990s.

CONCLUSIONS

In the spring of 1987 in the old motor industry capital of Coventry, the Museum of British Road Transport publicized an exhibition which would feature the city's two remaining motor car manufacturers – Jaguar and Peugeot-Talbot. One was a company which had started as a sidecar maker in Blackpool and had not moved to the city until 1928 – the other was a foreign multinational which had swept up the remains of a collection of different British companies.

It was a measure of the change, and failings, of the British motor industry. At the end of the 1980s, it was in much the same position as it had been over 70 years previously, before the start of the First World War and the long period of protection from outside competition which lasted for half a century.

The myth which had often sustained the industry from its very beginnings, that Britain could make cars better than anyone else, had been blown away, tested and found wanting. Even the glories of the race track could be put in context. As 30,000 British enthusiasts rose to cheer a lone works Jaguar home to fifth place in the Le Mans race, after a brave battle against the successful German Porsches, the legendary British successes by the gallant Bentleys, dented, battered and victorious in the 1920s and the Jaguar's own Big Cats or Aston Martin in the 1950s remained brief sunlit islands in a sea of foreign success.

Just as in the years before 1914, the British motor makers were running a balance of payments deficit, exporting less than most of their Continental counterparts, and depending on other countries and their equipment for their mass manufacturing techniques, and even some of the organization of their work force. New ideas

and changes had often come from the impact of the multinationals – the thorough disciplines of Ford and the more distant global
decision-making of General Motors and others.

British car manufacture was dominated by multinationals but
some of the enthusiastic handbuilding tradition remained. There
was still Morgan; the firm of T V R putting together sports cars in
Blackpool, Jaguar's old birthplace, and idiosyncratic sports cars
that recalled an earlier age were being assembled in a foreign-
owned Panther factory a stone's throw from the weed-grown
embankments of the historic Brooklands race track. The export
statistics continued to record Rolls Royces by the hundred, and a
few Aston-Martin Lagondas at over £70,000 each. The sports car
firm of Lotus, a new British legend on the Formula One Grand
Prix circuit in the 1960s had followed the almost traditional
British pattern of success followed by economic disaster, and was
now wholly owned by General Motors. It had plans for a major
increase in production to over 5,000 a year in the 1960s, levels not
seen much since B L killed off M G and Triumph. In late 1987
Ford too swooped to buy up famous names, swallowing both
Aston-Martin Lagonda and A C Cars.

In a way which both delighted and puzzled competitors, the
British industry had failed to make the transition from creative
backyard workshops to internationally aware and competitive
industry. Of those who had come closest, Morris' commercial
rigour had been overcome by a complacency and unwillingness
to let others press on when he flagged and lost interest, while
Herbert Austin, good engineer as he was, had never raised his
sights high enough. Above all perhaps, it was the feeling that
Britain was the centre of things, that we knew how to build cars,
and it was not necessary to look elsewhere – the divine right
would win through. As both managers and union activists put it
to me in the course of researching this book: 'We always felt we
could build cars better than anyone else.' For those who looked at
the export markets in 1914 or 1984, or the British public who
came to buy more than half their cars from foreign makers, there
was a different answer.

In 1987, as British-made cars once more managed to take just
over 50 per cent of the British market for the first time for years,
there were signs of revival, though it was more of an Indian

summer than a springtime of promise for what was no longer a sunrise industry.

A favourable and not to be underestimated shift in the exchange rate was one reason why Britain looked an increasingly attractive place to manufacture, but there were other more encouraging reasons too. The quality of both cars made in Britain and of parts supplied by the big component makers had improved – and so had productivity. Even so critical a judge as Bill Hayden, in charge of all manufacturing operations for Ford in Europe, saw improvements of which he said, 'I have to pinch myself to make sure it's happening.' In 1982 he and other Ford executives had returned from Japan thoroughly alarmed at the competition they were facing. Ford's AJ (After Japan) programme to get improvements in its plants brought immediate results on the Continent but nothing in Britain for two years. But now British productivity was improving faster than in Continental plants. Since the 1970–4 period productivity in British Ford assembly plants was up by 82 per cent compared with 52 per cent in the company's other European factories. Overall it is still behind but catching up and with currency movements assisting, it is now often cheaper to manufacture in Britain. In 1987 about 70 per cent of British Ford sales came from its British factories – the best figure for years – and a new engine intended originally for a German plant was switched into Dagenham because it could be made more cheaply. But progress was halted by the 1988 strike.

By the beginning of 1987, Vauxhall's Luton factory for the first time was turning out cars bearing the Opel badge for export, while Peugeot-Talbot's old Ryton factory, built as a wartime shadow factory, was starting production of lefthand vehicles for a new French-designed invasion of Europe. While Peugeot remained short of capacity at its Poissy factory near Paris, its prospects looked bright.

Meanwhile one out of three cars produced by Austin-Rover was being exported, and Jaguar hit new records with its new model.

Other structural changes were helping too. As the costs of development climbed, so the big international manufacturers started to change their approach. It seemed no longer economical to do all the development work themselves – the new thrust was to share the development work with component suppliers and to sub-contract it out to specialized independent design teams all over the world, keeping in instant touch through modern telecommunications.

For all the harsh words about British manufacturing performance, the quality of British engineers is recognized by their employment in motor companies all over the world, while British designers from universities or the special motor design course at the Royal College of Art have found employment throughout Europe.

The result of the new approach shows not only in the continuing strength of enterprises such as Lotus or Riccardo engineering, the engine specialists at Shoreham in Sussex, but also in the emergence of new, speculative design centres. A firm like Canewdon consultants on the fringes of Southend airport can call on the services of designers from the now disbanded British design teams of Peugeot-Talbot and General Motors, as well as recruits from Ford's slimmed down British operations, amongst its 200 or so staff. With closed circuit cameras monitoring arrivals, and often behind locked doors, its engineers create and model practical ideas for all three big American producers as well as the likes of Saab and Volvo, and others who may not be mentioned.

It is all far short of a rebirth of the industry and the hard fact remains that there is still a manufacturing overcapacity equivalent to two million vehicles a year in Europe, or a quarter of the cars produced; double the number of cars now made in Britain. With European car makers as a whole making losses, the market stagnant and more competition from the Japanese expected, British manufacturers are fighting for a share of someone else's cake.

As for exports, the old third world markets have been closed off by the Japanese and large scale sales in the United States' highly individual market have always proved elusive. For all Jaguar's race-track mystique two thirds of its American sales are to women, as the household's second car.

And so, from the standpoint of the late 1980s there are some hopeful signs for a sadder, smaller, wiser British motor industry with its protection largely removed. It has finally learnt to live with and to fight back against the international competition it scorned for so long though its struggle is never conclusively won or lost. Its cars will not sweep others off the roads of Europe or anywhere else. But it should remain a major manufacturing base although few of the companies which make cars here will be wholly British-owned.

APPENDIX I

The Topselling British-Made Cars

This is a list of the cars which were produced in the pre- and post-war years in the largest numbers by British factories. However, of all motor statistics, production figures are amongst the most contentious. It is not only a question of which models or variants to include but even manufacturers' own figures are sometimes inconsistent.

For this table, Ford and Vauxhall figures were supplied by the companies and the Rootes/Chrysler figures by the SMMT, with permission from Peugeot-Talbot. I am very grateful to Anders Clausager of the British Motor Industry Heritage Trust, which has many of the old BL and Rover archives, for a most painstaking compilation of numbers for the companies which were merged into them.

The division in the tables between post-war and pre-war is not quite watertight. Figures for the Austin Ten which was produced until 1947 and the Morris Eight are included in the pre-war list while the few 'upright' Ford Anglias and Prefects made before the war are lumped in with the post-war figures.

After discussions with Vauxhall I have included all three of the Viva models as one, because of their basic similarities, but have excluded the long-running Victor range because of the very major changes between the different models. The range reached 1,468,210 between the F of 1957 and the FE which ended in 1978.

I stress that these are production, not sales in Britain, figures. Some of the placings therefore reflect big export sales – most notably the modest Hillman Hunter which was the basis of the Iranian Paykan – Britain's best-ever export deal, and also, of course, the MG.

Conversely a car like the Ford Capri is not included, although over a million were made, because although it was first made in Britain, its production was switched to the Continent before it reached the half million mark which I have used as a cut-off point for the post-war listings.

The figures are those to December 1987.

PRE-WAR BEST SELLERS

Morris Eight (1934–53)	394,000
Morris Oxford and Cowley (1913–35)	390,000
Austin Seven	300,000 (plus)
Model T Ford	300,000 (approx.)
Austin Ten (1932–47)	283,000
Ford Model Y	157,668

POST-WAR BEST SELLERS

BMC Mini	5,065,220
Ford Cortina	4,279,079
BMC 1100/1300	2,132,980
Ford Escort (1968–80)	2,036,169
Morris Minor	1,619,857
Vauxhall Viva	1,597,063
Hillman Hunter/Paykan	1,486,643
Morris Marina/Ital	1,338,392
BL Metro	1,199,054
Ford Anglia 105E (1959)	1,083,955
Ford Escort (new series) from 1980	904,292
Austin Cambridge/Morris Oxford (Farina)	864,000 (approx.)
Ford Anglia/Prefect/Popular (1953)	843,832
Hillman Avenger	832,804
Ford Fiesta	681,164
Austin Allegro	667,192
Austin A40 (1947–56)	633,891

Triumph Herald	599,521
Ford Consul (1950–62)	581,481
Austin A30/A35	578,834
Ford (upright) Anglia and Prefect	537,913
Triumph 1300/Dolomite/Toledo	529,922
MGB	523,681
Ford Sierra	515,478
Vauxhall Cavalier Mk II	517,043

APPENDIX II

A Motor Industry Time-Chart

YEAR	POLITICAL EVENTS	BRITISH INDUSTRY	ABROAD
1886			Benz and Daimler make first cars in Germany
1888		Dunlop patents tyre	
1889			Daimler licence for French Panhard and Levassor
1890			Peugeot starts in France
1893			Benz Velo is first series production car
			Duryea brothers build first US car
1894		First car imported – a Benz	
1895		Austin and Lanchester experiment with first cars	
1896	Red Flag Act repealed	London–Brighton 'emancipation run'	Henry Ford builds first car

YEAR	POLITICAL EVENTS	BRITISH INDUSTRY	ABROAD
		British Motor Syndicate, Great Horseless Carriage Co, and Daimler Co (in Britain) founded	
		Austin and Lanchester build first cars	
1897		First factory-produced Daimler	
1899	Boer War begins	First four wheel Humber	
		Richmond exhibition	
1900		First Napier car produced	
		Thousand Mile Run	
1901		Wolseley and Argyll Co start	Daimler builds first Mercedes
		British Motor Syndicate patents challenged	
		Lanchester invents disc brakes	
1902		First Vauxhall, Sunbeam & Jowett engine	
1903	Wright Brothers make first aircraft flight	First Rover and Standard	Ford Motor Co established and first production cars made
		Ford imports first cars	
1904		Henry Royce builds first Rolls-Royces	
1905		Austin starts own company	

YEAR	POLITICAL EVENTS	BRITISH INDUSTRY	ABROAD
		First Jowett	
		Vauxhall move to Luton	
		Royal Commission on Motor Cars	
1906			United States overtakes France as world's biggest car producer
1908			Ford builds Model T
1909	Budget introduces tax based on horsepower so encouraging smaller British engines	Lanchester joins Daimler	
1911		Ford starts assembly in Manchester	
1912		3,000 Fords produced	
		Morris makes first car – the Morris Oxford	
1913		Ford production doubles to 6,000	Production: 45,000 in France 485,000 in US
		25,000 cars made in Britain	
1914	First World War starts		
1915	McKenna duty puts 33⅓ per cent on all motor imports		

YEAR	POLITICAL EVENTS	BRITISH INDUSTRY	ABROAD
1918	War ends	Month long strike at Austin	
1919		Moulders' strike	
1920	Economic slump begins Increased horsepower tax encourages small cars	General Motors bid for Austin	
1921		Austin calls in Receiver	
1922	Slump	Morris cuts prices Austin Seven First Clyno	
1924	McKenna duties lifted by Labour Government	250,000th Ford Ford buys site at Dagenham Merger talks between Austin and Morris	Morris buys Bollée plant in France Bentley wins Le Mans
1925	McKenna duties reimposed	Morris sets up export office	Ford starts manufacture in Germany
1926	General Strike	Morris buys Wolseley	GM takes over Adam Opel in Germany
1927		Pressed Steel Co set up Bentley wins Le Mans for first of 4 times	Austin Seven made under licence in Germany becoming first BMW
1928	Petrol duties reimposed	SS Cars (Jaguar) move to Coventry	Austin Seven made under licence in France

YEAR	POLITICAL EVENTS	BRITISH INDUSTRY	ABROAD
1929	New world trade slump begins	Edsel Ford starts Dagenham construction GM buys Vauxhall Rootes Group of motor dealers buys Humber and Hillman and become manufacturers	Austin attempts US construction under licence
1930		MG Car Co set up	Austin US production ends in fiasco
1931		Ford opens at Dagenham	Morris winds up Bollée
1932	Peak recession year	Ford Model Y Austin 10 Production falls by about 13 per cent	US production 75 per cent below 1929; German production halved; France loses one third
1933	Peak unemployment years		
1934		Morris Eight	
1935	30 mph limit	Ford cuts Model Y price to £100 First SS Jaguar Rootes takes over Sunbeam	
1936	Shadow factory scheme launched		
1939	Second World War starts		

YEAR	POLITICAL EVENTS	BRITISH INDUSTRY	ABROAD
1940		Heavy bombing of Coventry car plants; also at Vauxhall and Ford at Dagenham	
1945	War ends		More manufacturing being done in Australia, traditional large market; restricts imports
1946	Controls on steel supply – export drive		
1947	Horsepower tax ends	Factory power cuts	
1948		Morris Minor launched	
1950		First post-war Ford – the Consul	Britain world's biggest exporter overtaking US
1951	Korean War Steel shortage		
1952	Hire purchase restricted for first time – start of 'regulator'	Austin–Morris merge into British Motor Corporation	
1953		Big companies buy bodymakers – Ford buys Briggs and BMC takes Fisher and Ludlow	Jaguar's first win at Le Mans
		Ford Anglia, Prefect & Popular introduced	

YEAR	POLITICAL EVENTS	BRITISH INDUSTRY	ABROAD
1954	HP restrictions abolished		British exports stable – French exports up 30 per cent; W. German up 55 per cent
1955	HP up twice	Rootes takes over bankrupt Singer	First Japanese designed car produced by Toyota
1956	Suez crisis Petrol rationed HP restrictions tightened	Production and sales drop	W. German production and exports pass British
1957	HP restrictions tightened again		
1958	HP restrictions lifted	Production over one million	
1959	M1 opens	Mini launched Triumph Herald Ford Anglia 105E	Aston Martin wins at Le Mans
1960	Credit squeeze HP restrictions back		
1961		Jaguar takes over Daimler Leyland takes over Standard–Triumph Exports and production fall heavily	French car production passes British
1962		Ford Cortina	Honda builds first car
1963		Ford opens Halewood	

YEAR	POLITICAL EVENTS	BRITISH INDUSTRY	ABROAD
		Rootes opens Linwood	
		Vauxhall opens Ellesmere Port and (1964) starts Viva production there	
1964		Chrysler buys share of Rootes	
1965	HP restrictions tightened	Sales and production fall	Rootes signs Iran Paykan deal
1966	HP restrictions tightened Industrial Reorganization Corporation set up	BMC and Jaguar merge as British Motor Holdings Leyland takes over Rover	
1967	Pound devalued HP eased twice and then increased	Ford creates Ford of Europe Chrysler takes over Rootes	First Paykan produced in Teheran
1968	HP restrictions increased Import duties start to fall sharply from $25\frac{1}{5}$ per cent to 11 per cent in four years	Leyland and BMC merge to form BLMC First Ford Escort Exports rise sharply from 502,000 to 676,000	Japanese production passes both British and French going from 1.3 million to 2 million
1969		Imports up by half All-time export record of 771,634	
1971	HP restrictions abolished	Morris Marina	Japanese production at 3.7 million passes W. Germany

YEAR	POLITICAL EVENTS	BRITISH INDUSTRY	ABROAD
1972	Import duties down to 11 per cent	Record production year – 1,921,311 Imports at 450,314 are four times 1969 level	
1973	OPEC oil crisis starts slump HP restrictions back		Citroen in financial difficulty
1974		BLMC in talks with banks, asks for Government help	Peugeot takes over Citroen
1975		Ryder Report and reorganization of British Leyland	Talks between British and Japanese on voluntary restrictions of imports into Britain
1976		British Government rescues Chrysler UK	
1977		Strikes cost one third of BL production Michael Edwardes appointed Ford Fiesta	
1978		Peugeot takes over Chrysler Europe forming Peugeot-Talbot	
1979	Second oil price shock	Britain into red on motor trade – minus	Paykan contract disrupted by Iran revolution

YEAR	POLITICAL EVENTS	BRITISH INDUSTRY	ABROAD
		£287 million – first time for over 50 years	
1980		MG closes Metro launched Car production below a million for first time since 1957 New Ford Escort	Japan overtakes US as world's largest producer Big US companies make big losses
1982	HP restrictions lifted	Ford Sierra replaces Cortina British motor trade into red again – for good Minus £973 million	
1983		Peugeot-Talbot shift design out of Britain	
1984		Jaguar sold off Nissan signs deal with Government to set up plant	
1985		Record car sales – 1.8 million	
1986		Nissan starts manufacture in Britain Jaguar launches new car Rover Honda executive car launched as Rover 800 and Honda Legend	

YEAR	POLITICAL EVENTS	BRITISH INDUSTRY	ABROAD
1987		Lucas sells electrical lighting business to Fiat Ford buys Aston Martin-Lagonda and AC Cars	Peugeot-Talbot and Vauxhall building for export in Britain Rover Group exporting one third of output

REFERENCES

CHAPTER ONE (*The Beginnings*)

1. Laurence Pomeroy (senior) in a speech to the Institution of Automobile Engineers in 1914.
2. Quotations from W.O. Duncan come from his book *The World on Wheels* published privately in Paris in the 1920s.
3. *Dawn of Motoring*, E. Johnson, 1986.
4. S.F. Edge, *My Motoring Reminiscences*.

CHAPTER TWO (*The Pioneers*)

1. Quoted in P.W. Kingsford, *Lanchester, the Life of an Engineer*.
2. St. J. Nixon, *Daimler 1896–1940*.
3. S.B. Saul, 'The Motor Industry in Britain to 1914', *Business History 1962*.
4. S.F. Edge, *My Motoring Reminiscences*.
5. Articles in *Veteran Car Club Gazette, 1955*.

CHAPTER THREE (*Mass Production*)

1. Henry Ford in his autobiography.
2. H. Wyatt, *The Motor Industry*.
3. 'Policies that have built the Morris Motor Business' , *System 1924*, quoted in Andrews and Brunner, *Life of Lord Nuffield*.

CHAPTER FOUR (*The First World War*)

1. Quoted in W. Plowden, *The Motor Car and Politics in Britain*.

CHAPTER FIVE (*Interwar Years*)

1. Quoted in R.J. Wyatt, *The Austin 1905–52*.
2. Quoted in Andrews and Brunner.
3. Miles Thomas, *Out on a Wing*.
4. Article in *System*.
5. R.J. Wyatt, *The Austin 1905–1952*.
6. H. Wyatt, *The Motor Industry*.
7. Miles Thomas, *Out on a Wing*.
8. Andrews and Brunner, *The Life of Lord Nuffield*.
9. Brabazon of Tara, *The Brabazon Story*.

CHAPTER SIX (*The Specialist Cars*)

1. W.O. Bentley, *My Life and my Cars*.
2. Quoted in Lloyd, *Rolls-Royce – the years of endeavour*.
3. Andrews and Brunner, *The Life of Lord Nuffield*.
4. F. Wilson McComb, *The story of the MG sportscar*.
5. W.O. Bentley, *My Life and my Cars*.

CHAPTER SEVEN (*Component Makers*)

1. S.F. Edge, *My Motoring Reminiscences*.
2. H. Nockolds, *Lucas: The First 100 Years*.

CHAPTER EIGHT (*Workers*)

1. Quoted in P.W. Kingsford, *Lanchester, the Life of an Engineer*.
2. R.C. Whiting, *The View from Cowley*.
3. Ibid.
4. Jack Jones, *Union Man*.
5. Whiting, *The View from Cowley*.
6. P. Pagnamenta and R.J. Overy, *All our Working Lives*.

CHAPTER NINE (*The Second World War*)

1. Miles Thomas, *Out on a Wing*.
2. C. Barnett, *The Audit of War*.
3, Jack Jones, *Union Man*.

CHAPTER TEN (*The Forties and Fifties*)

1. Quoted in R.J. Wyatt, *The Austin 1905–1952*.
2. Interview for BBC 'All our Working Lives' series.
3. Pagnamenta and Overy, *All our Working Lives*.
4. Jack Jones, *Union Man*.
5. E. Wigham, *The Power to Manage*.
6. Quoted in G. Turner, *The Carmakers*.

CHAPTER ELEVEN (*The Sixties*)

1. Quoted in G. Robson, *The Rover Story*.
2. BBC Radio Interview, 1986.
3. Quoted in H. Nockolds, *Lucas; The First 100 Years*.
4. Interview for BBC 'All our Working Lives' series.
5. Quoted in G. Turner, *The Leyland Papers*.

CHAPTER TWELVE (*The Seventies (i)*)

1. Interview for BBC 'All our Working Lives' series.

CHAPTER THIRTEEN (*The Seventies (ii)*)

1. Quoted in Sir M. Edwardes, *Back from the Brink*.

BOOKS ABOUT THE MOTOR INDUSTRY

This is a selection of books about the industry which I have found helpful. Many of them contain further bibliographies and I would also recommend the article on 'The Documentation of Motoring History', by William Boddy in the August 1976 edition of *British Book News*.

On the Industry in General
H.G. Castle, *Britain's Motor Industry*. London, Clerke & Cocheran, 1950.
Noble and Junner, *Vital to the Life of the Nation*. London, SMMT, 1946.
Pagnamenta and Overy, *All our Working Lives* (Car industry chapter). London, 1984.

Economic and Industrial Histories
Maxcy and Silberston, *The Motor Industry*. London, Allen & Unwin, 1959. (A classic)
Rhys, *The British Motor Industry* (An economic survey). London, Butterworth, 1972.
K. Richardson, *The British Motor Car Industry; A Social and Economic History*. London, MacMillan, 1977.
Peter Waymark, *The Car Industry*. Bath, Sewells, 1983.

General Aspects
Two outstandingly interesting and useful books are:
W. Plowden, *The Motor-Car and Politics in Britain*. London, Bodley Head, 1971, and
G.N. Georgano, *The Complete Encyclopaedia of Motor-Cars*. London, Ebury Press, 1968, which is a dictionary of over 4,000 makes of car since 1885.

The Early Years

H.O. Duncan, *The World on Wheels*, privately published in Paris in the 1920s, is a wonderful, rambling, picaresque account by a man closely involved with all the early figures in the motor industry and Harry Lawson in particular. Treated with caution, it is an essential starting point.

As fascinating is S.F. Edge, *My Motoring Reminiscences*. London, G.T. Foulis, 1934.

Other books include:

E. Johnson, *The Dawn of Motoring*. Mercedes-Benz, 1986.

D. Scott-Moncrieff, *Veteran and Edwardian Motor-Cars*. London, Batsford, 1955.

P. Roberts, *A Picture History of the Automobile*. London, Ward Lock, 1973.

D.H. Aldcroft (ed.), *The Development of British Industry and Foreign Competition, 1875–1914*. London, Allen & Unwin, 1968. (See article by S.B. Saul)

S.B. Saul, 'The Motor Industry in Britain to 1914. (Article in *Business History*, December 1962, on which many other writings have drawn)

Hyamson, *David Salomons*. London, Methuen, 1939.

Brabazon of Tara, *The Brabazon Story*. London, Heinemann.

G. de Holden-Stone, *The Automobile Industry*. London, Methuen, 1904.

J.S. Critchley, *British Motor Vehicles*. London, Charles Clayton, 1913.

T.R. Nicholson, *The Birth of the British Motor Car 1769–1897*. London, MacMillan, 1982.

The Pioneers

Useful biographies include:

R. Church, *Herbert Austin – The British Motor Car Industry to 1941*. London, Europa, 1979.

P.W. Kingsford, *F.W. Lanchester, The Life of an Engineer*. Edward Arnold, 1960.

R.J. Overy, *William Morris*. London, Europa, 1976.

Andrews and Brunner, *Life of Lord Nuffield*. Oxford, 1955 (very much an authorized biography).

R. Jackson, *The Nuffield Story*. London, Muller, 1964.

Company Histories

R.J. Wyatt, *The Austin, 1905–1952*. London, David &
   Charles, 1981.

St J. Nixon, *Daimler. 1896–1940*. London, G.T. Foulis, 1946.

(Jowett), *Fifty Years of Progress – Jowett Cars 1901–1951*.
   Jowett, 1951.

C. Wilson and W. Reader, (Napier) *Men and Machines*.
   London, Weidenfeld, 1958.

Lloyd, *Rolls Royce – The Growth of a Firm and the Years of
   Endeavour*. London, MacMillan, 1978.

H. Nockolds, (Rolls-Royce) *The Magic of a Name*. London,
   G.T. Foulis, 1938.

G. Robson, *The Rover Story*. Patrick Stephens.

J. Davy, *The Standard Motor Car. 1903–1963*. 1967. (Privately
   published.)

St J. Nixon, *Wolseley*. London, G.T. Foulis, 1949.

Inter-War Years

C. Clutton and J. Stanford, *The Vintage Motor Car*. London,
   Batsford, 1954.

H. Wyatt, *The Motor Industry*. London, Pitman, 1921.

(Lord) Miles Thomas, *Out on a Wing*. London, Michael
   Joseph, 1964.

D.G. Rhys, 'Concentration in the Inter-War Motor Industry'.
   Reprinted from the *Journal of Transport History*. Leicester,
   1976.

Second World War

C. Barnett, *The Audit of War*. London, MacMillan, 1986.

Ministry of Labour and National Service Report, 1939–46.
   London, HMSO, 1947.

Specialist and Sports Cars

M. Frostick, *Bentley*. London, Osprey, 1980.

W.O. Bentley, *The cars in my life*. London, Hutchinson, 1961.

W.O. Bentley, *W.O. The autobiography*. London, Hutchinson,
   1958.

W.O. Bentley, *My life and my cars*. London, Hutchinson,
   1967.

A. Whyte, *Jaguar – The History of a Great British Car*. Cambridge, Patrick Stephens, 1980.

F. Wilson McComb, *The story of the MG sportscar*. London, Dent, 1972.

G. Houston Bowden, *Morgan – First and Last of the Real Sports Cars*. Wilton House Gentry, 1972.

W. Boddy, *The vintage years of the Morgan Three-Wheeler*. London, Grenville, 1972.

Ian Fallon and Srodes, *DeLorean: the Rise and Fall of a Dreammaker*. London, Hamish Hamilton, 1983.

The Component Makers

E. Tompkins, *The History of the Pneumatic Tyre*. Dunlop, 1981.

R. Storrs, *Dunlop in War and Peace*. London, Hutchinson, 1946.

Monopolies and Restrictive Practices Commission Report on the Supply and Export of Pneumatic Tyres. HMSO, 1955.

H. Nockolds, *Lucas: The first hundred years*. London, David & Charles, 1976.

Monopolies Commission Report on the Supply of Electrical Equipment for Mechanically Propelled Land Vehicles. HMSO, 1963.

T.C. Barker, *The Glassmakers*. London, Weidenfeld & Nicholson, 1977.

The Workers and Labour Relations

H.A. Turner, G. Clack and G. Roberts, *Labour Relations in the Motor Industry*. London, Allen & Unwin, 1967. (A classic study)

E. Wigham, *The Power to Manage*. London, MacMillan, 1973. (The official history of the Engineering Employers Federation)

Jack Jones, *Union Man*. London, Collins, 1986. (A union view)

H. Beynon, *Working for Ford*. London, Penguin, 1973.

R.C. Whiting, *The View from Cowley*. Oxford, OUP, 1983.

G. Turner, *The Carmakers*. London, Eyre & Spottiswoode, 1963.
P. Wickens, *The Road to Nissan*. London, Macmillan, 1988.

Post-War

After 1945 we enter the era of frequent official reports. The 'PEP Report – Motor Vehicles' – a Report on the Industry, 1950, was later followed by a string of Government and Parliamentary reports mainly concentrating on the problems of British Leyland. These included 'BL – the Next Decade' (the abridged Ryder report) in April 1975, which was quickly followed by the '14th Report from the Expenditure Committee on the Motor Vehicle Industry', Aug. 1975, which was highly critical of it, and the Central Policy Review Staff's 'Future of the British car industry' at the end of the year.

The BL saga was examined in books which included:

G. Turner, *The Leyland Papers*. London, Eyre & Spottiswoode, 1971, which described the merger.

L. Pomeroy, *The Mini Story*. London, Temple Press, 1964.

Sir M. Edwardes, *Back from the Brink*. London, Collins, 1983. The industry has continued to be the subject of further Parliamentary scrutiny. Reports include:

'The Eighth Report from the Expenditure Committee on Public Expenditure on Chrysler UK'. 1976.

'The Third Report from the Industry and Trade Committee on Finance for BL'. 1981.

'Trade and Industry Committee Report on the Motor Component Industry. 1987'.

The problems of the industry have been analysed in books including:

K. Williams, J. Williams and D. Thomas, *Why are the British Bad at Manufacturing?* London, Routledge Kegan Paul, 1983.

B. Elbaum and W. Lazonick, *The Decline of the British Economy*. Oxford, OUP, 1986. (See chapter by W. Lewchuk)

The Economist Intelligence Unit continues to issue a string of illuminating reports on the industry, notably recently,

'A financial assessment of the West European Motor Industry', A.T. Lowry, 1986.

A detailed union view is set out in a pamphlet by TASS.
The Way Ahead: New Technology and the UK Motor Industry,
 1986.

Statistics
The best sources for these remain the annual statistical
 yearbooks of the Society of Motor Manufacturers and
 Traders.

INDEX